# SYRIA'S SECRET LIBRARY

# SYRIA'S
# SECRET LIBRARY

*Reading and Redemption in a*
*Town Under Siege*

## MIKE THOMSON

**PUBLIC**AFFAIRS

*New York*

PublicAffairs
Hachette Book Group
1290 Avenue of the Americas, New York, NY 10104
www.publicaffairsbooks.com
@Public_Affairs

Printed in the United States of America

Originally published in the United Kingdom in 2019 by Weidenfeld & Nicolson, an imprint of The Orion Publishing Group Ltd.

First US Edition: August 2019

Published by PublicAffairs, an imprint of Perseus Books, LLC, a subsidiary of Hachette Book Group, Inc. The PublicAffairs name and logo is a trademark of the Hachette Book Group.

For additional copyright information, please turn to page 305.

Print book interior design by Input Data Service, Ltd, Somerset.

Library of Congress Control Number: 2019938981

ISBNs: 978-1-5417-6762-1 (hardcover), 978-1-5417-6761-4 (ebook)

LSC-C

10  9  8  7  6  5  4  3  2  1

I dedicate this book to the people of Daraya, whose courage, resilience and love of books has brought light to a country in darkness.

And to Leo and Holly.

# Contents

# A Note on Place Names and Spelling

When translating Arabic names into English, there are several options for how to form the name. In this book, I have opted for translations that are consistent with each other in style, to allow a smooth reading experience. Similarly, with place names in Syria, there are multiple correct English spellings. Daraya, for example, can also be spelled Darayya. I have chosen to spell these places in accordance with how the people of Daraya spell them: these places are their homes, I will take their lead.

On a separate note, I refer to the terrorist organisation known to the world variously as IS, ISIS, ISIL, Daesh, and many other names besides, initially as the so-called Islamic State and IS thereafter.

Some people's names have been changed in order to protect the individuals and their families from possible arrest or ill treatment by Syria's security services.

## Introduction

As dawn breaks, the crack of rifle fire echoes through empty streets. Yellow mist, a sulphury haze of exploded barrel bombs and burning plastic, hangs over shattered homes, their warped, crumbling roofs splayed forward. Here and there charred electric cables dangle down, limp lines of debris over a prone, bleeding city.

Picking his way through the lifeless landscape, defying the rotten smells and prolonged, rumbling explosions, a teenage boy slips through the half-buried entrance of a gutted building. After shutting the outside door, its weathered surface pockmarked with cracks and holes, the boy descends. Down, down he goes, step by careful step, into the darkness. One palm touches the wall steadying his passage, the other hand grips his precious bundle of books. As he nears the foot of the concrete stairs, the sounds of war fade into silence, broken only by the echoes of his sandalled feet.

In the gloom, the boy gropes for a light switch. With electricity now a rarity, he does so more in hope than expectation. A naked bulb flickers into life, illuminating a large basement room with generous high ceilings.

Books, long rows of them, line almost every wall. Grand volumes with brown leather covers; tattered old tomes with barely readable spines; pocket-sized guides to poetry; classic and contemporary novels; religious works with gaudy gold-lettering; a range of reference books: all rub shoulders in well-ordered literary lines, their neat, regimented rows marred only by occasional kinks in the handmade shelves.

Setting his books on a table, fourteen-year-old Amjad bustles about, preparing for the day ahead, stopping here and there to align the chairs and rehome the odd stray book. It is early and this is *his* time. The only sounds, the shifting of books, the rustling of paper and the faint hum of a small rusty generator. A cloth in hand, Amjad makes for a narrow bookcase. Carefully, he takes the volumes down, then lovingly dusts each and every one, before buffing the shelves to a hazy shine.

In a few hours' time the secret library will open for business. Between twenty to thirty people arrive every day. All make treacherous journeys across the shattered city, braving snipers, bombs and missiles. Their reward – a few precious moments quietly choosing books, reading and exchanging news. Then they return to the streets and warily, block by block, inch their way home.

The books Amjad so lovingly tends were not bought from shops or delivered by publishers. Most were bravely gathered from burning homes and bombed council offices, often under shelling and sniper fire. Filling this library was a dangerous business.

Amjad meticulously signs every book in and out, each one handled like a priceless treasure. Names, addresses and return dates are logged. He smiles and nods, while advising on the merits of one book or another. Not that he ever has bad words to say about any of them. As choices are made and titles bundled into bags, everyone is told to keep safe and come back soon. Though whether Amjad is thinking as much of his beloved books as the person borrowing them, is hard to say.

There is only one thing more important to Amjad than the thousands of books on the shelves and that is the secrecy of the library itself. Everyone is told to reveal its location only to those they trust. Otherwise, he warns, pro-Assad planes will destroy it. That, the teenage tells me, in a near-starving city that is slowly dying each day, 'would be the end of hope for us all'.

As a Foreign Correspondent for the BBC, I am no stranger to war zones. From Somalia, Iraq and Afghanistan to Sri Lanka, Myanmar and Colombia I have seen the horrors of what man can do to man, and of course women and children too. Every war has its share of horrors and depravity, but one conflict in particular sticks in my mind. I will never forget the extraordinary brutality to women during ongoing unrest in the eastern Democratic Republic of Congo. Many were not only raped by militia groups and sometime government soldiers, but also violated with rifle barrels and other implements, in many cases in front of their children. I remember asking a doctor who was treating survivors of sexual violence in the town of Bukavu in 2007 why he thought people did this. After all, these were men with mothers and often wives, sisters and daughters of their own. He told me that he had come to believe in a chilling explanation voiced by a former militia member he had treated. The man had told him: 'If you can destroy a woman's ability to bear children, while also destroying her mind, you melt the glue that binds your enemy's community together. You kill his will to fight.' I have never been able to forget those awful words.

In 2011, when President Bashar al-Assad's security forces opened fire and killed several pro-democracy protesters in the southern city of Daraa, I watched events on an ancient, spluttering television, in northern Congo. I was covering the murderous march of what was left of the notorious Lord's Resistance Army, or LRA, through large isolated swathes of central Africa. I had been in Damascus only a few months before and remembered the tensions and rebellious spirit of many I had talked to there. Much of this was expressed to me in furtive whispers in cafés and hotel lobbies, or in scribbled notes on scraps of paper. But these had not in any way prepared me for what was to follow. Damascus, with its attractive tree-lined streets and pretty flower-adorned restaurants, did not look a likely war zone capital. Yet the deaths in Daraya would soon ignite an uprising against President Bashar al-Assad and his regime, which would spread across the country. Nearly eight years of war and untold suffering that continues to this day.

I knew nothing of the town of Daraya until it came to my attention in the summer of 2015 when I was compiling a news report for the BBC. At the time around half a million people were living in cities and towns encircled by pro-Syrian government forces, though a few had been besieged by rebel groups or so-called Islamic State (IS) fighters. By all accounts it was a grim struggle to survive in all of these places. Yet, to me, the dire situation in Daraya stood out because it had received no aid of any kind since being surrounded by pro-Syrian government forces back in November 2012. How, I wanted to know, were people there surviving?

I called my contacts inside the country, hoping that one of them could put me in touch with someone in Daraya. At first this proved difficult. Those who knew people there needed to talk to them first, before passing on names – all normal etiquette in most parts of the world, but absolutely essential in Syria. This is a country where one day it is safe to speak out against your enemy, the next your town is overrun and you face arrest or worse.

Finally, I managed to get in touch with some people in Daraya. Thanks to their candid and revealing testimonies I was able to complete my reports on the latest situation there. But the more I found out, the more interesting the people and their town became. In particular I was trans-fixed by rumours of a secret underground library that, I had been told, was full of books, books that had been gathered, and were being read, in the most harrowing and dangerous of circumstances. It seemed almost unimaginable. Battles were usually over things like money, women or power. Yet here was a love of books, a passion for literature and learn-ing that ran so deep that people were willing to risk their lives for it. Here in a time of war, when feelings of hatred and lust for revenge grew as casualties mounted, a group of young men were dedicating themselves to learning and culture. All this while their town was being attacked on all sides and they were living on little more than a cup of watery soup each day.

At first it was hard to believe. Given that I could not get into the besieged town to verify what I was being told, I wondered whether it was true. Could there really be a secret library filled with thousands of books rescued from the rubble of war? An underground literary sanctuary filled with lovers of poetry, science, history and art, who held book clubs while bullets flew above? It defied every brutal image I had of the Syrian war, and I was determined to find out more.

*

The story of Syria's Secret Library was first broadcast as a documentary by BBC Radio 4 in late July 2016. It got a heart-warming reception and won two major awards. Among the correspondence I received after the broadcast was a tweet from a Washington-based lecturer on the Middle East. The secret library, he wrote, had given him his first glimmer of hope for the country in many years. This was something that deeply resonated with me. In all the time I had been reporting on Syria, I had never come across a story like this. One that inspired rather than depressed, and showed how a love of literature, learning and culture had somehow survived, amid all the cruelty and bloodshed. And I realised there was so much more to say.

# Chapter One

Until 2011, Daraya, a town of around 90,000 people on the southern doorstep of Damascus, was a thriving, vibrant community. Life carried on pretty much as normal in its broad, tree-lined streets. Convoys of farmers' trucks laden with rich varieties of locally grown crops; small furniture factories producing the town's speciality – hand-crafted bedroom pieces; crowded markets and shops, decked with brightly painted placards and elaborate shop windows.

Daraya is often referred to as a suburb of Damascus, but it is a separate town, with its own identity and history, and is said to be the site of Paul the Apostle's Damascene conversion.[1] Daraya was initially a Ghassanid Christian village, full of monasteries, but with the rise of Islam in the seventh century, it soon became an important site for Muslims and the monasteries were replaced with shrines to the companions of Muhammad who lived and died there.[2] Bilal, one of Muhammad's closest companions, is believed to have settled in Daraya. Born in Mecca, he is considered to be the first ever muezzin chosen by Muhammad and, as such, is one of the most significant figures in the early history of Islam.

Throughout the early Islamic period, Daraya was a bustling but modest village. Its proximity to Damascus, which became the capital of the Umayyad Caliphate in AD 680, meant it was always in the shadow of its wealthy, illustrious neighbour. Nonetheless, Daraya was not completely out-shone. Having been host to the Prophet Muhammad's companions and their descendants, it became a sanctified location and was soon renowned among scholarly circles, said by some to be the 'place to go for anyone seeking knowledge'.

Daraya was also well known as an agricultural area, revered for its fine orchards and fertile soils. One of its crops – the grape – has long been prized above all others, not just locally, or nationally, but right across the world. In 1862, an article appeared in the British publication *Once a Week,* extolling the virtues of a 'white grape, large and long, very fragrant, sweet and juicy, and with a hard skin which enables it to bear packing and carriage without injury. It is cultivated in a village near Damascus called Daraya, on the old Roman road south-west of the city, and there only, for often though planted elsewhere, it has always obstinately refused to thrive.' The article went on to quote a story, translated by London's then-Consul, named only as Mr Rogers, involving the Prophet Muhammad and a follower of his who, one afternoon, followed Muhammad in an attempt to discover where the Prophet said his afternoon prayers. According to the legend, after Muhammad prayed:

The heavens opened, and a ladder was let down to the earth, up which Muhammad proceeded to climb. His friend followed close, and when the door of heaven was reached, he contrived, by hiding himself behind the skirts of the Prophet's dress, to enter with him unperceived. He found himself in the immediate presence of Allah. Allah was seated on a magnificent divan, in all the celestial splendours. He was evidently waiting for the arrival of Muhammad, whom He at once recognised, called him to his right hand at the corner of the sofa, and commanded Gabriel and the other attendants to bring coffee, pipes, sweetmeats etc. Meantime the friend had been enabled, in the bustle of the entrance, to creep behind the divan, from whence he watched all that happened. After a time, conversation flagged, and a game of chess was proposed. To this Muhammad – who was perfectly at his ease, and apparently well used to his company – would only assent on condition that the game should be for some stakes worth winning. It was at last settled that the stakes should be a banquet, to be furnished on the spot by the loser. The Prophet won the game without difficulty, and the banquet at once appeared. One of its chief delicacies was a cluster of magnificent grapes, such as no mortal vine ever bore, beautiful in form and colour, and of celestial fragrance. At the sight of the grapes the friend could resist no longer. He stole out of his hiding place while the Prophet and his Host were busy with the feast. He contrived, by mingling with the attendants, to break off a portion of the bunch, which he hid in his bosom, and then darted off down the ladder.

Once on the earth again, he waited quietly in the neighbourhood, and on the Prophet's reappearance congratulated him on having played his part so well. Muhammad was at first indignant, and professed not to understand his meaning, till the production of the grapes showed him that his follower had really witnessed all that had passed. He then bound him to secrecy: 'As for the grapes,' said he, 'do not waste such precious fruit by eating it, but take it to Daraya, near Damascus, and there plant it, so that the earth may benefit by your visit to heaven.' This his friend did. Now, all men know that the earth of the plain of Damascus is that out of which our first father Adam was created, and that in all the world there is not so fine or productive soil: but of all that plain Daraya is the richest. The grapes grow there to this day in abundance, for though thousands and tens of thousands eat of them, there is never any lack. But the vines will flourish nowhere else, as many can affirm who have planted them elsewhere. And this is the story of the grapes of Daraya, which will grow nowhere but in their own soil.[3]

In 1953, nearly a century after this story was published, a festival of grapes was held in Daraya. More than thousand different varieties of the fruit were displayed and the occasion was attended by the then President of Syria, Adib Al-Shishakli.

The magnificent quality of Daraya's grapes continues to be celebrated. Photos of them adorn websites mentioning the town and the fruit was even used as a symbol of the uprising there on rebel posters and in campaign literature. Locals I have talked to have their own theories on what has made their grapes so particularly special. Most put it down to the area's rich red soil and the life-giving waters of the Western River, which sates the thirst of the bounteous vines. One man I talked to described Daraya's grapes as 'sweeter, bigger, tastier and more colourful than any others'. He even believed that there is a spiritual explanation, telling me that, 'The farmers who plant the vineyards do so with the most noble and good intentions. They grow them for all the community, for pleasure rather than profit. Their celebration of this special gift from God is infused in the flavour of the fruit.'

Indeed, the grape has been a source of great pride and celebration in the town, adorning websites and local literature. But, this being a Muslim country, wine has never been something that has fuelled the locals. Instead, in early 2011, for those in Daraya seeking refreshment and shade during the heat of a baking summer's day, when temperatures often top forty degrees, there were a multitude of coffee houses, restaurants, Internet cafés and computer game shops to choose from.

But it was in the relative coolness of the evening that the town was most alive. Older people gathered to play backgammon, chess or cards, while the young whiled away the hours in tea houses near much loved football grounds. One of the most popular of these was the Champions Café. Its walls were covered with big-screen televisions which streamed the most important football matches, many of them international. On sultry summer evenings crowds would gather around wooden tables in the café's garden area, many dressed in the colours of Barcelona or Real Madrid, easily the most popular teams. Their exuberant, near deafening cheers and shrieks would fill the evening air, briefly masking the roar of motorbikes pelting through the dusty streets, the riders accelerating hard until their front wheel rose into the air. Similar sounds would engulf the football ground next to the café from 2 p.m. every Friday afternoon. This was when the hotly contested local league matches were played. There was no Ronaldo or Messi here, no luxury stadium with directors' boxes and thumping pop music, but the crowds were every bit as passionate.

Only one other kind of event in Daraya could compete with football matches when it came to decibels: weddings. Even if you were not getting married yourself, or actually attending, you would soon know if one was happening, such was the scale and pageantry of these events.

As in many Islamic countries, traditional weddings in Syria take place in two halves, divided according to gender. The men hold one ceremony, often in public, and the women attend another, in some kind of ceremonial indoor venue. And to put it into colloquial terms, the idea was to 'large it' as much as possible. The man's family would aim to stage the biggest and brashest event possible. Those attending would be regaled with mouth-watering food and luxury cakes. Ideally the event should appear to be costing a lot of money, which it probably was. Meanwhile, over at the women's ceremony, competition was the order of the day. If your neighbour or friend looked stunning, then you needed to look even better. It was the time to roll out your most beautiful dress, stylish shoes and most opulent jewellery. And if you had a daughter, she was to do the same – for this was the ideal occasion to show her off. After all there would be other mothers there, on the look-out for prospective wives for their sons. Yet despite all the mind-blowing expense, preening and posing, everyone at these events seemed to have a thoroughly good time. No slinking off straight after the knot was tied; these boisterous occasions would often carry on into the early hours.

For those without a wedding to go to, there was always Koushak. This gleaming, modern ice cream café was a favourite haunt for many. Walking through its doors, customers entered a dreamworld of elegantly arranged ices, sweets and desserts of every colour and flavour. Strawberry red iced lollies, chocolate brown tarts, tangerine lollies and cream cakes. Housed in the centre of town, this temple of temptation drew customers from all over the area, even from neighbouring Damascus. Those who lacked the money to buy would come to look, such was the draw of Koushak. The shop's recipes were a tightly guarded secret – so much so, that the proud owner would often draw the curtains and lock all the doors when concocting his ice creams.

A short walk down the road from Koushak, just past Daraya's busy clothes market and a popular hummus and falafel store, was the Central Toaster shop, which sold all sorts of delicious-smelling toasted nuts and seeds. The aroma would drift down the road, enticing helpless people through its doors. On returning home, the shop's customers would lay out these moreish snacks in small ornate bowls, and nibble them while watching television – this was evidently Daraya's answer to popcorn.

Daraya was clearly a very tightly bonded, close-knit place where many people were related and so just about everybody knew each other. It was also a town with many natural attractions. On Fridays and Saturdays Darayans often sped off to the town's western fringes. There, among the area's scenic orchards, they could rent attractive and in-expensive farmhouses. Young and old would enjoy relaxing in the shade, chatting, playing card games and holding bar-becues. In an environment such as this, they could forget about the many irritants of daily life, like the haphazard electricity supplies. Blackouts were common, sometimes lasting for many hours at a time. The mains water supply was often unreliable too. The provision of some public services was also rather threadbare. Until shortly before the war, there was no public hospital in Daraya, so anyone needing treatment had to go to a private one. These were not so expensive, but many families on lower incomes still struggled to pay their bills. Another thing that pushed up the cost of living, not to mention everyone's blood pressure, was corruption. If you wanted something done by the local council services, you usually had to pay; somebody, somewhere would demand a 'facilitation' fee.

Though perhaps unfamiliar in its landscape and customs, Daraya in the early twenty-first century was, in its fabric and soul, little different to the average European or American town. People shared the same busy lives, families, responsibilities and preoccupations. The same often tiring and time-consuming commute into work. Rents and house prices were much cheaper than in central Damascus, so Daraya had become a bit of a commuter town for many on lower incomes. Although the national economy was growing each year and inflation stood at a fairly low 4 per cent, most local families had to work hard to get by. Whether they laboured on a farm, in a government office or in one of the town's many furniture factories, money was tight. Not that this dented Daraya's strong sense of community; its people took great pride in a town some had lived in for generations.

But this apparently peaceful life was about to change.

Daraya is a town with a proud and fascinating history of protest and a strong will to survive. From around AD 730 the town was already acquiring a rebellious reputation. Its inhabitants had developed strong grievances against the Umayyad authorities, who they believed favoured a rival tribe.[4] Daraya also played a prominent role during the Crusades. Following a clash between two Muslim armies there in 1139, a large number of local fighters, who were on the losing side, were put to the sword.[5]

By 2011, the vast majority of the town's population were

Sunni but Daraya was also an important place for Shi'ites. In 2003, a holy Shi'ite shrine was established there and the town was then added to pilgrimage routes. Until recently, there was also a Greek Orthodox Church in Daraya and a strong Christian presence, church bells ringing out in solidarity with the anti-regime protesters in March 2011.

In recent times, Daraya had become best known for its non-violent protests. When, for example, in 1998 a group of twenty-three young men and women were thrown out of a local mosque for studying the Quran with a progressive cleric, instead of giving up and going home they simply sat on the ground outside and carried on with their meeting.[6] Within a short period of time, the Majmu'at Shabab Daraya (Youth Group of Daraya) grew to around fifty members. They held open debates, screened films and called on people to take responsibility for their own destiny. Obviously intent on practising what they preached, the group decided that it was up to them to clean the streets of Daraya and with brooms in hand, they set about sprucing up the town. They decided that it was also their responsibility to clean up corruption too, and each month their members published charts revealing their next targets.

Daraya Youth Group believed that reading and learning were essential if they were to truly change society for the better, yet getting hold of the right books had not been easy. Most young people could not afford to buy from bookshops so their main source of literature was their local mosque where the choice of reading material was limited. There were several small libraries in the town but these were often not accessible to the general public. In response the young radicals collected hundreds of books donated by people all over Daraya and created the town's first free public library.

A placard outside proudly labelled it the 'Paths of Peace Library'. Keen to do things properly, they knocked on the doors of various government offices, asking for a licence for their new endeavour. They were told to go ahead with their plans while the relevant authorities considered their request. Yet almost as soon as the Paths of Peace Library opened, the police closed it down and confiscated all its books.[7]

On a wider scale, one of the group's political campaigns involved demonstrating in solidarity with the Palestinians who, at the time, were being attacked in the Jenin refugee camp in the West Bank. Their biggest demonstration took place in 2003, against the US invasion of Iraq, when the group's young members marched, one hundred strong, through the centre of Daraya in silent protest. Given that Syria's government also opposed the invasion they might have thought that such an action would have been applauded by the authorities. Instead, many were jailed for failing to seek official permission for the march.[8]

Discontent with the ruling regime simmered on in Daraya, but it was to be another eight years before local passions were ignited again by the extraordinary Arab Spring.

# Chapter Two

S hortly after the demonstrations in Daraa and Damascus in 2011, pro-democracy protesters took to the streets of Daraya. Despite growing tensions caused by the deaths of the four demonstrators in Daraa, activists in Daraya were, as befitting the town's long history of non-violent protest, committed to keeping their rally peaceful. They called for widespread reforms, respect for human rights and democracy.

As was often the case in Daraya, and elsewhere in Syria, protesters had gathered first at a central mosque before pouring onto the streets after prayers. Given the large numbers, the protesters had initially wanted to meet at two much bigger mosques nearby, but were told that those were being watched by the security forces. Among the crowd that day was, Anas Habib, a twenty-eight-year-old former civil engineering student. Tall and slim, and dressed, when I first spoke to him, in a sober-looking khaki jacket and jumper, it was hard to picture him in the thick of the protests. But this seemingly reserved figure, who came across as being older than his years, evidently was in the thick of things. He told me how determined those around him were, despite the very real possibility that the security forces might react violently. 'When we left Al Abbas mosque,' he told me, 'my heart was beating like a drum and my hands were shaking.

Other young people soon joined us and before long we had a group of around fifty protesters, all shouting the words: "Syria is free. Freedom only!"'

Anas and his fellow protesters began to take comfort from their numbers and shared sense of purpose. Their chanting grew louder and louder, as they called for democratic reforms, their confidence growing. Before long a rival crowd of government supporters began massing in front of the protesters, yelling pro-Assad slogans. Some of these people were possibly plain-clothed security officials but many others would have been from religious minorities, be it Alawite Muslims like President Bashar al-Assad, or Shia Muslims, Christians and secularists. Many of these groups might have had little intrinsic love for Assad himself, or for many of his policies, but they believed that he did at least allow them to continue practising their faiths in peace. They feared that if he was toppled, rebel Sunni Muslim extremists might take control, and bring religious freedom to an end. Many of the young protesters at that time were not initially calling for the president to step down, however. They were demanding major reforms, such as fully democratic elections, as well as freedom of speech and other civil rights.

Anas remembered: 'We wanted to encourage more people to take part in the demonstration and break the wall of silence and fear that had kept us quiet for so long. This barrier of oppression had been built up over half a century, and we were determined to knock it down.'

Like many others in the anti-regime crowd, Anas relished the chance to protest – not just against the current injustices in Syria but past ones too. Back in February 1982, President Bashar al-Assad's father, Hafez, had used extreme violence to put down an uprising by the Muslim Brother-hood in Hama, which had left hundreds of his loyal troops dead. In retribution, Hafez al-Assad's soldiers had gone on an orgy of blood-letting, levelling entire neighbourhoods of the city. As many as 20,000 people were thought to have been slaughtered. Nobody is sure of the exact total because few, if any, independent journalists were able to witness what had happened. But over the following years the scale of the massacre began to emerge. Although protests now focused on the deeds of the son, those of his father had not been forgotten. This memory had left a festering wound in the minds of many across the country that had been passed down from one generation to the next.

It soon became clear that the anti-Assad protesters were winning the shouting match. The more they yelled, the more bystanders joined their fast-swelling ranks. At one point, Anas told me, more than 1500 protesters, most of them young men and women, marched together, dwarfing the two hundred or so Assad loyalists before them. But, although heavily outnumbered, the pro-regime crowd maintained their defiance. Some, sensing they were losing the war of words, tried to start a physical fight. Missiles and fists began to fly, all in an attempt to goad the chanting protesters into fighting back. It was around this point that Anas's father arrived at the scene. He insisted that his son come home immediately, and reluctantly Anas did what he was told. 'When I got home, my mother was crying. She had seen my face among the crowds on television. My dad said this was very dangerous because the regime's people would recognise me. I would be arrested, maybe jailed for life.' Indeed, Anas's father had good reason to fear for his son; he had only narrowly avoided arrest himself during the

Hama massacre of 1982 and knew that this regime was just as savage. Torture was common and some who went to jail were never seen again.

Later that evening, as Anas's adrenalin began to subside, his feelings of euphoria morphed into dread. Maybe his father was right, he thought. 'I started fearing for my life. I wondered about all the awful things that might happen to me in jail and what this would do to my parents. But at the same time this had been some day, one of the most important of my life. I knew I had to act, that I had to be true to my principles and in the end I decided there was no going back. I had chosen my path and would have to continue, whatever the price.'

The protests in Daraya were being led by Yahya Shurbaji, a thirty-two-year-old political activist and admirer of India's pacifist former leader, Mahatma Ghandi. Shurbaji had been campaigning for non-violent change with the Daraya Youth Group since 1998, and he practised what he preached. When pro-Assad soldiers were sent in to suppress the marches using increasingly violent methods, he and his brother Maan called on protesters in Daraya not to retaliate. Instead he brought bottles of water and flowers for them to give to the soldiers. This led Shurbaji to be nicknamed 'the man with the roses'. He insisted that the regime's security forces should be treated as human beings, even in a police state such as Syria.

Among the many in Daraya to be impressed by Shurbaji and his methods was fellow activist, Ghiath Matar, a twenty-six-year-old tailor. Sceptical at first, Matar had been won over after he noticed that following the gifts of water and flowers, pro-Assad soldiers behaved differently, making eye contact with the demonstrators and treating them better. He believed that this could truly change things and Matar soon became closely associated with Shurbaji, acquiring the nickname 'Little Ghandi'. His dreams, however, were not to be fulfilled and over the next couple of months, the violence meted out by government troops got worse rather than better. Several activists were reported to have been killed in Daraya and many more died elsewhere in Syria.

This did not deter a group of local women from setting up a civil grassroots movement which they named 'Daraya's Free Women'. Their first act was to stage a sit-in, demanding the release of prisoners of conscience. But any notions the women had of peacefully persuading the regime to cooperate were soon dashed. Instead of listening to them, the security services opened fire, leaving many of the women in fear of their lives. Still, as the weeks went on, in the spirit of the town's history and philosophy, demonstrators in Daraya continued to express themselves peacefully.

But the regime responded with increasing oppression, and it wasn't long before they came for the rebels' peaceful leader. On 6 September 2011, Ghiath Matar, Yahya Shurbaji and his brother, Maan, were arrested. Four days later, Ghiath's mutilated body was returned to his mother and pregnant wife. The man whose last words to his friends were, 'Remember me when you celebrate the fall of the regime and . . . that I gave my soul and blood for that moment', had paid with his life.

The reverberations following Ghiath Matar's death and the disappearance of Yahya and Maan Shurbaji, were felt across Syria and around the world. As a mark of the esteem in which 'Little Ghandi' was held, his funeral was attended by the ambassadors of the United States, Japan, Germany,

France and Denmark. The UN called on the Syrian government either to release Yahya and Maan or explain their fate. Neither request was, or ever has been, granted. In one of his last posts on Facebook, Ghiath Matar had written: 'We chose non-violence not from cowardice or weakness, but out of moral conviction; we don't want to reach victory by having destroyed the country.'

As time went on, the government forces responded with increasing ferocity. On some occasions demonstrators were fired on using live ammunition, and there were also cases of people being beaten to death. Without their inspiring leaders, peaceful defiance became difficult to sustain and rebel resistance in Daraya grew increasingly hard-edged. Former students who had been devoted to non-violent revolution were beginning to take up arms, many seeing this as a necessary form of protection from the Syrian security forces.

Rateb abo Fayez, a fresh-faced eighteen-year-old economics student with an immaculately cropped short, dark beard, was typical of many protesters at that time. He had been convinced that non-violent protest was the best way to bring positive change to the country, but, he told me, the brutal actions of the security services he witnessed during the demonstrations were putting this policy under growing strain. One incident in particular sticks in his mind: 'One protester was trying to get away and ran into a butcher's shop. A group of government soldiers rushed in after him. A few minutes later they all came out, dragging the protester with them. His body was covered in blood. I'll never get that awful picture out of my head, I'll never forget it.' After that incident, Rateb said, the security forces went from attacking protesters with wooden sticks to using weapons and many people died. 'This,' he said, 'was the turning point. The violence had escalated to the point where it had become a war.' For Rateb and his friends, there was no going back from here.

Within the next few days Rateb joined the Free Syrian Army (FSA), a country-wide force comprised of a hotch-potch of armed anti-regime groups. His younger brother Raed also joined several months later. Conscription to the Syrian military is compulsory for all men from the age of nineteen. University students are allowed to postpone their enlistment, but must still serve on finishing their studies. Many of the young men in Daraya would have been conscripted to the government forces, but escaped this fate because from late 2012 it was beyond the regime's control. Rateb's father, a carpenter, had been shot in the arm by a sniper, so was unable to join the rebels. Instead, he volunteered to work with the medical teams who treated the mounting number of injured civilans, while his wife looked after the family home.

In November 2011, the Arab League suspended Syria from its ranks and imposed sanctions on the country, accusing its government of failing to implement an Arab peace plan. This brought a renewed mood of optimism and defiance in Daraya. The town's history of peaceful protest, combined with the recent death of 'Little Ghandi' and the disappearance of his colleagues, had got it noticed around the world.

Around this time Anas started a diary. On 1 January 2012 he wrote:

Today for the first time, the flag of the revolution flies above the main palace. The regime's flag was earlier taken down. It is such a beautiful and indescribable feeling to see our flag flying over the city. A delegation from the Arab League visited us. This is the first foreign delegation to come here. It makes me realise that it is down to us alone to explain the revolution to the world. I usually spend this month of the year preparing for my exams but I've decided to skip some of them and get authorisation to postpone my studies. This way I can avoid being conscripted into the army that is killing our people. For now, things look very unclear and no one knows what will happen to us. But we are hopeful the regime will fall soon.

Also still hopeful that the world was listening, was a group of mainly 'citizen journalists' in Daraya, around half of them women. At the end of January 2012, they published the first issue of a weekly underground revolutionary news-paper, *Enab Baladi* – Grapes of my Country, in honour of Daraya's famous grapes. The paper's stated aim was to peacefully advance a democratic society via credible, in-dependent and in-depth reporting. Before long, however, one of the publication's most prominent founders, Nabil Shurbaji, was arrested in Daraya by the security forces and is believed to have died in jail. These were his last reported words: 'Dear Lord, exonerate us from any blame for any bloodshed or killing in Daraya, for any reason or justifica-tion, and exonerate us from blame in any act of torture or injustice perpetrated against any human being whomever they may be.' Despite Shurbaji's death and the ongoing conflict, more than a million copies of *Enab Baladi* have been distributed since the launch of the newspaper.

In February 2012, the conflict escalated from an ongoing series of skirmishes to all-out war. On the third of that month, President Assad's forces began shelling the city of Homs. The bombardment lasted a month, before regime troops took control of part of the city. But by July the fighting had spread to Aleppo, Syria's biggest city. International efforts at mediation continued to fail and in August 2012 Kofi Annan quit as the UN/Arab League's Envoy.

The military situation in Daraya was deteriorating by the day. As Anas recorded in his diary:

the regime's forces have been deployed right across Daraya. The government has erected checkpoints in front of mosques. When people began demonstrating after prayers they started shooting at them.

And the very next day:

The funerals of those killed yesterday were held early so that the martyrs could be buried in the morning. These did not go as planned. Government forces showed up and shot at protesters. I am horrified to say that now twenty-four of them have been killed in just two days. My dear cousin was among them. He was nineteen years old. His death represents a disaster for both myself and my family. We are so very sad and fear the same fate may await us all soon. We have called this Black Day.

The use of brutal force by President Assad's security forces to crush the uprising was now rebounding on his regime. In July three of his senior security officers were killed by fighters from the FSA. The following month a member of Assad's own regime spoke out against his ruthless suppression of those who opposed him. The Syrian Chargé d'Affaires in London, Khaled al-Ayoubi, resigned saying that he was no longer willing to represent a regime that had committed such violent and oppressive acts against its own people.

And then the eyes of the world returned to Daraya. Austin Tice, a former US Marine working in Syria as a free-lance journalist, vanished three days after his thirty-first birthday. The last place he had been seen was Daraya. As a younger man, Tice had risen to the rank of second lieuten-ant in the Marines, but after two deployments he left the military, enrolling in law school at Georgetown University in Washington. However, this didn't work out for him and he re-enlisted as a reservist. But after seeing active service in Afghanistan, he left the army for a second time. Rather than going back to his law studies, Tice decided to pursue a career as a freelance war photographer and journalist, making his own way to Syria via Gaziantep in southern Turkey.

This was Tice's calling and he went on to report from many areas of Syria, including war-ravaged Homs, pro-viding copy for the *Washington Post*, the BBC and NPR. He travelled the country in the company of a Syrian fixer and translator to whom he had been introduced in Turkey. During this time Tice met fellow US journalist James Foley, who was later captured and beheaded by IS fighters. Just four months on, Tice himself suddenly vanished.

Nobody knows for sure what happened to him, but it is widely believed that Tice was abducted by the Syrian secur-ity services. Most of his work had, after all, been done while embedded with rebel fighters and he had also reported on human rights abuses allegedly committed by the regime, so he would probably have been viewed by Damascus as anti-government. However, the Syrian regime swiftly denied that it was holding him. The following month a grainy video appeared on YouTube, in which a convoy of vehicles driving across a barren and hilly landscape suddenly comes to a sudden halt, and a group of men in what looks like traditional Afghan dress and black headbands approaches. Armed with automatic rifles and rocket launchers, they jump out of a white pickup truck shouting 'Allahu Akbar!' while manhandling a bearded hostage, closely resembling Austin Tice, and then disappear from view.

No group has claimed responsibility for Tice's abduction and some experts who have studied the video believe it was staged. They point to the fact that the Afghan-style dress seen in the film was not something worn by Syrian rebel groups at the time, and they even suspect that the video could have been made by the Syrian security forces in order to deflect accusations of his abduction from themselves.

Soon after the disappearance of Tice, Daraya was surrounded by tanks. Then, following reports of renewed attacks by the FSA on the nearby Mezzeh air base, the town's electricity supply was cut off. Anas became increasingly alarmed. He noted in his diary:

Although traditional visits to the tombs of the martyrs have gone ahead, as usual worrying news is coming in from outside the city. We hear that the regime has taken control of much of Western Ghouta and has started attacking Kafarsousa and al-Moadamyeh. The Free Syrian Army of Daraya is helping its al-Moadamyeh branch and victims of the fighting were carried all the way to our village for treatment. I was in the house when my cousin's husband was brought to us. He had been shot in the back. It's a really bad injury and we've been told that he is going to be paralysed from the waist down. We are all sad and very worried about him.

On Monday, 20 August, Daraya was shelled for the first time. This was followed, the next day, by a lengthy artillery bombardment. Abdul Basit al-Ahmar, a former business and economics student at Damascus University, who had quit his studies during the protests that year, was in Daraya at the time. This tall, sensitive and idealistic young man told me: 'It all began when the Syrian regime started ordering civilians in Daraya to hand over the names of any activists or peaceful protesters who were opposed to the government. When we told them that we weren't prepared to do this, the security forces went wild and began attacking people.'

When news of the growing number of casualties reached Abdul Basit, he went to a recently set-up field hospital to offer his help. Even though he had no medical training, the staff there were so overwhelmed they immediately took him up on his offer. He was staggered by what he saw – patients, so many of them covered in blood and some with limbs missing – filled the corridors.

Soon after Abdul Basit began helping out at the hospital, government forces launched another attack on Daraya. Rebels in Homs and Aleppo had been bombarded earlier that month, now it was Daraya's turn to be repeatedly bombed. The town, with its long history of resistance to many of the policies of both Bashar al-Assad's regime and his father's government before that, was a particular irritation for the ruling family. It also lay on the very doorstep of Damascus. Insurrection so close to the seat of power had to be contained. Many of those injured in the offensive were badly hurt and the doctors were so deluged with casualties they simply could not cope. Abdul Basit watched on, desperate to help, 'But I didn't have enough experience at that time to treat most of them, and that really distressed me,' he told me. 'I remember a badly injured child being brought in to the hospital. Even experienced doctors couldn't do anything for him. He was in a terrible state and they just didn't have the medicines and equipment they needed. I watched his life slowly ebbing away. It was the first time I had seen anybody die like that, never mind a young innocent child.'

As the bombardments continued, Abdul Basit found he was unable to leave Daraya's makeshift field hospital, due to the constant stream of casualties being carried in. 'The scene at the hospital was awful,' he recalled. 'There was blood and suffering everywhere. It was made even worse by the fact that the hospital was housed in what had once been a school. So alongside the blood and screaming people with terrible injuries were bits and pieces from the classrooms. Places where innocent children had so recently been having their lessons. Instead of caring for these children and protecting their school, the government's soldiers were destroying it and trying to kill all those inside.'

There wasn't much the doctors could do for the many casualties brought in, and it soon became more a case of delaying death rather than preventing it. Volunteers like Abdul Basit used the limited skills they had learned so recently to try to stop bleeding and to dress wounds, but the makeshift hospital was in absolute chaos. Staff did their best to cordon off areas for those needing intensive care, desperately trying to send those less severely injured to other, better equipped, hospitals. But government soldiers simply turned them back, leaving Abdul Basit and his colleagues with no choice but to deal with them. He told me: 'I won't forget the smell of blood until the day I die. It seemed to be everywhere. But people did what they could for each other. Every now and then I would stand amid all this horror and ask myself: how can the government kill its own people like this, just because they asked for reforms?'

Abdul Basit was witnessing both the very worst of what humanity could do, and also the very best – a precursor to the ways in which the citizens remaining in Daraya would help each other. In those early days, those less badly injured would support others while they waited for a doctor; local residents risked coming in to give food to both patients and doctors and, after seeing the terrible overcrowding in the hospital, many offered to house those still able to walk. Nobody knew how long the situation would last, yet people were willing to share what little they had with the injured.

Abdul Basit told me that during this period, a doctor he was working with at the hospital heard that his mother, sister and niece had been badly injured. They were all brought in for treatment, yet even though they were his relatives, the doctor did not prioritise them over others. There was a triage rule: patients were given treatment according to who would benefit the most, as some patients had little chance of survival. When their time came, the doctor did what he could for his relatives, but his young niece was beyond saving. Abdul Basit recalled: 'There wasn't really anything he could do for her. I'll never forget that. She died just a few hours after being brought in. He knew he couldn't save her but could prevent others from dying. After she passed away, he kissed her before giving her body to the burial team. He then carried on with his work.'

*

That offensive was the precursor to what is alleged to have been one of the worst massacres of the Syrian civil war.

In August 2012, hundreds of pro-Assad soldiers backed by helicopters and armoured vehicles poured into Daraya and sealed off all escape routes. Rebel fighters in the town withdrew, in what they said was an effort to help limit civilian casualties.

Adel, a cousin of Anas Habib, recorded much of what he witnessed over those terrible days:

> Soon after arriving in Daraya the regime's forces arrested fifty people. I was among them. Local civilians came out onto the streets to see what was happening and could hear people being killed. They all then waited for their turn to come. Among them was a twenty-year-old man who was with his fiancée. They executed him right there on the spot in front of her. Then they took his fiancée to a place nearby and raped her. She complained to an officer but he just shrugged and laughed. He didn't care. She had wrongly assumed that he had no idea what was happening and would have stopped it if he did.

Adel went on to tell me that a cousin as well as his neighbour and their baby had also been killed by the soldiers. Pictures of their bodies were broadcast by the pro-government Addounia TV channel. He had only found out what had happened to them after talking to two young men who had managed to flee the carnage.

Anas's father was distraught. He decided to get his son and the rest of the family out of the town and head to their farm in the neighbouring village of Jdayde. Everyone packed quickly and jumped into their battered old car. They took side roads in the hope of avoiding army checkpoints but as their car turned a corner, soldiers started shooting above their heads – a warning to them not to try and drive away. Anas's father approached the checkpoint slowly, then stopped the car. Everyone feared the worst after witnessing what had been happening over the previous few days. But, fortunately, after searching the family's car and finding nothing incriminating, the soldiers let them go.

By around noon that same day, pro-Assad soldiers had taken control of the whole town. They chased away the last remaining FSA fighters and began to clear the streets. That done, they pushed into people's homes as part of a door-to-door search and arrest operation. While all this was happening other members of Anas's extended family fell victim to random attacks: 'We heard news that a missile had hit an apartment block near my cousin's house,' Anas told me. 'My aunt and her daughter and nephew tried to take refuge in their basement, but were hit by another missile as they made their way down there. It was terrible. We didn't find out what had happened to them until we reached our farm. It was heartbreaking. No one was able to bury them, so their bodies were moved to a no-man's-land where they were finally buried with a group of other people who had been killed.'

The army continued to arrest people in large numbers and soldiers searched the city looking for weapons, as well as anti-regime activists. By all accounts this first group behaved comparatively well. But, as Adel recalled, the second wave of soldiers that arrived were very different: 'They were savage. They arrested lots of people and executed some of them in groups. People were just shot where they stood.

Others were tortured in front of their families. We heard reports of massacres happening all over Daraya. These carried on the next day too. It was horrific, there were bodies everywhere. It was very hot and the city began to stink. To be honest, we were all petrified. We heard horror stories about gruesome killings taking place all around us. It felt like a terrible nightmare that would never stop.'

Abdul Basit, who had stayed in the hospital throughout the killings, told me that when the streets suddenly went quiet, he and some colleagues went outside for the first time in several days. 'After the massacre was over the government forces left Daraya. It was only then that many of us discovered the full scale of the horror. There were corpses everywhere. We started piling up bodies and taking them to the cemetery for mass burial. The atmosphere was so sad, so terrible. I remember that it was raining much of the time. It felt as if the heavens were crying with us.'

Reliable statistics are difficult to come by, and are hotly disputed, but according to local accounts as many as 700 bodies were discovered after the soldiers went on their door-to-door search. Men, women and children were said to have been dragged from their homes and executed. Local activists released video footage which purportedly showed five mass graves. In other videos, dozens of bodies are shown, piled up in a mosque.

On 25 August, government forces pulled out of the town, leaving behind an orgy of death and destruction. On arrival back in Daraya, Anas's family were greeted by relatives who were overjoyed that they were still alive. But he was later to write in his diary that many, many others had not been so fortunate:

I'm told that this massacre has led to the killing of more than 700 people, 514 of whom we can name. The dead includes 39 women and 62 children. 219 others were arrested and 115 people have disappeared. These are terrible days. They are like ones I had previously only heard about in history books. But one thing is for sure, this makes us more determined than ever to get rid of the regime.

Other reports put the number killed at less than 200. Claims that pro-Syrian government troops were responsible for all the killings were also disputed. When the journalist Robert Fisk, of the *Independent*, arrived in Daraya a few days later, he reported that according to some locals, FSA rebel fighters had carried out some of the killings because of a failed prisoner swap. Naturally, the Syrian state media blamed the rebels for the massacre, adding that Daraya had now been 'cleansed of terrorist remnants'. Yet such claims, fiercely denied by the rebels, were inconsistent with other detailed testimonies given by its civilian inhabitants. There were widespread reports that the few people left in Daraya who supported the regime had been tipped off before the massacre that troops were about to move in.

Over the days that followed the horrific killings, tens of thousands of people, especially the old and those with families, decided to flee the town in case the Syrian army came back. Within a few weeks, Daraya's population fell from around 80,000 to less than 8,000. Those who chose to remain were mostly dissidents, men escaping conscription from the army and others who had decided to fight the regime. All were now well aware what the consequences of their stand were likely to be.

Abdul Basit's family were among the hordes of fleeing

civilians. They, like many others, made for the homes of relatives near by. Although entering an area controlled by the regime, they would be unknown to the security services there. He told me:

> My family decided to leave because they were worried about the safety of my brothers and sisters. They left after four days, but I decided to stay. My dad didn't try to dissuade me, in fact he encouraged me to remain. He told me, Son, you are doing the right thing. My mum was clearly very worried about me, but she didn't actually ask me to go with them. I remember, as if it were yesterday, the last time I saw her. I kissed her hand and she looked up at me and said, Are you sure you don't want to come with us? I replied, Mother, in your heart, deep down, you know I should stay here. She didn't shake her head or disagree. That was the last time I saw her or any of my family. I can't think of any words, any sentences that can describe what I felt when they left. I had such a happy and stable life and suddenly it was gone, torn apart by the Assad regime.

Having got to know Abdul Basit, I knew how difficult this parting must have been for him. A dreamy-eyed, gregarious, generous soul, he had lived all his life in Daraya, growing up on a small farm, helping in his father's household goods shop, going to school and praying in the local mosque. As Anas told me: 'Abdul Basit is a very social person who loves talking to people and having all sorts of interesting conversations. He is always interested in anything to do with the news, politics, the economy and he loves sport. He is very open-minded and strong-willed and always aims to do the very best he can in anything he undertakes.'

Like many Syrians, Abdul Basit was very family-oriented. He would take family members to the doctor if they were ill, go shopping with his mother, help his younger brothers with their homework, even buying them a computer with his savings. 'But,' he once told me, 'I suppose I am most proud of teaching my mum how to read and write. And, feeling like a friend to my dad, as well as being his son.' Watching them leave their home was one of the saddest moments of his life, though he consoled himself with the thought that at least they should be safer away from the battleground that Daraya was becoming.

Abdul Basit's family's instincts were right. The regime now pushed ahead with efforts to seal off Daraya from the outside world, cutting off the town's supplies of food and medicine. Efforts were also made to isolate the community by disrupting mobile and Internet networks there. There was a fear that calls to relatives in government-controlled areas might be monitored, so those remaining were reluctant to contact their loved ones, lest they be targeted by the security forces. Anyone who tried to flee or forage for food in the surrounding countryside risked either being arrested by the regime's soldiers at checkpoints near the town or being shot at by snipers.

The long and terrifying siege of Daraya had begun.

# Chapter Three

The siege was quick to take hold. On New Year's Eve, 2012, a light mist hung over Daraya, partially obscuring the scarred countryside beyond. The few civilians on the streets walked briskly in the chill air, listening for the sounds of planes overhead. But the fearful noise people began to hear was not coming from above. Instead the distant rumble of engines and metal-tracked wheels, which shook the ground, came drifting across the fields. As the din grew louder, accompanied by shouting and the squawk of military radios, there came the whistle of shells and then sickening booms as they hit their targets. The Syrian regime was launching another full-scale attack on Daraya. Over the following weeks, its forces pushed further towards the town, threatening to overrun it. Yet the few hundred or so rebel defenders, easily outnumbered and outgunned, stubbornly clung on.

By 17 February 2013, the UN high commissioner for human rights announced that the death toll in the Syrian civil war had passed 70,000, and that the figure was climbing rapidly. So, too, it seemed, were the levels to which the Syrian government would go in its efforts to win this conflict. In April that year the US Secretary of Defense, Chuck Hagel, announced that his government had assessed 'with some degree of varying confidence' that the chemical weapon sarin had been used on a small scale in the war – a charge denied by the Syrian regime. But just four months later, on 21 August 2013, as many as 1400 people were killed when shells loaded with that same poisonous gas rained down on Eastern Ghouta, a rebel-held area just to the east of Damascus. More than 700 people were also injured by the attack on nearby Daraya. In the wake of international outrage, the Syrian government again denied it had used such weapons. But a UN investigation team, which was allowed into the Ghouta area a few days later, found 'clear and convincing evidence' that sarin had been used. In his remarks to the UN Security Council, Secretary-General Ban Ki-moon declared that this was the 'most significant confirmed use of chemical weapons against civilians since Saddam Hussein used them in Halabja in 1988'. Global calls for action against Assad's regime followed, though just over a week later the UK Parliament voted against the use of any military action. It was just the first of many occasions on which the outside world said much, but did little.

At the outset of the conflict, Daraya's rebel force belonged to a bewildering assortment of groups affiliated with the FSA. They were, as Rateb abo Fayez put it to me, 'simply a bunch of young men who had opted to fight to protect our town from the regime's attacks'. Astonishingly, with limited help from elsewhere, just a few hundred of them continued to fight the comparatively mighty Syrian army into a standstill. It was not just their lack of numbers that made this surprising. It was also the fact that their members were not, at this point, a trained force. Nor were they initially cohesive in terms of allegiance. As the siege progressed most came to belong to just two rebel forces: The Martyrs of Islam Brigade or Ajnad al-Sham. These two groups in turn became allied to two larger coalitions – the Army of Conquest and the Western-backed Southern Front.

Rateb had never experienced war and was surprised when the conflict went quiet for a while after the first couple of attacks. But, he told me, this gave him and his fellow volunteers time to recruit and become better organised. Many of those Rateb fought with were locals, but others came from Damascus and elsewhere in Syria. They didn't look much like a regular army because none of them wore uniforms. Firstly because, being under siege, they did not have access to the materials needed to make these. Secondly, it was not a priority, given the numerous other urgent tasks that faced them, such as finding food, caring for the injured and, most crucially, fighting a vastly better-manned and equipped enemy. There was another significant reason too, as Rateb explained: 'We were all really just civilians, former university students. We didn't want to dress in camouflage like the Syrian army soldiers. Most of us hated the regime's forces and the last thing we wanted to do was look like the soldiers of a regime that had oppressed us for so long.'

According to Rateb, the rebel force in Daraya differed from many others across the country in the way that it was run and the relationship he and the other recruits had with their officers, in that it was much less hierarchical. Many of the FSA's leaders came from the same community as the men beneath them, had done similar jobs, and often lived in the same neighbourhoods. The biggest difference between rank-and-file soldiers and their commanders, it seems, was that the latter had more responsibilities. 'The relationship between ourselves and our officers was more of a brotherly one,' Rateb told me. 'It simply wasn't like a hierarchy. We lived in the same houses, talked about the same things, we even swapped clothes with each other. Our leaders didn't talk down to us, they were never patronising.'

In those early days, he and his comrades fought a hit-and-run style of warfare. They were not yet trained or equipped to take on the regime's forces in a more conventional manner. When government soldiers launched ground attacks on the town, Rateb told me: 'We hid in abandoned homes, opened holes in the walls or sat and waited for them to come within range of our guns. We had to fight this way because we only had simple weapons. They had tanks and all sorts of sophisticated arms.'

When there were no houses to hide in, they would either lay booby traps for the enemy or conceal themselves in ditches they had dug. This way, while unable to break the siege, they managed to stop further major advances by the government forces. Nonetheless, from late 2013 onwards, bombs, rockets and shells continued to bombard Daraya almost relentlessly. Both forces were well dug in, although the front line was rarely fixed. One side would advance and capture a few buildings, or even a street or a stretch of farmland, but would then be beaten back again when the other counter-attacked.

In urban areas, Rateb told me, the front line would often be just a street. On either side of the road snipers, whether rebel or regime, would crouch, out of sight. Some would hide on rooftops festooned with charred, twisted pipes and cables, or lurk behind peepholes in the walls of crumbling buildings. Sometimes, in more open areas, both sides would build a barricade of dirt and sandbags to screen themselves from the enemy. The front line in the fields around Daraya, however, was totally different and often difficult to decipher. Fighters, whether rebel or regime, often infested innocent-looking farm buildings, or would lie unseen in shallow trenches dug into the fields. Large areas of no-man's-land often separated both sides, filled with tempting swathes of fully grown crops swaying gently in the breeze. But such crops would be in the crosshairs of hidden snipers, so to harvest them would mean certain death.

Despite these minor advances and retreats, the government forces fought a war that was often static. Why risk casualties by trying to advance across the ground, when your forces had command of the skies? Let your planes destroy your enemies' homes and businesses, shattering morale, while your tightening siege slowly starved them into submission. If the bombs did not kill them, hunger eventually would. One of the first buildings to be flattened in central Daraya in the summer of 2013 was the iconic Koushak ice cream parlour and soon after that, just a few doors down, the once-lively Central Toaster store. Koushak's owners escaped with their lives. Sadly the family who ran Central Toaster were not so lucky.

From the outset of the siege, Syrian government forces would not allow international or local relief convoys into the town. At first Daraya managed to struggle on, thanks to the rich farming tradition of an area that had been the breadbasket of Damascus. But as the regime's forces slowly edged nearer, annexing farmland on the way, growing crops became more difficult. Even when the locals did manage to grow something they often could not harvest it due to the constant threat of snipers. The only option left for the resourceful people of Daraya was to grow food anywhere they could within the town, even though such efforts could never be enough. Hunger quickly became a fact of life and continued unabated. Smuggling supplies through rebel lines worked for a while but became increasingly dangerous.

There were, at least, brief ceasefires during which the bombs and shells stopped falling. While these did not mean that all snipers put down their rifles, it did give residents an opportunity to harvest crops or hunt for food, as well as a merciful break from the carnage.

It was during one of these treasured windows of calm that a group of young men, nearly all former students, began discussing more positive ways to spend their time. All had treasured their education, yet few had been able to graduate from university before the chaos took over. Most had initially thought that the unrest and then the fighting that followed would be over in a few months, and they would then be able to go back to their studies. When it became clear that peace was unlikely to return in the near future, they asked themselves what they should do in the meantime. How could they both keep their minds sharp and do something useful for their besieged and battered community? As Abdul Basit put it to me: 'The first couple of months were perhaps the toughest of all. It was hard to think of anything other than simple survival. So we began by planting vegetables, but soon realised that we needed to feed our minds too.'

This educated group of young people, most of whom were not currently involved in the fighting, did not want to sit around doing nothing but dodging bombs and watching their vegetables grow. They were brimming with ideas on how to make life more meaningful. One suggestion was that they should set up a centre where people could learn foreign languages. Many of those who were fluent in English or French had left Daraya when the fighting started, and language skills were needed to communicate with the outside world. There was still a handful of linguists who could provide lessons. Others suggested they could construct some sort of community centre, where talks could be given on everything from the Quran to history and sport; some proposed appointing a community scribe, who could record what was happening in Daraya as the siege went on. But the suggestion that ignited the biggest spark among them all was the creation of a store to help keep books safe from all the bombing and destruction.

These former students had studied a wide variety of subjects but they all had one thing in common – a love of books. Whether these dealt with chemistry or economics, poetry or physics, self-help or literature, it made little difference. The joy of gaining knowledge, understanding and empathy through books transcended such boundaries. Nor, I later came to discover, was the pleasure of reading the preserve of dedicated bookworms. Reading, learning, discussing the content of books was enjoyed by almost all who could read, irrespective of class, occupation or education. When Daraya's much-loved former town library had been destroyed by fire, the community at large had been distraught. Now this group hoped to create one that was even better.

When I first heard rumours of a secret underground library in Daraya, I thought it must surely be an exaggerated account of events. Yet over the months that followed I interviewed dozens of people there, some of whom sent me photographs, and it became clear that this really was true. Young people there were risking their lives each day to preserve books of all kinds, in the hope of using them to help build a better tomorrow. I was hugely inspired. I realised that this extraordinary story could more than fill a documentary, never mind a brief report in the news. Happily the BBC agreed and the project was commissioned. However, there were obvious obstacles. Such an in-depth programme would require on-the-ground interviews, copious sound recordings as well as photos and videos of those taking part. Yet, Daraya was surrounded by heavily armed Syrian government soldiers and even if I did come up with a plan to get into the town, the BBC would never allow me to go there, as an assignment of this sort would be viewed as near suicidal.

A colleague suggested I interview people over the phone, but that was a non-starter. After years of carnage much of Syria's mobile phone network was in tatters and there were few working landlines. And even if these were repaired, nobody left in Daraya could afford to make international phone calls or texts. While Skype, WhatsApp or other social media calls were free via Wi-Fi, this too was clearly only a partial solution. I had interviewed people in Syria over Skype before, and connections were often dire. Sometimes people could not get online for days and I had only limited time to make this documentary.

One factor greatly in my favour was the ingenuity of the people I was getting to know, remotely, in Daraya. Most were young, energetic and technologically savvy. Take the ever-resourceful, Malik al-Rifaii, Daraya's very own Mr Fixit. What many would say was impossible, was a mere walk in the park for this twenty-four-year-old former wedding-card vendor, turned media activist. At times, Malik, whose family owned a local petrol station, would disappear for days or even weeks at a time, leaving me wondering if he would ever return. But I soon learned there was no need to worry. Malik, who was constantly juggling numerous media tasks, always got back in touch in the end. So, one chilly but sun-blessed day in March 2016, I put a suggestion to him. When the Internet went down, might it be possible for local people to write or record answers to my questions on their mobiles, then send the recordings to me when the connection came back. Of course, Malik replied, without the slightest hesitation and in a heartbeat, my problem was just about solved.

Over the following months I got to know a number of people from different walks of life in Daraya. Most were involved in creating the town's secret library including fourteen-year-old Amjad, the self-declared Chief Librarian; Anas Habib, a dynamic, hard-working, former civil engineering student; Abdul Basit, former business and economics student, and now helping hand at the hospital; Ayham al-Sakka, a book-loving ex-dental student; Homam al-Toun, a former pharmacy student; Sara Matar, who was to become a courageously dedicated teacher, and Rateb abo Fayez, a rebel fighter who not only took his loans from the library into battle, but held a book club on the front line. Each of them took enormous risks in talking to me, each of them was impassioned, determined and utterly devoted to their secret library. All were to become my much treasured, long-distance friends.

When the Internet was working we would talk via Wi-Fi, sometimes managing long Skype and WhatsApp interviews, which gave me a valuable window into their everyday lives. When the Wi-Fi went down, which was often, they recorded audio diaries, or patiently tapped out messages to me on their phones. Sometimes I waited days for answers that I feared might never come. But just like

Malik, they always turned up. And it was this group who told me how they had transformed their dream of building a library into a reality.

The group received word that there were many valuable books in some of the homes that had been hit by bombs. Rain, sun and wind were fast destroying these as the shattered buildings that housed them often lacked windows, walls or even roofs. The group were told that some of these books were in small private libraries, of which many in Daraya had known nothing before the conflict. Weeks of enquiries followed, with all involved asking everyone they knew to suggest buildings where such endangered titles might be found. Then, armed with a long list of likely locations, the young men organised teams of volunteer search parties. They set out to rescue as many books as they could find, both for the sake of the absent owners and the community as a whole.

In the weeks and months that followed a treasure trove of books was retrieved from gutted homes, libraries and other buildings. Sadly, it was too late to save some, which had already been ruined by falling masonry or the weather. But day after day prized titles were pulled from the rubble, dusted off and carried back for safekeeping. Among these was a battered copy of *The Alchemist* by Paulo Coelho, Muhammad Imara's Marxist interpretation of Islam, compilation works by Syrian poets Adonis and Maram al-Masri, and somewhat aptly, an Arabic edition of Agatha Christie's *The Body in the Library*. The piles of rescued books also included complete sets of encyclopaedias, religious tomes, textbooks, novels and pamphlets.

As Abdul Basit and his friends began to appreciate the quality and quantity of the treasure they were amassing, they were inspired by a new idea. Rather than just store these rescued books, why not let people read them? That way the precious books could also provide knowledge and pleasure. Former students could use the books to continue their education, especially if they could find somewhere peaceful and safe to house the collection. Others could come and read simply for pleasure.

This was met with universal approval by the group, but there were concerns. Given that these books did not belong to those who had collected them, people couldn't be allowed to just come and take them away. The group would need to introduce a method of recording who had borrowed what, as well as where the books had come from. Then, as Anas told me, someone shouted: 'What about running the book store like a library?' And just like that, the idea was born.

Nobody can quite remember whose voice made that suggestion. Perhaps its owner was simply too modest to stake a claim to an idea that was to give hope and inspiration to so many – not only to the people of Daraya, but also to people around the world. The naturally poetic Abdul Basit, who could turn even the most mundane memory into a literary feast, hoped it would become a library for everyone. One for the benefit of the whole community, not just educated people such as himself and his friends. He told me: 'We believed that a place like this could store part of our heritage as well as the keys to our future. It would not only help us to continue our education but be there for anyone who loved reading. We also hoped to use the books we gathered to create a curriculum for local youths. This way they would have some sort of guidance, like we had at university, rather than just randomly reading any books they came across. In short, we wanted the library to become a minaret for Daraya.'

Another person who played a big part in setting up the library was a warm-natured, good-humoured dental student, Ayham al-Sakka. He was involved in many of the earliest efforts to find stock for the library. Whenever we spoke, I was struck by the infectious smile in his voice: 'Many of the books we rescued are treasured volumes, ones that their owners would have hated to lose,' he told me. 'Not only that but the wider community will gain much from reading them. They help us understand the outside world better. This is a golden opportunity not only to educate ourselves but to be able to take our minds off the death and destruction around us. By building the library we are creating a place where people can come and read, continue their education, or just relax. It is an oasis of normality in this sea of destruction.'

One priority, then, was to decide where to put the proposed library, in a besieged town where nowhere was completely safe. Ayham told me: 'We decided to place the library in a small street in one of the worst affected neighbourhoods. It was a road where nobody lived any more and all the buildings had been extensively damaged. Broken masonry littered the area. After looking around we discovered that the basement of one building was usable, even though the upper floors had been destroyed. This meant there was no sign of life, making it an unlikely target. So this, we decided, was where we would put our library.'

The basement was in a block on the corner of what had once been a busy street near the centre of Daraya. The white stone building that had stood above it was newer than the others nearby, but due to the extensive damage around it and the dust that covered everything, it no longer looked any different. The entrance to the basement was through a big black door at the rear of the building. No signs marked its existence and there was nothing to suggest that what lay below was any less barren than the shattered concrete corpse above it. Yet down those dusty stairs, beneath the terrible destruction, busy young hands were transforming the dingy, dusty space into a literary sanctuary. Overseeing it all was Abdul Basit. His voice danced as he told me: 'When we had finished converting the basement, our next task was to place a few sandbags around the entrance to help protect the library further. Despite all our efforts the doorway later become quite damaged, though thankfully not enough to stop us getting in.'

The often risky gathering of books had already begun in late 2013, but it would be several months before the library was ready to open. It needed shelves and seats and tables for those who come to read, and a system to keep track of who has borrowed what, and when. It is difficult to overstate the challenges that faced the secret library pioneers. First off, securing the raw materials and tools to make and assemble shelves; then ignoring nagging hunger in order to be able to function, let alone build anything. With only small amounts of food being smuggled into Daraya, hunger was a constant. One bowl of watery soup a day was often all anyone had to eat. Coping with the weather was another challenge – in summer, temperatures can top forty degrees and in mid-winter plunge to near freezing.

Then there were the bombs to contend with. To minimise this risk, most book-collecting missions were carried out in the early hours of the morning, when the regime's bomber planes were rarely in the sky. But there was no escape, whatever the time of day or night, from snipers.

Homam al-Toun was part of the secret library project from the start. He told me: 'The fear of being shot by snipers is with us twenty-four hours a day. We have to be very careful wherever we go. The biggest danger is to stand out too much, particularly against the skyline. That means we rarely go through open spaces, because they leave us very vulnerable. Instead we try to find routes through damaged buildings. These are usually quite enclosed which makes it hard for snipers to spot us. We have to think about this all the time. Become a target and you will be dead in seconds.'

I got to talk to Homam a little later than most of the group, but I soon felt that we had known each other for years. His warmth and helpfulness in response to my constant barrage of questions was touching. Like his friends, his love for the library infused everything he said, but there was never any sense of bravado creeping in or colouring his stories. In fact, I sometimes had to push Homam for more details of the daring exploits he and his friends had got up to during the early days of the siege. Many of these centred on getting books out of buildings that lacked usable doors, without being shot by snipers. 'I remember really wanting to get into one particular building that had lots of books inside,' he recalled, 'but its entrance was watched by snipers. We worked out that the only way to get in safely was by knocking a big hole through the wall at the back of the building. From there we made another hole in the ceiling and climbed up through that to the floor above where all the books were stored.'

Fortunately, this treacherous trip turned out to be well worth the trouble. Homam and his team were greeted by a glorious sight – rows and rows of books stacked neatly along the back wall. Some of them were large and very heavy, others lovingly bound with ornately lettered spines. Their next challenge was how to get this enticing collection back to the secret library. It had been hard enough for them all to get into the building, through holes in the wall and ceiling, when empty handed. Now they had to go back the same way clutching piles of weighty books. But having come this far, Homam and his friends were not about to be defeated by such logistical trifles. He told me: 'We wrapped the books in blankets, knotted them with ropes and then lowered them through the hole in the floor to the level below. Then other members of our group passed them through the gap in the wall at the back of the building. We escaped, laden with books, along the route we had come in.'

Sometimes the book-collecting parties brought ladders with them, given the difficulty of entering many bombed buildings via the ground floor. Piles of rubble frequently blocked doors and windows and it was often impossible or unsafe to climb over these to the floor above. Teams also brought along a large hammer or metal bar which they would use to knock entry holes in the walls. Anas told me how he and his friends would sometimes go through the side of one building straight into another, to avoid being seen by watching soldiers: 'Using this method we never actually went outside. We could stay inside the shells of the bombed buildings, using their walls as cover. But we had to be extremely careful. Snipers sometimes followed us in their sights, anticipating the next step we'd take, waiting until we crossed an open area.'

When it was impossible to take a route through the gutted buildings, the library teams had to cross open land. They did this in large groups so they could look out for snipers and give warnings of any danger. They also needed plenty of people to carry the books back, as some were very large. From time to time, the team managed to get access to a car despite the extreme shortage of fuel. To help counter the threat posed by snipers, the driver would hurtle through the streets as fast as possible, making the vehicle harder to hit. There were occasions when the older cars broke down or ran out of fuel, leaving their occupants with two options: either to leave the vehicle and run for cover, or to get out and push it out of sight. Going by what Anas told me, I got the feeling that abandoning their haul would have been a very last resort. 'I'll never forget the thrill of having a car full of books,' he told me, his eyes alight. 'That beat everything! Absolutely everything!'

Cars, unreliable as many of them were, were essential when rescuing books from more distant places, such as farms on the outskirts of Daraya. Such open places would often mean driving for hundreds of metres within range of snipers or even Syrian army positions. Yet, amazingly, such collections still went ahead. I find it hard to imagine how these young men were able to cope with the mental stress of putting themselves in such danger on such a regular basis. After all, most of those involved were not fighters and some had never even held a rifle. This was what Homam told me: 'We've gradually become more used to the dangers as the siege has gone on. When we get nervous, which is often, we do our best to see the funny side of the situation we are in and laugh about it. If we couldn't do this, I don't think we would be able to carry on. Also, it is always easier to do dangerous things when you are in a group. Somehow being able to share the fear lessens it. I suppose it is a case of safety in numbers.'

I asked Anas, the former civil engineering student, whether collecting books, however valuable, was really worth risking his life for. 'We have no intention of endangering anyone's life unnecessarily for the sake of gathering these books,' he replied, 'however much we want to get them. We always weigh up the risks and try to minimise them as much as possible. If you were to ask me whether we would carry on with a collection if it became clear that there was a 60 to 70 per cent chance that one or all of us would die, I would say no.'

Anas pointed out that when the local library was destroyed he and his friends had tried to rescue books from inside the remains of the building, but despite several attempts they'd had to give up. The risk of being hit by snipers was just too great. This, though, he told me, was one of only a few occasions when the team had been forced to abandon their plans. 'We believe that building this library is very important, not just for our minds but also for our souls. We are convinced that knowledge rarely comes when you sit doing nothing. It usually follows hard work and sometimes taking great risks.'

Soon after the siege began, a special council was created in Daraya. It aimed to keep all sorts of public services running while bombs and shells rained down. Unusually for a war zone, this civilian-run body had authority over the FSA fighters defending the town, and the two often worked together. From time to time the fighters would volunteer to come along on book collections, particularly when such trips involved going near the front line. Sometimes they even lent their cars to the group, if it was thought that a large number of books could be rescued.

Abdul Basit remembered one rather frightening trip that

he and his friends made with the help of local fighters. Their destination was the home of a local teacher who had built up an impressive collection of books. His house had been badly damaged and parts of it were in such a precarious state that they feared the rest might soon fall down. The team had wanted to retrieve books from this house for several months but had been stopped from doing so by the FSA, who thought the task was too dangerous as it was close to the front line. But after much persistence they finally got the go ahead on the condition that some experienced fighters went with them and no lights were used. Abdul Basit told me that while he understood the reasons behind the second condition, it brought problems of its own: 'We went late at night when the chances of being spotted by snipers were lowest. The trouble was that in the pitch-black we could hardly see our hands in front of our faces, yet we couldn't use torches or any other kind of light in case they were seen by the regime's soldiers.'

His group approached the derelict building from the third floor of another house on the left-hand side. This position was less visible to the nearby soldiers of the Syrian army. They could see that getting in to what was left of the house was going to be difficult. The doorway had been destroyed and the lower windows were buried in debris. But, on the advice of the fighters, the group gathered long planks of wood that were lying on the ground. 'We pushed a plank out through the window of the building we were in,' continued Abdul Basit, 'and then guided it through the open window of the teacher's house opposite. After several attempts, we managed to get it securely in place. As we were on the third floor it was high up and we could see that walking along that plank was going to be scary.'

So scary in fact that the FSA fighters who were with them insisted that only they should try walking across it. Abdul Basit and his friends were told to stay where they were. Two of the fighters then scrambled along the plank and managed to make it safely through the open window opposite. As soon as they were across they started gathering up the books in preparation for bringing them back across the wobbly plank. Abdul Basit watched, heart in mouth, as they struggled to keep their balance: 'It was all a bit like some sort of nerve-jangling action movie. As they walked along the plank it wobbled so badly that we were convinced they would fall. And it wasn't only their safety we were worried about. One loud noise would alert the soldiers and that might have been the death of us all.'

Then in a moment of forgetfulness, one of Abdul Basit's friends, unable to find the books he had been given to carry, broke one of the cardinal rules. He absent-mindedly turned on his powerful torch. Everyone froze. They might as well have had targets pinned to their chests. A light that bright made them sitting ducks for Syrian snipers. The FSA fighters were furious but knew that shouting at the man to switch off his torch would only make their plight worse. Instead they rushed towards him, intent on snatching the offending light from his hands. But by now the offender, having realised what he had done, was busy burying the torch deep in his pocket. Knowing they must all have been visible from hundreds of metres away, each man belatedly took cover behind the rear wall. They waited and listened for the crack of rifle fire. Eventually, having concluded that they had somehow not been seen, the men, now drenched in sweat, resumed their rescue of the books across the perilous wooden bridge.

Once they had finally managed that job, they went on to the next one. This task looked even more difficult. The books that needed to be rescued were on the fourth floor of a tall, battered building. The problem was it had no usable stairs. It was one thing climbing up the crumbling exterior clinging to wires and shattered masonry, quite another coming down again with a pile of heavy books. But after a fair bit of thought, a solution was finally found after one of them spotted some blankets in the rubble. They tied these around their waist before slowly clawing their way up to the fourth floor. Then, after gathering up the books, they wrapped them inside the blankets, tied a knot around their haul, and then lowered the bundles through the holes in each floor. Arduous and hair-raising though it was, Abdul Basit remembered it as being a good night's work: 'Some of the books we got were quite amazing and very valuable. We were delighted.'

But how, I wondered, did they choose which books to take? Or did Abdul Basit, Anas and their friends just collect whatever they found? 'To be totally honest with you,' Anas told me, 'when we first started setting up the library we were more after quantity than quality. We felt like the more books we had the better, even if some of them were duplicates of ones we already had. But since then we've got fussier and now only take ones that we haven't seen before. Among the books we value most are those which describe how people in other countries have dealt with traumas like ours. We hope that by reading these we can learn the best ways of rebuilding our nation when the fighting has stopped. They give us hope in dark days like these.'

And of course there were surprises along the way. Anas remembered one particular mission when, in the midst of gathering the books they were suddenly brought to a halt. 'One of the people with me shouted out, Hey guys, I've found treasure here! We all thought he must have come across a really interesting book and we turned around waiting to see what it was. But instead of proudly holding up some cherished work of literature, he was pointing to a large glass object on the ground. Look, he said, I found a jar full of honey! We all thought that was really funny. He had apparently found the honey jar carefully hidden behind some books.'

Sometimes rather than having to go out and rescue books from all sorts of dangerous locations, the books would come to the secret library. This did not happen much at first, because only a small number of people knew of its existence, but Abdul Basit told me that when word about their literary sanctuary started to leak out, more and more books began to arrive at its door. There were many people in Daraya who shared the same view; that it was better to take their books to a place of safety, than to leave them at home where they were likely to be destroyed by bombs or the weather. 'Many people have collections in their homes that they would like to share with others,' Abdul Basit told me. 'Most have few visitors now because it's so dangerous to go out, so their books just sit there not being read by anyone. We assure all donors that meticulous records are being kept of where all the library's books have come from and who their owners are. We put an identity number on the inside cover so they will be traceable if they are ever found outside the library and so whatever happens, we will always know who each book belongs to.'

Some of the books in the secret library belonged to Abdul Basit's family. His love of libraries stemmed from childhood, when friends and relatives would come calling, books in hand, at his family's home. They would lend their favourite ones to his parents, who would lend them theirs in turn. Now Abdul Basit was determined to donate some of his family's collection to the new library. Their old home had been bombed a few months earlier, but he went back and sifted through the ruins, putting any books that had survived into a large box. Some of the ones he found had belonged to his grandfather, whom he had always been close to, and it was to his home that Abdul Basit went next. His grandfather had left Daraya with his parents before the siege began, but they had managed to speak on the phone. 'I asked my grandfather if I could take some of his collection to the library so that others could benefit from them. I promised that they would all be well cared for. He didn't just agree to this, he was overjoyed. He praised all those involved with the secret library and said it would be a privilege to have his books there. I remember he once told me that one of the main measures of a person is how much they have learnt in life.'

Many of these books were more than thirty years old, but were in very good condition. Abdul Basit told me how proud he felt, knowing that the entire collection had been read by all his family. First by his grandfather who had chosen to buy them, then his mother and father, and most recently by Abdul Basit and his three brothers. And now, he said proudly, 'all in Daraya can read them too.'

Having seen photos of the secret library sent to me by Abdul Basit and Malik al-Rifaii, I was interested to know where everything in it had come from. For instance, what about the rows and rows of shelves I could see in the pictures? Some were of dark polished wood, while others appeared to have been hewn from a rougher material. Anas told me that much of the wood had been pulled from walls, ceiling struts and the staircases of gutted public buildings, shops and other businesses. In fact, in many cases, the wood had come from the very shelves that the collected books had been sitting on when they were found. Abdul Basit was particularly keen on this, telling me: 'We tried whenever possible to bring with us the shelving that the books were on when we rescued them. It felt right to do this because it meant the books would continue to be displayed in the same way their owner had stored them. This, of course, helped solve our shelving shortage but we also did it out of respect for the people from whose homes these books had come.'

In the early days of the library, the group was very hesitant about taking larger items from people's houses, even though they had been abandoned and lay in ruins. They felt guilty because the furniture did not belong to them, but then they decided they could treat the furniture like they had the books. The names and addresses of owners were written or carved underneath, and the group did their best to contact the owners to tell them what they had done, and check they were happy about it.

I asked Anas how he and his friends had managed to transport these, often-large, pieces of furniture to the library. He told me that when possible they borrowed any car they could get and loaded the tables and chairs onto it. This left me with the rather surreal picture of various dilapidated old cars being driven around war-torn Daraya with couches, comfy chairs and desks piled on their roofs. One can only presume that some of this activity must have been spotted by the regime's snipers, who infested parts of the town. What would they have made of it all?

What too, I wondered, did others in Daraya make of this devotion to collecting books? In a town whose inhabitants were virtually starving, did some not think that these young, dynamic men should be putting their energies into collecting food instead? I put this to Anas who looked at me down the flickering video link as if I had asked the most ridiculous question possible: 'Mike, I haven't come across anyone who has said that,' he told me. 'And had they done so, I would have told them that just like the body needs food, the soul needs books.'

Not, I thought, an answer I could argue with.

# Chapter Four

The creation of Daraya's secret library at a time when Syria was being torn apart by civil war may seem bizarre. Yet writing and a love of literature have infused the region's cultural history for thousands of years. A passion for poetry and prose and the exploration of just about every subject known to man can be traced back millennia. And, perhaps even more significantly, what is now Syria was once home to the world's first library, established around 4500 years ago – the Royal Library of the ancient kingdom of Ebla.[9]

This grand, early library was not home to books as we know them. Paper was only used for such purposes from around the second century AD in China. Instead, the first ordered collections of literature were engraved on clay tablets. Thousands of these were discovered in the palace archives of the ancient city of Ebla, in what is now northern Syria.[10] They were found in the mid-1970s by an Italian team of archaeologists during excavations at Tell Mardikh, about thirty-five miles south-west of Aleppo. The team unearthed a collection of more than 1800 complete clay tablets as well nearly 5000 fragments. Each one had been carefully arranged, kept upright on wooden shelves and appeared to have been grouped by subject. Clay tags found with the tablets suggest that this reference system was quite sophisticated. The library consisted of two rooms – one housing bureaucratic records, while the other was home to religious writing, literature and texts used for teaching scribes.[11]

The tablets were produced using a *calamus*, a triangle-shaped instrument able to make characters in moist clay. They revealed a wealth of information about trade and the production of goods that were exported at the time, including different kinds of beer. Soon after 2250 BC, the world's oldest recorded library was engulfed by fire but fortunately, the heat of the blaze acted like a kiln, preserving the writing on those tablets that hadn't already been baked. Once discovered, the tablets were moved to museums in Idlib, Aleppo and Damascus.

Yet preserving life and literature in Daraya in the summer of 2013 was increasingly difficult. As autumn approached, life under siege grew harder by the day. Many had thought that after bombarding their town for months, the pro-Assad forces would pack up and leave, having had their revenge. Yet the surrounding sea of green-uniformed men showed no signs of retreating.

When, during a brief ceasefire, thousands decided to flee to the neighbouring town of al-Moadamyeh, just to the west, many never made it to safety. Local residents told me that those who passed through government checkpoints – mostly young men of fighting age – were harassed, attacked and detained. The old city of Homs and towns in Eastern Ghouta near Damascus were in a similar situation. Not that pro-government forces were the only ones using siege as a tactic. For more than three years, mainly Sunni Muslim rebel fighters besieged the Shia towns of Foua and Kafriya, to the south-west of Aleppo. As in Daraya, this blockade prevented most food, medicines and other aid reaching tens of thousands of people. They too were regularly shelled, though the rebels had no planes to bomb them with. Meanwhile opposition fighters inside Aleppo, which was split between government and opposition forces, sometimes prevented supplies from reaching regime-controlled areas of the city. In an effort to stop such practices the UN called on all sides to allow the transit of food and medical supplies to civilians. This plea was to fall on deaf ears.

For those who remained in Daraya, life was grim and unrelenting. And yet, there was a formidable sense of resistance to the besieging army, and a huge collective purpose in keeping the town going. Many local men had stayed behind when their families had fled after the massacre, and the younger ones had joined the rebel fighters, taking up front-line positions against the far more powerful besieging government forces. Others set up classes for children, worked on local farms to help alleviate the increasing shortages of food, or did whatever they could to help keep water and electricity supplies running. And there were those who dedicated themselves to alerting journalists such as myself to what was happening inside their beleaguered town.

Among this group was a former English teacher, Muhammad Shihadeh. I first came across Muhammad on social media and his comments stood out as particularly measured and articulate. There was a gravitas and weight to his words. This impression was further borne out by a photo I saw of him: a man in his mid-thirties, with a small beard and thinning black hair, his eyes filled with a steely determination. He had the look of the kind of teacher you liked and admired at school – kind and good-natured, but not a person to cross. And in the early days of the siege, he had indeed taught English to both children and adults and became widely known as 'The Professor', though this sobriquet applied to his approach to life rather than his job. He was a man people of all ages would come to for help and guidance. 'I would describe Muhammad as a very mature person,' Anas Habib told me. 'He is very far-sighted in the way he sees and understands life around him. He's an extremely calm person. He even walks calmly and sits calmly. He's the sort of person who wins your respect as soon as you meet him, it's almost automatic. He's got this sort of vibe around him.'

It was that vibe that made me a little wary of contacting Muhammad at first. I worried that he might find my investigation into the town's secret library rather inconsequential, given the bombs and mortars falling from the skies and the hunger plaguing his community. With that thought in mind, I began our first conversation by asking him how the people of Daraya were coping with the ongoing siege. In a surprisingly relaxed and friendly tone, Muhammad told me that many of the town's best educated citizens had chosen not to cope with the situation at all, and had 'got out' while they could. 'Many people chose to leave,' he said, no hint of recrimination in his voice, 'but I'm not going anywhere. I don't want my town to be cleared of all its people. That is what has happened elsewhere. People have been forced out by starvation and siege, the same weapons that are being used against us. So although it's very hard, although it's very dangerous, I have to stay. There are many strong people, beautiful souls, who are carrying on here, despite everything we are living through.'

Muhammad feared that if everyone like him left, Daraya

would be changed for ever – not just the fabric of the town, its shops, schools, homes and farms, but the very spirit of the place. And as every aspect of life *had* been stripped to its most basic, his admiration of, and pride in, the strength of those remaining, particularly the farmers, rang clear. 'Many farmers have been killed or injured going into their fields to harvest herbs or crops,' Muhammad told me. 'A lot of them are shot dead by snipers or blown up by shells. Many are maimed, often having to have their hands or legs cut off because of shrapnel wounds.' And yet, he continued, many farmers still went to their fields, often under the cover of darkness, to harvest whatever they could. The monumental risks they took were helping to keep the town's people alive.

Those remaining in Daraya just tried to cope and get on with their lives, no matter how dangerous it was. So children would be sent off to school in the morning even though their mothers know they might not come back. Muhammad Shihadeh spoke about the extraordinary resilience of local people. How during even the most desperate times they carried on, sometimes with the most amazing good cheer: 'Often when we get back with the body of someone who was killed during the day, we have to wait until it's dark to be able to bury them. It is a very long wait for their grieving loved ones, but on many occasions that time is filled with laughter as well as tears. We all remember the best things about our departed relative or friend, and sometimes we laugh out loud. Maybe it's the only way to cope with what we are going through.'

Food, of course, was an ongoing problem. More so, as the siege went on. In the early days of the war, most families had been able to stockpile reserves of food in their basements. The new town council, created to help the community cope with the siege, also built up large public food stores. Various grains were poured into sturdy containers to make them less susceptible to rodents, some fruits were dried and delicious dates were preserved in salty water. These supplies were aimed especially at helping those locals who had little money and no family links to local farmers. But, as Muhammad explained, by the summer of 2013 these food banks had begun to run dry. Meals had become rare and diminutive, and most people would eat no more than once a day. As stomachs grew ever more empty, people began adding grass and leaves to their meagre brews. Such supplements lacked any nutritional value but they gave people the temporary illusion of being full. Seven people had already died from malnutrition-related conditions, a fact that brought Muhammad close to tears when he told me. When I asked him how people were managing to survive, he replied that, in their characteristically resourceful and defiant way, the inhabitants had turned Daraya into a sort of giant allotment. 'Just about everyone grows crops wherever they can,' he said. 'They spread soil on balconies, rooftops, back yards and even the floors of their homes when there's enough light from an outside window. Lots of people have also planted parsley, mint, coriander and vegetables in small areas of open land around the town.' Sadly, he told me, where once the most sought-after grapes in Syria had grown in abundance, there was now nothing but withered vines.

Defiant and determined people came up with ways to grow food, and to stretch or supplement what was available. But the growing lack of medicine and medical equipment presented an even greater challenge. The rising number of

injuries from the bombing and fighting was already stretch-
ing Daraya's medical services to the limit and basic materials
such as blood, antibiotics, anaesthetics and even bandages
were fast becoming unobtainable. This was exacerbated
when pro-Assad forces bombed a medical storehouse; a
tactic used by the regime against other besieged areas in
Syria, along with the targeting of hospitals. This, as well its
refusal to allow aid agencies into Daraya, was designed to
help break the morale of those who had stayed.

It was a dreadful situation to watch, week after week,
month after month, year after year. Through my contacts, I
could listen to people telling me about the nightmare they
were living through, and relay that to the outside world, but
it seemed to be doing little, if anything, to help them on
the ground. I talked to various aid agencies, as well as the
UN, reminding them of the plight of all those besieged in
Daraya, but the answers were always the same. We cannot
take food or medicines into besieged towns, they would
tell me, unless the Syrian government agrees to allow the
convoys through their lines. And this was something that
Assad's regime rarely did. They had deployed this medieval
tactic with the simple aim of starving and bombarding their
opponents into submission, and so allowing aid in would
defeat that very purpose. Yet the majority of people living
in Daraya – and other besieged towns – were civilians,
not fighters. At the end of conversations with people like
Anas, Abdul Basit and Muhammad Shihadeh, I could only
say inadequate and somewhat meaningless phrases such
as 'look after yourself' or 'keep safe'. There *was* nowhere
safe in Daraya. Sometimes I could hear bombs and shells
exploding in the background, but those I spoke to just
carried on and made little of it, and the distance between

us seemed to melt away. Yet we were living in two very different worlds.

Another tactic used by the regime was to do what they could to limit access to something everyone needs: clean drinking water. Before the siege, almost every home in Daraya had been connected to the mains water supply but the government wasted no time in wrecking that. When word got around that the water was still flowing in one neighbourhood, people from all over Daraya would rush there with barrels, buckets, bottles and every kind of receptacle, before staggering off home with their precious cargo. Most made frequent trips knowing that such good fortune was unlikely to last for long, which indeed it did not. The government would soon cut supplies to the lucky area, leaving locals with nothing but water from wells. Many of these had been hastily dug and their water, though good for washing in, was dangerous to drink without boiling first. And to boil water, you need electricity and by now there was rarely any available because the mains supplies had also been cut. Some people, too thirsty to wait, drank the well water anyway, only to come down with all sorts of stomach problems, some of them serious.

Without power or fuel, it was impossible to run much-needed generators. Without these, the besieged town's hospitals struggled to care for the injured and sick. But the ever-inventive people of Daraya managed to come up with their own solution. Anas, who had studied civil engineering during his all-too-brief student days, told me: 'We made a kind of fuel from melting old plastic containers, most of which were too full of holes to carry water any more. We broke them down into small pieces, put them into a barrel and then heated the contents on a fire to a very high temperature. After a while it would turn into a kind of oil which we could use for fuel.'

I could imagine the terrible smell, and the thick black smoke that would have accompanied this process, but such factors must have seemed a price well worth paying in order to get the generators going. These enabled well water to be boiled more easily and provided a few hours of heating and light for hospitals and homes during the long, grim nights under siege. We mostly think of Syria as a hot country, where keeping cool is the prime necessity, but that is only half the story. In winter, temperatures can drop below freezing and life can be very hard without any heating. Anas told me about a day earlier that year when he had been forced to shelter from the bombing in a ditch near his home: 'I had been in the ditch for the whole day,' he said, discomfort etched on his face, 'and I had to stay there because of the heavy shelling. When the bombardment finally stopped, I crawled out and went back to my house. It felt like my limbs had frozen. I lay under three blankets but I couldn't warm up. Hours later my feet were still like ice; the cold seemed to have penetrated right into my bones.'

Under such ferocious conditions, it would have been easy for the people of Daraya to fall into a dog-eat-dog type of existence, where only the strong survived. Yet there was clearly a concerted effort among those remaining to watch out for each other; for the children, the elderly and the badly injured. Inevitably, some people, who had friends or relatives working on farms, had more access to food than others, yet from what I heard, most shared their supplies with those who were struggling. And when the planes halted their orgy of destruction, neighbours would come out of their basements and help clear up the streets, removing debris from people's kitchens and front rooms – a scene of devastation that was a sad reminder of calm and settled family life blown apart in seconds. Clearing up put people in extreme danger, but that didn't stop them trying to make homes and streets safer for each other. And while they were out, people would also look for places to plant seeds, even if few of them ended up growing.

Living under ongoing bombardment was unbelievably stressful. At any moment, you, a loved one or friend, might be killed. But, as Muhammad told me, people developed ways to help keep themselves calm at such times: 'Some people try to control their fears with little exercises that keep their minds busy, such as counting how many shells they hear each day. Others guess what time the helicopters will come over their homes, or when they think bombs are about to drop, which they judge by listening to the sound the helicopter's engine is making. We all try to deal with this nightmare in our own different ways. Otherwise we would go insane.'

These individual efforts to look after the community helped give everyone a sense of purpose, but as life became more fractured and fraught, a more co-ordinated plan was needed to keep the town running. As mentioned before, Daraya had created a new town council. This example of wartime civic democracy was in itself unusual, as its leaders had been democratically elected, a first in Syria for more than four decades. In addition, the council's 120 members and representatives were selected by ballot every six months. And despite the siege, despite the incessant bombing and snipers, despite the lack of food, fuel and medicine, the council somehow managed to carry on functioning. Not only that, but it also worked in partnership with the FSA, whose fighters reported to the council, so in Daraya, it was the civilian leaders who were making most of the local decisions, not the men with guns. A rare situation in times of conflict.

Daraya's council had various departments, each with its own responsibilities, although they all co-operated with one another. In this way the roads were regularly cleared of debris; goods from bombed shops were distributed to those in need; rubbish was collected and, when possible, safe drinking water was delivered to people's homes. The council ran workshops that taught people how to repair their cars, though with little fuel for vehicles these became somewhat redundant; a sewing service for repairing clothes; a relief registration office; a soup kitchen; three primary schools and a medical clinic. All pretty remarkable at the best of times, never mind during a siege. I think that what surprised and touched me most was the work the council carried out in repairing the windows and doors of bomb-damaged homes. An estimated 60 per cent of Daraya's buildings had already been either totally or partly destroyed, and that number was growing every day. Yet here were dedicated council workers busily replacing the windows and doors of homes that might not even be standing the next day.

Daraya's council also ran its own media department, watched over by Muhammad. Its primary job was to document human rights abuses by the regime, and to spread word of the town's plight. With his excellent English, Muhammad was able to alert the outside world to what was happening – when it was willing to listen. The hope was that international outrage might persuade President Assad to stop the bombing and allow aid convoys in.

The Syrian government would doubtless have liked to cut Daraya's communications with the outside world. In fact, I had often wondered how people there had been able to stay online, given the terrible destruction all around them. From what Abdul Basit told me, their secret was down to an odd combination of luck, ingenuity, silver foil and a pan lid. 'In areas of Daraya that are close to three nearby towns,' he said, 'we can get the Internet because of the mobile phone networks operating there. But unfortunately these barely reach central areas of the town, so we've had to invent a technique of boosting the very weak signal we get. This involves taking the top from a pan, covering that in silver foil and then drilling two holes through it. We then place the lid on the roof of a building and feed a silver wire through each hole, before trailing the wires all the way down to the basement. We then place our phone next to the silver wire and this is how we manage to get online.' All I can say is that it certainly worked. Although there were many times when I could not get through, on some occasions the line was so good we even managed to talk over video links. I don't think this book could ever have been written if it weren't for the ever-resourceful Abdul Basit's silver foil and pan lids.

But despite the council's attempts to reach out, few in Daraya still had much hope of outside help as 2013 drew to a close. After all, nobody had intervened the year before, after one of the worst massacres of the war. The rebel cause was dealt another blow on 11 December 2013 when the United States and UK suspended 'non-lethal' support for the Western-backed FSA in northern Syria after reports that an alliance of Islamist rebels had seized some FSA bases. The fear was that arms given to moderate FSA rebels might now fall into the hands of extremists linked to al-Qaeda. Despite this, Muhammad showed no signs of bitterness. Instead he busied himself with the council's website, putting up photos of the devastation that he had taken with his much-prized SLR camera. He told me: 'At least I feel I am doing something useful to help the situation.'

The work of the council was vital, ensuring there was at least some food to eat, water to drink and emergency fuel for the hospital. While these were vital to keep people alive, other less practical things were also needed to boost morale, especially among children and young people. With this thought in mind many locals volunteered to get the town's mini football league running again. The people of Daraya had always been passionate about football, but the league had become yet another casualty of the siege. All that changed when local youngsters decided to start playing again. They split themselves into a range of different teams and then drew up a fixture list. Most matches were held at the town's largest school, even though it was badly damaged and did not have a grass pitch to play on. Muhammad told me that the games would take place – bombing, shelling and snipers permitting – on a large, hard surface just behind the main building. There was even a trophy for the winning side.

Football-mad youngsters often used breaks in the bombing to resume their roadside matches, and school yards echoed with the sound of running feet, excited yells and balls being kicked. Nor were the people of Daraya going to let bombers and snipers keep them from getting fit. One well-attended gym near the centre of town provided a range of basic equipment including dumbbells, weights and a treadmill. For less sporty children there were singing classes in both Arabic and English and, movingly, some of these sessions were videoed and posted online.

Muhammad told me how he and his friends also did their best to enjoy themselves whenever possible. When there was bombing, they would spend evenings gathered together in somebody's basement, or chatting outside when the skies were clear. Sometimes they would sing old pro-democracy chants dating back to the 2011 protests, or belt out traditional folk songs. This, he explained, helped people rekindle memories of life before the siege, generating 'a mixture of nostalgia, excitement, sadness and happiness, all at the same time. It is another thing that helps our people get through.'

Like Abdul Basit, Muhammad wasn't medically trained, but in between his work for the council and the community, he too spent much of his time helping out at the local hospital, doing what he could for the surgeons and doctors. The rest of his time, it seemed, regardless of the carnage around him, was spent doing the usual household chores. 'I live with around ten people in a shared house,' he told me. 'I do the washing, which is always piling up, and then spend time in long queues to get food for our daily meal. We all take it in turns to do the cleaning, washing-up or repairs to the house. We have to do most of these things during the hour or so a day when we have electricity from the generator.'

It is strange to picture everyday life carrying on as normal in times of siege and war. Obviously it has to, although the mundane tasks are hardly the sort of scenes you read about in historic accounts. When I mentioned this to

Muhammad, he didn't react. All I heard was silence. Just when I was beginning to regret having made such an apparently silly comment, he smiled and said: 'War is only the superficial face that you see first. Underneath that, there is so much humanity, so much else taking place. There may be death but there is also normal life here too.'

Muhammad was a great supporter of the secret library and helped on many of the trips to rescue books. He had experienced the repressive censorship of the Assad regime when at primary school. He and his classmates were only allowed to read officially 'approved' books, and even these were in limited supply. The situation had improved when he reached high school, but even then certain subjects, or elements of them, were kept off of the syllabus. 'We had plenty of history books,' Muhammad told me, 'but these all dealt with ancient history. There was nothing about more recent events in Syria. In the classroom, we would learn about the glorious old days of Islam, but when it came to questions about contemporary history, there was complete silence. We would never get answers to our questions. The teacher would just pass over the subject very quickly.'

Even when he reached university, Muhammad continued, it was impossible to study recent Syrian history or politics properly. Books on such subjects were simply not available and lectures on them non-existent. The government had informants all over the university who looked out for anyone reading 'subversive' books, or involved in what were considered subversive activities or conversations. This kind of surveillance was backed by the secret police who kept photographic evidence of those taking part. Many students were later arrested and Muhammad knew of others who were refused their graduation certificates after completing their degrees. They were never given any explanation, effectively making their several years of intensive and demanding study worthless.

The censorship didn't just apply in schools or universities, but permeated society; so much so that, 'unfortunately, it became self-censorship,' Muhammad said. 'People knew where the line was and would therefore not buy or sell books that clearly crossed it. They simply avoided publications that would not have been approved by the regime. This was the case whether the books were Syrian or foreign.'

Like Muhammad, members of the secret library group had mostly known only repression and censorship, so it was important to them that their library contained a wide range of books. During a call with Anas, he told me: 'We don't ban any books. We are open to those on all subjects. We believe that by excluding books we may not agree with, we would just be helping to raise ignorance. If we want to sharpen the intellect of our generation and their understanding of the world, we need to let them think for themselves. We even have some "explicit" books here, containing information on sexual interaction and how sexual intercourse takes place.' Such literature, he explained, was kept on the highest shelves for married couples or those who were officially engaged. If readers wanted to borrow these books, they would need to speak to one of the library staff first. Presumably, I thought, not fourteen-year-old Amjad, who at less than five foot tall would struggle to reach them.

Abdul Basit, who had joined the conversation, expressed pride in one particular book-rescuing mission at a Christian church in Daraya: 'Some of the building was still on fire when we got there. The flames had become so fierce that the firefighters with us had to stop to deal with the blaze. When we eventually managed to get into the main part of the church we found a room in the back filled with boxes and boxes of assorted religious books, many of them bibles. Despite the fire we managed to get all of them out of the church to safety. Some are now in this library. It doesn't matter to us that they are Christian books rather than Muslim ones. Whether they were in a church or a mosque, we were just pleased to save them.'

I was delighted to hear this story. I knew that Abdul Basit and his library friends were all religious, and I feared that their generally very tolerant attitude to life might not extend to this issue. But clearly this was not the case. Divisions over religion in Syria, as has been the case in so many other parts of the world, have been the cause of so much bloodshed. Whether it's Sunni Muslims against Shia Muslims in the Middle East, Protestants against Catholics in Northern Ireland, or Christians against Muslims elsewhere in the world, the result has been the same.

The discussion I'd had with the men about censorship also resonated deeply with me, especially Muhammad's regret that after a time people began to self-censor, avoiding publications they might previously have had access to. Given the brutality of the Syrian government's security forces, it did not surprise me that most people behaved in this way. Decades of repression were bound to have had a huge impact. I still marvel at the courage of the hundreds of thousands who took to the streets right across North Africa and the Middle East during the Arab Spring, bent on deposing all-powerful dictators. They must have known what would follow if their protests failed, yet they still went ahead.

As the people who compiled Daraya's secret library told me, being found with a book disapproved of by the Syrian government could lead to a jail term or worse. That is part of the reason they all so enjoyed being free to read whatever they liked, even though gathering the books under fire could have cost them their lives.

History has some stirring examples of how societies combated the censorship of literature. In Germany during the 1930s, Nazis tried to confiscate all Jewish books and newspapers, as well as anything critical of their ideology. They did not destroy them all, however, as Hitler planned to create a museum filled with books and artefacts of what would be the extinct Jewish race.[12] In response Jews set up secret libraries in the ghettoes of occupied Europe, many of which were underground. The secret library of the Theresienstadt ghetto had over 60,000 books.[13] And in Vilna (Vilnius), teenager Yitskhok Rudashevski wrote with great pride about the day the library loaned its 100,000th book, on 13 December 1942: 'Today the ghetto celebrated the circulation of the one hundred thousandth book in the ghetto library. The festival was held in the auditorium of the theatre. The reading of books in the ghetto is the greatest pleasure for me. The book unites us with the future, the book unites us with the world.'[14]

After decades of military rule, Myanmar's jails were full of political prisoners – men and women who had often done little more than criticise the military government, or read books by others who had done so. It was for this reason that when a thirty-one-year-old Yangon bookshop owner, Ye Htet Oo, began collecting non-approved English language titles, he did not dare stock them openly.[15] Instead, he put in an official application to open a library. Permission was denied but rather than given up his project, Ye Htet put the volumes, which he lent out to local students, in a locked room at the back of his premises. Customers entering his shop had no idea that behind the padlocked door at the back was a secret library, full of foreign books such as *Oliver Twist*, *Animal Farm*, *Hamlet* and *Sherlock Holmes*. Few among them were seditious or threatened the military government, but Ye Htet faced a lengthy jail term if the room was discovered. So, when he was summoned by phone in June 2010 to discuss the issue of his library, he thought the game was up. The official penalty for possession of an unauthorised library is three months in jail for every book. He had 6000 of them. But instead of being thrown in jail, Ye Htet Oo was told that he was, after all, going to be granted a licence for his secret library. About a year later, he met the minister responsible for licensing libraries at a conference in the capital Naypyidaw. He asked him how officials had first become aware of his hidden library. The minister is reported to have told him: 'My kids were in your library before me. I was really interested. I thought it was unbelievable, it's not possible. And I got in there and I loved your library.'[16] Ye Htet Oo's once-secret book room is now called 'The Tharapar Library' and operates openly below an English school, also run by him. It now has more than 15,000 books on its shelves and three other satellite branches elsewhere in the country.

It is this spirit of finding a way that motivates the people of Daraya and their treasured secret library. While these are accounts of very different places, times and faiths, nonetheless the shared love of books transcends national boundaries and defies the calamitous events of history.

In the final days of December 2013, a Syrian air force helicopter gunship released a host of small bombs over the city. This was nothing new, but as the devices continued to fall their bulbous, tell-tale shape caused a whole new level of alarm. When the first one hit the ground the explosive roar was followed by a cloud of flying metal fragments which shattered windows before embedding themselves in walls, roofs and anything else in their path. The Syrian air force had unleashed barrel bombs on Daraya for the first time.

The barrel bomb – often a gas cylinder or oil drum filled with a combination of explosives, nails, metal and concrete – had become synonymous with the war in Syria but until now had not been inflicted on the people of Daraya. Designed to allow shrapnel to fly in all directions as it explodes, these bombs vastly increase the chances of death or injury over a wide area. Inherently indiscriminate, and nearly impossible to target accurately, these bombs expose civilians anywhere near the explosion to lethal pieces of metal flying through the air. The use of barrel bombs marked a significant escalation of the Syrian government's brutality in Daraya.

But not even the continued use of these horrifying weapons over the months that followed could prevent the long-awaited official opening of Daraya's secret library in May 2014. Thousands of books lined the walls of their new basement home, covering almost every subject under the sun. This uncensored literary treasure trove was finally ready for all. Not that the average passer-by would have noticed a thing from the outside. Given the certainty that the library would be bombed if the regime knew where it was, there was no ribbon-cutting fanfare, nor signs on the door.

Inside, however, it was a different story. Beneath the shattered streets, down a steep flight of stairs, celebrations were in full swing. Surrounded by brightly coloured posters and improvised paper streamers, a throng of excited book lovers scanned the shelves, swapping plans on what they would read first. Months of rescuing books, building shelves and finding furniture had finally come to this. To avoid attracting attention the visitors had arrived at intervals, by themselves or in pairs, and that is how they would leave. Not that anyone would even think of going for some time yet. Daraya's biggest source of inspiration, the beating heart of its besieged community, was born. 'It was a wonderful occasion,' Muhammad told me. 'Even the leader of the local council was there. I don't know how they managed it, but somehow the organisers got hold of some special food. They baked this delight with sugar and flour and coconut and served it in small bowls. We all loved it. This turned what was already a very special occasion into something magical.'

Others talked of their joy at witnessing an occasion they had once thought would never come about. After many months of rescuing dusty, damp and dirty books from burnt-out houses, here they were surrounded by the fruit of their labours. Restored to their former glory, books that had so recently lain forgotten in mud and rubble, now graced the polished shelves. Abdul Basit told me how he was so moved by this special occasion that he was lost for words. While those around him rejoiced, some even moved to song, he just stood there, quietly taking it all in. 'I felt so happy, looking at what we had all achieved. I knew this was a very special moment. I just stood there, soaking up the memory of it all, hoping that I would remember it for ever.'

From this moment on, a new optimism took hold in Daraya. This literary haven offered more than an escape from bombs and boredom. It was to become a portal to another world: one of learning, one of peace, and one of hope.

# Chapter Five

In the early days of the siege there had been much optimism that the international community would step in and stop the carnage. Surely, the people of Daraya thought, organisations such as the United Nations would not simply stand by while they were being bombed and starved to death. They must be aware of what was happening to the town, if not from reports of those who had fled, then from those who were still inside Daraya including Muhammad Shihadeh and Malik al-Rifaii who spent countless hours posting videos and photos online. So when news reached the town, in late 2013, that new UN-brokered peace talks in Geneva had failed, there was bitter disappointment. The two sides had not been able to reach an agreement: the Syrian government had refused to discuss the possibility of a transitional government being formed to negotiate a path to peace, while the rebels repeated their insistence that they would never agree to a deal that left President Bashar al-Assad in power.

With no break in the deadlock, concern grew for the safety of children still living in Daraya. Most had left with their mothers and elderly relatives in 2012, but hundreds remained, their parents assuming that the president would call off the horrifying siege as soon as his forces had flexed their military muscle. Now, however, it was becoming clear that his goal was absolute victory, and this realisation led some in the community to reassess the long-term welfare of their children. While keeping them as safe as possible was the first priority, now that the siege was likely to last, the goal was to find a way to resume their education. Many schools had been forced to shut due to the constant danger from shelling, bombs and snipers, and fears were growing that a generation of local children might grow up not being able to read or write.

One teenager, however, had landed on his feet. Fourteen-year-old Amjad, a small slim boy with dark, neatly cut hair, had all the books he could ever want to read. Indeed he had virtually made his home in the secret library after coming across it by chance. I had been introduced to him when talking via a WhatsApp call to Anas and Abdul Basit in the library. Amjad told me that although he lived very close to the library, he had never heard of it until being directed there by two local men. They had spotted him in the street frantically searching for cover as a round of shelling and sniper fire erupted. They told him he would be far better reading books in the underground library than dodging shrapnel outside. But they had warned him that it was a secret place so he should never tell anyone where it was. 'When I first walked into the library,' he said, his vibrant brown eyes aglow, 'it was exhilarating and a complete surprise. There were so many books. Some were piled high on top shelves that I couldn't reach. I made up my mind to try and memorise every single book. But there were so many of them that I didn't know where to start, so I just began by leafing through the one nearest to me. I said to one of the men in charge: I want to stay here. They agreed and have looked after me ever since.'

Amjad's infectious enthusiasm never failed to touch me. 'We have all different kinds of books,' he told me. 'We have science ones, medical ones, literary ones, just about everything really. As Chief Librarian, I have a number of duties. My main one is to look after the running of the library. I also take down the names and addresses of people who borrow books and record them in that large file over there. I also do a lot of dusting, mainly of the books themselves.'

The other striking thing about the secret library, he continued, was the furniture in it. This was something that Amjad was particularly proud of. After telling me at length about the comfortable chairs with blue floral seats, richly patterned dark-red magnolia carpet and wooden dining table, he added with a flourish: 'I even have my own office at the back of the library – it has a sign saying "Management" on the door. In there I have my own desk. It's small, just like me. I also have another seat in the middle of the library. This means that people can easily see where I am when they want to borrow books.' Young Amjad did not only have a chance to educate himself, the fourteen-year-old had also found a job he loved in a place of comparative safety. I cannot think of anyone more deserving of such good fortune.

Sadly, many other children could not reach the library, which was in a dangerous area of town not far from the front line. Most of them had little access to books or any kind of formal education. The problem was that there were very few teachers left in Daraya, and almost nowhere safe to school the remaining children. That is, until two young local women got together and came up with a solution. Sara Matar, a tall, slim woman in her late twenties, with striking nut-brown eyes, was one of them. Sara had been a housewife since graduating from Damascus University and marrying her husband, Bashar, who worked for the council. But she was soon to play a very valuable role in life beyond her home. Over the months and years that followed I came to greatly admire Sara's warmth, intelligence and vision. The fact that she was by nature quiet and reserved made the courageous role she played in children's lives especially remarkable.

I should say here that Sara is not her real name. When we first began to talk, she told me that her parents, brother and three sisters all lived in an area controlled by government forces and that although it was nearby, the siege meant she had no way of seeing them. When the rest of the family fled from Daraya in the late summer of 2012, she and her husband decided to stay on, both determined to support the uprising there. Sara couldn't even phone her relatives as the regime monitored all phone lines and considered anyone still living in rebel-held Daraya to be either a terrorist or at least somebody with sympathies for them. Sara feared that contacting her family would lead them to become suspects too and for this reason she asked me not to reveal her identity.

Sara's close friend, Amena, a teacher for thirteen years, asked if she was interested in organising some education for mainly primary-school-age children in Daraya. At the time, Amena had just been released from prison. She had been jailed twice by the Assad regime, the second time for two years, on terrorism charges, after being arrested while taking part in anti-government demonstrations. After her release she had arranged to be smuggled back into Daraya by a local guide who knew a way around the military checkpoints. An ardent supporter of the revolution, she was determined to help like-minded civilians under siege, even though this would put her at risk of being arrested again, or even killed.

Not long after her arrival, she talked to Sara about the lack of schooling for children in Daraya. Although she had no teaching experience, Sara shared her friend's concerns and they decided to set up a classroom together. Due to her command of the language, Amena thought Sara would make an ideal English teacher. Sara later told me that she had learned to speak it by watching English-language films on TV, so her teachers had included Angelina Jolie, Kate Winslet and Arnold Schwarzenegger.

After much searching they found an apartment in a quiet backstreet. Its inconspicuous location meant that it was unlikely to be targeted by bombers and before long they had moved in, cleaned it up and were ready to go.

Both Sara and Amena had high hopes that the schooling they offered young children would in many ways be much better than what they had had before the siege. Before the year 2000, the school system in Syria was split into three stages: elementary, preparatory and secondary. Elementary was from first to sixth grade, preparatory from seventh to ninth and secondary, where children studied for their baccalaureate, was tenth to twelfth grades. Elementary school was compulsory, but education after that was optional and many children dropped out. After 2000, the system was changed to just two stages. Primary, which was compulsory, went from first to ninth grade and secondary schooling was optional, though pupils could not leave until they were fifteen years old. Under the country's education system, the curriculum was based strictly on the regime's and the Ba'ath party's views of the country and its history. Pupils were made to memorise statements by Bashar al-Assad and his father Hafez al-Assad from compulsory text books. And at the beginning and end of each school day they had to repeat an oath of allegiance to the regime. All schools, as well as government buildings, businesses and shops, were required to display statues and pictures of the Assads. Pupils were discouraged from ever questioning what they were taught, or from giving personal opinions on political issues, especially regarding civil rights and freedom of speech. Parents were also under pressure, not only to ensure that their children conformed to these rules, but also to display loyalty to the regime themselves. For instance, those who owned shops were encouraged to paint their window shutters in the colours of the official Syrian flag.

Sara remembers that she became increasingly resentful about the pressure put on children and was determined to do things very differently on becoming a teacher herself: 'I don't want this new generation to have their intellectual development held back in the way that ours was. So I try to teach them to think for themselves and express their own emotions. Since the uprising this is much easier. We are now free to criticise the regime here in Daraya.'

In the chilly days of early 2014, that criticism became even more vociferous, as barrel bombs and missiles fell all around the children's new makeshift classroom, though Sara insists they never tried to indoctrinate the children about the revolutionary cause. As had previously been the case in many Syrian schools, there was no segregation along gender lines, with boys and girls sharing the same classes. In all, around seventy children, aged between five and twelve, went to Sara's little school. They came from a wide variety of religious backgrounds – Muslim, Alawite and Christian.

The same applied to those who taught them. At first, the school had only three teachers: Sara, her friend Amena and another colleague. But after posters went up around the town advertising the school, class sizes slowly grew, along with the number of staff. Before long, lessons were moved to the basement of the building to help keep the children safe.

Whenever Sara spoke to me about her young charges, her tone would markedly soften. She clearly adored the children and the work she did with them. Her anguish over the dangers they faced each day was palpable. Peace talks in February brought some relief, as the almost constant bombardment ceased. But, as Sara told me, this respite was only temporary:

When the peace talks were happening we were able to take the children out of the basement at last. We then set up our classes in the demolished school. They loved it there. There was natural light everywhere and they could see out of the windows. But then the shelling started again and we were forced to take the children back to the basement. They virtually have to live there now. Sometimes, if we suspect there is going to be bombing in the afternoon, we let the kids go home early. We send them in pairs, not in groups. The hope is that if the planes arrive overhead before they get home the pilots won't target them, because they usually only go for large groups of people.

It was not only daylight that the children were deprived of in their basement classroom. The school had little in the way of pens, pencils and crayons, nor any kind of paper on which to write and draw. But the biggest problem of all was the lack of textbooks. Sara and her fellow teachers had tried to have some brought in from a neighbouring country, but these were seized at the border and burned. Thankfully they managed to retrieve a few books from abandoned local schools, especially science texts. But Sara told me that they decided to cut pictures out of some of these before giving them to their near-starving pupils. 'Some of these science books had large photos of food and vegetables which were there to teach children where nutrients come from,' she told me. 'I didn't want them to see images like these, it would only stir emotions. It just wasn't fair on them.'

It's a haunting image. Children so hungry that they had to be protected from even *seeing* pictures of food. Many must have arrived at school with groaning stomachs, and left the same way, not knowing what, if anything, they would get to eat at home. It's amazing that any of them managed to come to school at all, never mind have the will to concentrate on their studies. As in all wars, these children were innocent victims of the conflict. They suffered the consequences, but had no say in how it started, or how it might end.

After the bombing forced Sara and Amena to move classes down to the basement, they were plagued by a lack of light. Being underground, there were no windows, and with little or no mains electricity available, the lights could only be powered by a generator. Although the school did have one of these, they had no fuel to run it. This meant the children had to struggle in near darkness to read any of the few books they had. I asked Sara whether she had considered taking her pupils to the secret library. She shook her head and sighed deeply before telling me that as the library was situated in a very dangerous area of town, only those who lived nearby could go there. And while most families might have known that the library existed, she said, many wouldn't have known exactly where it was due to the need to keep its location secret. Also, even if they had known, it would not have crossed the minds of most parents to take their children there, as such a journey would have meant putting their lives at even greater risk than they were in already. Sara was clearly frustrated at being unable to take her pupils to a place she knew they would love: 'One of the first school outings we thought of arranging, after moving the class into the basement, was to the secret library. We knew the children would really enjoy it there. They dreamed of sitting quietly in a place filled with books. But unfortunately because of the heavy shelling we had to postpone the trip.'

At least Sara had been able to go to the secret library regularly herself since it opened. She was ecstatic on first hearing of its existence, having been an avid reader all her life. Since the siege started, she had been unable to get her hands on many books, yet the library enabled her to choose from a plethora of titles, and all for free. Initially, given the fact that the library was in a dangerous area of town, Sara's husband, Bashar, who worked for the council, would walk with her, but he was often too busy. As a result, she later made this perilous, but rewarding journey alone. 'I will never forget,' she told me, 'how exciting it was to walk in there and see all those wonderful books.'

At first Sara felt uncomfortable when she saw that the library was mainly being used by men. Sometimes, she told me, she was the only woman there. Although she was always made to feel welcome, she was relieved to hear that special visiting hours for women were being organised. The only other downside to her visits was that the more she saw of the secret library, the more she realised how much the children were missing out. Here were books on just about every subject you could think of, all kept in such a safe place to read. Yet the journey there was just too dangerous for the children.

During one of our chats about the library, Sara went on to recount how she regularly saw a 'very lovely and hard-working' teenage boy there. He would sit, head down, engrossed in his books, silently mouthing the words he was reading. Sara recalled how his head would move from side to side as he followed the words on the page. Now and again the small, wiry figure would be interrupted by people looking for a particular book, or returning one they had borrowed, but he would soon be back in his seat once more, reading. One day, intrigued, Sara sat down beside the boy and introduced herself. Delighted to be in the company of a school teacher, he told her that his name was Amjad and that he was fourteen years old. He explained how the bombing meant that it was very hard for him to get to school, so he spent much of his time in the secret library, either reading or helping to run it. The beaming Amjad clearly loved spending time there and believed that other children would too. Sara remembered him telling her what he often said to his friends: 'Just come and visit! It is so much better than staying at home looking at the walls. I say to them, you don't have TV now anyway, so why not come here and educate yourself? It's fun.'

Amjad told Sara how worried he was about having fallen behind with his school work. 'He was quite upset about this,' Sara recalled. 'He said to me, "Miss, I want to be able to read just as well as you in the future, but I'm not

learning much any more. I used to do so well in school.'"
Sara's school, though not far from where Amjad lived, did
not cater for older children, so he had become reliant on
using the secret library's books to teach himself. Evidently,
much as he enjoyed it, it was proving an uphill struggle.

During one conversation with Sara, a close friend, Aysha
Fayyad, came into the small, dimly lit room at the back
of her house. Not wanting to interrupt our conversation,
Aysha, a teacher in her early forties, sat quietly in a chair
a few feet away. But, after being encouraged by Sara, she
began telling me that she too had founded a small school
in the town. Aysha had set it up around the same time as
Sara had set up hers, soon after the siege began in November 2012. She called her makeshift little centre, 'The Hope
of the Nation'. Like Sara, Aysha had kind, dark eyes and
a ready smile, but she also exuded a steely determination.
It turned out that her decision to start the school was
motivated not only by the desire to ensure that Daraya's
children were educated, but also by a personal tragedy in
her life. At first she chose not to elaborate on what had
happened. I felt reluctant to pry, sensing that she was still
struggling to cope with the memory. But after a deep sigh,
Aysha broke the lengthening silence, her voice laced with
sadness. 'My fifteen-year-old son left school when the violence first started and he joined rebel fighters on the front
line. Before long he was dead. This made me think of all
the other children who take this path. Might they suffer the
same tragic end?' While Aysha chose not to dwell on the
fate of her son, it was clear that she felt unremitting sadness
and frustration at having been unable to save his life. 'The
situation was so bad at the time that I could not stop him.
The regime's forces were making big advances, so I had no

choice. I watched him walk away and join the rebel fighters. They gave him only brief training before putting a gun in his hand and sending him to the front. I simply couldn't do anything about it. There seemed to be nothing I could say.'

The rebel fighters were always on the look-out for new recruits, telling the inhabitants of Daraya that young people were urgently needed to help defend the town. Aysha told me that many youngsters had answered the call to battle, some even younger than her son. Fortunately, some mothers were luckier than Aysha. Their sons, many of whom had fought alongside her boy, survived and eventually came home. Tears welling up in her eyes, Aysha recalled how she often pleaded with her son not to enlist. But he would always reply that if everyone did what their mothers asked, the regime's soldiers could simply walk into Daraya. 'Who will stop them if I do not?' he would ask her. 'You have to let me go.'

This made me think how this had to be a situation faced by so many mothers – not just here in Daraya, or elsewhere in war-ravaged Syria, but around the world, throughout history. Then I thought of Anas and Abdul Basit, and the other young men who had chosen to build a library rather than fight a war. Perhaps their love of books and reading, their joy in creating rather than destroying, was unusual. Aysha seemed to agree: 'I would say nearly every boy's dream is to fight. Most of them witnessed the massacre here in 2012. They saw cold-blooded murdering by government soldiers. Some even saw their parents being killed right in front of them. So I'm sure they all had this dream of revenge and joining the fighters who are defending us all. But I think some go to war without really knowing why.'

Aysha added that she hoped others had managed to

think things through, and truly understood what they were fighting for. No soldiers, she insisted, whether young or old, should ever bear arms without knowing why.

Following the death of her son, Aysha became increasingly concerned that, without education, children might prove easy recruits for extremist groups such as al-Qaeda and IS. By January 2014, IS had already taken over the Syrian city of Raqqa in the north of the country and would go on to sweep across vast areas of Syria and Iraq. Every day, large numbers of young men, local as well as foreign, flocked to join them. Many parents had no idea what their sons had done until it was already too late; others feared that defying such extremists might endanger their whole family. A few even encouraged their sons. IS did, after all, pay those who joined them, in a shattered country where there were few jobs to be had. An even bigger number, especially in the early years of the war, approved of their children joining moderate rebel forces, like the FSA. Filled with bitterness at what the Assad regime had done, this at least gave them the satisfaction that their family was fighting back.

It was not as if boys who went off to battle were leaving happy, settled lives. From personal experience, Aysha was concerned that many of these boys would end up with weapons in their hands, perhaps thinking that it was better to kill than be killed. She did her best to encourage children to continue with their studies, getting them to help her pin up flyers advertising the schools that existed. 'While bombs were falling,' she continued, 'I would pass children playing in the street and think how much safer they would be back in school. It seemed to me that we had a basic choice. To stand by and watch our children be killed or pushed into the arms of terrorists, or set up a school to help stop this.'

At first, some children did not adjust to school life and thought only of joining the war. But Aysha was relieved to find that most soon came to be appreciative and enthusiastic about being able to resume their studies. 'Some of them said to me, If we're going to die in this war, we would rather do so in school, studying for a better future, than be killed wandering the streets.'

The older children were particularly important as the younger boys looked up to them for guidance. If the older boys stayed in school and resisted the call to fight, most of their little brothers would do the same. Aysha added that if her pupils chose to enlist after they had finished school, then at least they would be better equipped to understand what they were fighting for. In fact, by the summer of 2016, several rebel groups did promise to stop recruiting youths under eighteen years old.

Like Sara, Aysha had had great trouble finding books for the children in her class. She and the other teachers began by going to abandoned schools to look for some, but while they managed to find a few this way, there were not enough for her pupils. In the end, her school's most fruitful source was her father's private library – a vast collection of books on religion, education, human development and literature, many penned by famous Muslim writers. 'I can still remember how beautiful many of these books were,' Aysha told me. 'Some of the smaller ones had really nice animal stories for children and lots of interesting drawings. One of my favourite books was *The Gold Sutures* by Sharh Ibn Aqeel, I read that several times. I also loved looking through his many medical books, or others on space and historical titles about the Ottoman Empire and the two world wars.'

Aysha told me that many of the books seemed huge and very heavy. One tome she picked up was more than fifty centimetres long and thirty-five centimetres wide, perhaps the local version of *War and Peace*. Smiling, Aysha told me more about her literary father, who had let her take whatever titles she wanted. He had had to leave Daraya just after the massacre because her mother had cancer and needed specialist medical treatment. Initially they had settled in a suburb of regime-controlled Damascus, but her father felt constantly in danger there. He and his wife had to travel to hospitals around the city and feared they would be arrested at one of the many checkpoints. Their identity papers showed that they were from rebel-held Daraya, and that fact alone was potentially enough to get them arrested. As Aysha's mother's health deteriorated, her father became ever more desperate to get her the care she needed. Finally he gathered all the family's savings and flew her to Saudi Arabia for treatment. Sadly, she could not be saved and died two years after leaving Daraya. With the town still under siege, there was no way that Aysha could go to see her mother and comfort her in her dying days. It was also five years since she had last seen her book-loving father. 'One of my fondest memories was of him sitting there with his glasses on, holding as many as five books in his hands at a time. He would comment on each of them, switching from one to the other. This is always the vision that comes into my head when I think of his library. He would sit there happily, surrounded by books to his left and to his right. I can still picture him sitting there so clearly.'

Aysha told me that her father's library had taken up more than one room. While the bulk of it was housed in a large room downstairs and a smaller one next to that, many more books were to be found in his bedroom, and still more littered shelves in the family's spacious guestroom. Their house had been home to this vast library for as long as she could remember, as her father had started accumulating it before he met her mother. Each week it would grow, and as shelf space ran out, piles of books would spring up elsewhere. Not that Aysha and her brothers and sisters ever thought that there was anything odd about this – after all, the library had been there as long as they had.

The only category of books that Aysha had found it hard to find were those on science. Unwilling to accept defeat, she had turned to the Internet and whenever the signal was good – which from my own experience was not often – she would download science papers and articles for her classes and construct lessons from them. I found it difficult to imagine how it was possible to teach often terrified young children, when bombs were falling all around. How could the children concentrate on their lessons when the ground and the walls around them were shaking and in danger of falling in? How did parents cope with seeing their children off in the morning knowing that they might not make it back? How much of a struggle was it for teachers, watching their young pupils set off on their dangerous journey home? They must have been constantly listening for the dreaded sound of approaching planes. Aysha nodded, saying: 'There are days where there is continuous heavy bombing and shelling. Sometimes it hardly stops. During days like this we open the school for only one or two hours at most, usually from six to eight a.m. in the morning.'

Those hours were usually among the quietest times of the day. As Aysha had mentioned, school hours often varied from day to day, according to how much shelling and bombing there was. And, as was the case in Sara's school, all lessons at Aysha's school were held in a sandbag-barricaded basement. It seems strange to think that in the UK, a few inches of snow or stormy winds can lead schools to close their doors. Yet in Syria, where children might be bombed or shot at without warning, they often stayed open. And what is more, Aysha believed this was not just to keep parents happy: 'What most inspires us is the fact that despite all the dangers we've been talking about the children really want to come to school. Some days, when there is heavy bombing and shelling, I arrive at school expecting to find the classroom empty, only to discover that most children are there.'

Aysha was also convinced that school helped ease the trauma of children during wartime, by enabling them to share their worries with each other. This belief helped motivate her and the other teachers to continue their jobs on such dark and dangerous days. Their aim was to try and make life as near to normal as possible for the children, at a time when all they otherwise knew was chaos, fear and loss. To this end, they arranged special entertainment days, when the children could all play their favourite games together. During rare ceasefires, they were taken on day trips to farms on the edge of town. Aysha described how they loved to see the animals. Sometimes she let them stay behind after class for an hour or so, to play with their friends. But of course there were the bad days too. 'The worst times are when children or their parents have been killed. Every child in this school is like our child. So whenever one of them is killed I feel like I've lost one of my own children. Thank God none has been killed at the school, but at least twenty of them have died in bombings at home. Others have been killed while out playing in the streets. Some of the dead have been newborn babies. It causes me such pain.'

Sadly, much more pain was to come. By March 2014, more than 300 barrel bombs had been dropped on Daraya since the beginning of the year. And on the twenty-fourth of that month yet more were to die, when Syrian government tanks briefly broke through some of the rebel defences around the town. Parents faced the agony of not knowing whether the sons and daughters they had sent to school that morning would return home alive.

I called Sara one cold March morning. In London, a week of bright, sunny weather had come to a bone-chilling end. Flurries of sleet lashed the windows of my first-floor study. Outside the gusting wind was bullying some loose canvas sheeting on the roof of my garden shed, punctuating the gloom with eerie whistles and moans. As usual the Internet connection in Daraya was problematic, the scratchy pops and whines on the line not all that dissimilar to those of my wind-battered garden. Finally, on what must have been my sixth or seventh attempt, I got through. Sara, who was normally so positive, whatever was happening, sounded deeply depressed. There was no school that day. 'I feel dazed,' she told me. 'It's like what is happening around me now isn't real. I've stopped reacting much to it. Yesterday I was told that the bomb which hit the building next to me here weighed 500 kilograms. I don't know how anyone knows that, but it was certainly a huge explosion.'

Then came silence, interrupted only by the sound of distant explosions. I waited for Sara to continue but the silence went on. Was she still there? Had I lost the line? I looked down at my mobile. The connection was not strong enough for a video link, but I could see a symbol saying my voice call was still active. Then, at last, to my great relief she spoke again:

This barrage is getting worse. I should go down to the basement, but I haven't moved yet because I feel numb. Many of us are like this now. I've been getting violent shakes. After these I can't remember anything. I even forget what my family looks like. I actually can't remember their faces. I think it's the fear, it's the shock. Whenever there's a barrel bomb or heavy shelling my instant reaction is to escape that particular moment. So I forget the faces I love. I forget what I am doing. I even forget what my husband looks like.

Given the terrible danger Sara was in, it was obvious that our conversation could not continue. She needed to get to the comparative safety of her basement as quickly as possible. Sara had told me several times how much she hated the pitch-black darkness down there. Unable to read, she could do little but listen to the distant sound of exploding bombs, hoping all the time that her home would be spared. Given that she was unlikely to get a Wi-Fi signal in her basement I asked if she could record a voice message for me on her phone, and then send it to me when the bombardment had stopped, so that I would know she was OK. Then, before she had a chance to reply, the line went dead. Even though I knew Sara to be tough and resilient, a worrying few hours followed. I got out my laptop and checked WhatsApp, Facebook and Twitter, my usual channels of communication with the people of Daraya. There was nothing, no messages of any kind.

Finally, in the early hours of the following morning, my mobile phone pinged. I had a horrible feeling that this was going to be bad news and hesitated to check the message, even though I had nervously been waiting hours for it. I had a WhatsApp voice message from Sara. After the line had gone dead earlier, I had regretted asking her to record a message for me, as she surely had enough to contend with without having to bother with that. But true to form, the indomitable Sara had managed to do it. In fact she appeared to have begun recording as soon as we had finished talking: 'I'm walking down into the basement now. I hate it down here, it is too dark and I can't see anything. I feel like I am suffocating every time I come here. It is a different world, isolated from everything above. I can't wait to get out again. But sometimes, when the bombing is bad like it is now, I spend the whole night in this basement. I wish it wasn't so terribly dark.'

Unfortunately for Sara, over the years to come, she and the children she taught would face many more days and nights in such basements. There was to be no quick end to their ongoing nightmare. Yet even in the very worst of days there was light in the darkness, fuelled by an extraordinary resilience, a determination to carry on, come what may. Not just to survive but to prosper, through education and books. People like Sara, Aysha, Abdul Basit, Anas and little Amjad, led the way, through their unfaltering dedication and passion. And I was about to meet another who helped keep the flames of hope alive. Not through reading or writing, but with the help of a paint brush.

# Chapter Six

Daraya's secret library was an extraordinary creation. Its thick walls, deep underground, provided sanctuary from the horrors above. A peaceful place to read, learn and talk. To celebrate literature, poetry, science and history. A place to plan a future without bullets and bombs. But perhaps the most remarkable factor of all was not the building itself, nor the many thousands of books within it. It was the people who created it. Those who risked their lives to fill its shelves, arranged lectures and book groups, logged its titles and scrubbed its floors. The people who never lost faith in the value of culture and humanity in such terrible times.

On 3 June 2014, despite being loathed by many who were busy fighting his rule, President Bashar al-Assad was re-elected to office with a staggering 88.7 per cent of the vote. Assad's fortunes on the battlefield had also improved the month before, when 900 rebel fighters in Homs, Syria's third most populous city, had agreed to leave after being besieged by the government forces for two years. This was a highly significant defeat for the rebels. Homs had wholeheartedly joined the uprising and the city had once been dubbed 'the capital of the revolution'. Yet despite such successes, Assad's hold on power continued to be precarious, and few outside observers thought he would be able to hang on to power much longer.

Then, a week later, came news that the much-feared and despised IS had taken Iraq's second city, Mosul. The following day they went on to capture the Iraqi town of Tikrit. These victories, which followed their conquest of Raqqa in north-east Syria six months before, shocked the world. Long convoys of machine-gun-toting men in black, faces covered with balaclavas, roared along dusty roads, their Islamist flag held defiantly aloft. IS, which had split from al-Qaeda in February 2014, was led by Ibrahim Awwad Ibrahim al-Badri, better known as Abu Bakr al-Baghdadi. On 29 June he rebranded ISIS as Islamic State and declared the return of the 'caliphate', a state to be run under strict Islamic or sharia law. This now stretched all the way from his proclaimed caliphate capital of Raqqa in northern Syria, to Mosul in northern Iraq. IS was opposed to anyone who did not share their beliefs, especially Shia Muslims and those of all other faiths. As a result, their targets included Assad's regime, the Western world and even moderate Sunni Muslim members of the FSA. When IS began flooding the Internet with videos showing the gruesome executions of orange jumpsuited hostages, many of them kidnapped Western journalists and aid workers, the international media focused on little else. To the watching world this was the very incarnation of evil. Yet there seemed to be no way to stop this grim, ragtag army, whose jihadi recruits had come together from all over the globe, all united in their lust for hatred and violence. In the midst of this, the plight of Daraya received little attention. But this was soon to change.

On a clear and humid night in August 2014, the town of Daraya lay asleep. For the first time in weeks, the skies were clear of bomber planes and shells, and the streets below were quiet. But on a small side road, near the centre of the town, a shadow moved to and fro, its presence betrayed by the light of the moon. A tall, slim figure clutching a paint-brush was hard at work. In the near darkness, it was hard to make out who he was or what he was doing. All that could be seen was the shadowy shape of a ladder propped against a wall and the movement of his hands arcing from left to right. When dawn came he was gone, but the result of his night's labour remained for all to see. There on a large concrete slab, hanging from a shattered building, was the image of a little girl. Standing on a pile of skulls, she was writing the word 'hope' high above her head.

Later, this simple image, with its one word caption, in-spired people across the world. I was one of them. I was sent a photo of the picture by a contact in Daraya, not long after it was painted. The version on my phone had no text beneath, no message, just the picture of the little girl and that single word, 'hope'. I remember crying when I first saw it. Not tears of sorrow, but of relief, joy and deep ad-miration. This was a country at war, a town under siege, a people starved, yet here was the image of a child, writing about hope, not hate or revenge. It gave me hope too. Hope for Syria's future. What a riposte this was to the posters elsewhere in Syria of men in masks, pointing guns, endless drawing of explosions and soldiers, arms aloft, basking in the death of those who opposed them. It reminded me of seeing an interview on BBC television several decades ago. In 1987 a young nurse, Marie Wilson, was killed by an IRA bomb in the town of Enniskillen, Northern Ireland. Before she died her father, Gordon Wilson, had held her hand as they both lay in the rubble. When asked of his response to the bombing by a reporter, he said simply: 'I bear no ill will. I bear no grudge,' and he called for forgiveness and recon- ciliation between both sides of the conflict. His words were reported around the world and came to symbolise what was coined the 'spirit of Enniskillen'.

I was so captivated, so moved by the image in Daraya that I set out to contact the artist behind it. Initial enquiries brought little success. Many of the people I spoke to there knew about the painting but not the person responsible for it. Some appeared to know a little more, but had heard that the artist wanted to keep his identity secret. That didn't surprise me, given that many supporting the uprising against Assad feared, not only for themselves, but also for their families. But finally I did manage to make contact with the mysterious painter, and we began a conversation by email. In answer to my question as to why he had chosen to put the young girl at the centre of his painting, he wrote: 'To me, she symbolises much of the Syrian population. Al- though most are innocent, so many of them are suffering. Yet despite the war, despite the deaths, despite the terrible siege we live under, we still have hope.'

Over the following weeks, the young artist sent me photos of other work he had done around Daraya. He was in some of the photos himself, though he always wore a mask over his face in order to keep his identity secret. Overnight, this sensitive nineteen-year-old youth had helped transform the image of Daraya. The Syrian government had long insisted that the town was a hotbed of terrorists, who threatened the survival of all decent people living in Syria. Yet with one painting the artist known as Abu Malik al-Shami – not his real name – had shown what a lie that was. Abu Malik's gentle image spoke of life triumphing over death, and hope over hate. But while his painting became recognised around the world, few know much about the artist himself, not to mention his dozens of other works dotted around Daraya. Largely because of this fact, the Western media labelled the town's mysterious, fly-by-night creator, the 'Banksy' of Daraya. It is a nickname that stuck.

Abu Malik told me he had been worried that his art would not go down well, especially with locals. 'In the beginning I was very afraid of what people would think about my drawings on the walls,' he explained. 'I mean, many of them have had their homes destroyed, and here I was drawing on the shattered remains of where they had once lived. I felt this would look rather cruel and heartless. So I did these murals after dark, usually in quieter streets where few people pass by. I didn't want anyone to know who I was in case it made them angry and they stopped me from doing any more.'

For these reasons, as well as concerns about his safety, Abu Malik wanted his identity kept secret, although he did agree to tell me a little about his background. He is from Damascus and one of a very large family of seven brothers and three sisters, all of whom had studied at university. While none of them had ever picked up a paintbrush, art had always been a central part of Abu Malik's life. He first used his creative skills in 2011 after joining demonstrations against President Bashar al-Assad, aged just sixteen. 'I was a great believer in what the people were calling for and decided to join the rallies on the streets. Back then, these protests were all peaceful. I soon worked out the best way I could help was by using my artistic skills. I contributed by drawing illustrations for the revolution as well as writing many slogans.'

As the security forces became more violent, several of Abu Malik's friends were arrested and later tortured. He carried on protesting on the streets until police seized him too, along with one of his brothers. Although he was later released, this spelled the end of both Abu Malik's studies and life with his family in Damascus. Convinced by this point that peaceful protest was getting nowhere, he decided, with great reluctance, that Assad's regime could only be defeated by force. Early in 2013 he joined the FSA. 'I felt the time for shouting at the regime was gone,' he told me. 'Now I had to fight them.'

Abu Malik chose to join the FSA in Daraya for two reasons. Firstly, he greatly admired Ghiath Matar, the prominent non-violent revolutionary, who had been arrested alongside his brother, Hazem, and then killed by the security forces. Secondly, one of Abu Malik's older brothers, who went by the *nom de guerre* Abu Omar al-Shami, was already in Daraya, having joined the FSA some months previously. Before the war Abu Malik had been to the town occasionally with his father to visit relatives. Even back then it wasn't easy to get to Daraya from Damascus by public transport but in March 2013, with the town surrounded by hostile pro-Assad forces, it was almost impossible. Making sure he was carrying nothing that might reveal his links with anti-government groups, Abu Malik chose what looked like the best route. This took him through the neighbouring town of al-Moadamyeh, just to the west of Daraya. He wrote: 'I vividly remember the regime checkpoint I had to go through to get to Daraya from there. It was one of the most feared checkpoints in the whole area. The post was run by local committees who were known for being very cruel to civilians. They're reported to have killed on the spot anyone they suspected of being involved in the FSA. Women were often raped. They had a terrible reputation. So I was really lucky to get through and make it to Daraya.'

Abu Malik was deeply shocked when he got there. The level of destruction was beyond anything he had imagined; the whole town seemed to have been completely destroyed and a couple of days after he arrived, Daraya came under ferocious attack. During this airstrike, thirteen out of fourteen members of one family were killed. The building they lived in was near where Abu Malik was staying. 'It was the first time I had seen blood splattered everywhere and people dying right in front of me,' he told me. 'Never before had I walked though streets littered with fragments of people after air raids and mortar fire.' He then told me that some members of that family might have been saved if it had been possible to get them to hospital quickly. But the building they were in was so badly damaged that it had taken hours to get them out. After a long silence, he added: 'I'm still overwhelmed by those first memories of Daraya. It was all so terribly shocking to me. I had never seen anything like it before.'

After being introduced to his FSA unit by his brother, he began his military training. Given that the town was fighting for its very survival, Abu Malik imagined that thousands of fighters would be defending it. But when he got to the front line, he was surprised to find that there were only a few hundred, and many of them seemed very young and inexperienced. On seeing this he felt that he had been right to choose to fight here, as they clearly needed help, although, he told me, 'I have to admit, I did occasionally think of getting out of the place and saving my skin. But with so many people dying here and so few fighters defending the city, I felt I had to stay and help.'

Abu Malik was part of a group tasked with defending Daraya. The job of launching attacks against Assad's forces was, at that point, left to others. The front line was a scary place, especially for a young man not yet out of his teens who had only recently picked up a gun. In some areas, the two warring sides were only a few metres apart. Nothing had quite prepared Abu Malik for this. 'I had been at college,' he recalled, 'studying books, going to lectures and living with my family. Yet here I was now, just a stone's throw away from people who were trying to kill me.' Every day Abu Malik witnessed death and destruction. He admitted that at times he found it difficult to cope with. But there was no way back. He feared that had he returned to Damascus, he would have been arrested and killed.

It was during the summer of 2014 that Abu Malik first picked up his paintbrush in Daraya. 'I hadn't done any artwork, including graffiti, on walls before I moved to Daraya. In fact, I didn't start doing this until around a year after I got here. It was when the fighting calmed down for a while that I suddenly got the opportunity. With time on my hands and surrounded by such terrible destruction, I decided to do my first painting on a wall in the town.' He modestly described one of the first paintings he had done as graffiti. Working in the darkness of a summer's night in 2014, he painted the flag of the revolution with his rifle next to it, adding some poems he had written alongside the image. After that, he painted copies of art he had seen and admired in other besieged towns in Syria. His main aim, he told me, was to help cheer up the people who were living in such a terribly depressing environment. 'Most of the town was completely destroyed. It's devastating for people to live amid all this destruction. Nothing but crumbling debris and pale, fading colours. I thought I could make life much more colourful with my big, bright paintings. Above all, I wanted to remind everyone that there was life here as well as death.'

On 2 December 2014 pro-Assad forces broke through rebel lines and captured four blocks of the city. Rebel forces then counter-attacked and swiftly took all but one back. Although positioned a fair way back from the front line, Abu Malik admitted to finding it all 'very frightening'. Intense fighting carried on for just over two months until, suddenly, the guns fell silent once more. A ceasefire deal brought the people of Daraya a welcome respite from the carnage. For Abu Malik it presented the opportunity to get back to work. Before too long he was once more painting and drawing on the walls of Daraya, though just as before, he only did this at night.

It was at this point that Abu Malik began to realise the importance of his art to the local community. Though valued for his courage in joining the FSA, in that role he was just another man with a gun. But when it came to using his paintbrush to promote the revolution against Assad, Abu Malik was in a league of his own. His work was beginning to spread the message of the rebellion around the world. It was also lifting local morale. Seeing his paintings daubed on walls around Daraya, people felt that at last somebody was articulating their thoughts, as well as brightening their environment. It was the same for the work done by Anas, Abdul Basit, Amjad and their friends in creating and maintaining the secret library. Had they decided to join the FSA and fight full time, their extraordinary sanctuary would never have existed. The inspiration this provided, the encouragement and will to carry on that it gave to so many, would have been sorely missed.

One day a local photographer, Majd Mouaddmani, nicknamed 'the eye of Daraya', noticed one of Abu Malik's drawings on a wall. Impressed with what he saw, he asked one of the artist's friends to introduce him. At their first meeting, Majd immediately suggested that Abu Malik should do more of his painting and poetry around town to help make demoralised Daraya look a much brighter place. Sensing that Abu Malik still felt a little nervous about doing the paintings openly, Majd, who was known for his fearless photography on the front line, suggested that they work together. He offered to get the materials they needed and to act as Abu Malik's assistant. When the paintings were finished, he would photograph them and then post them online. That way people in the town would get to see them too, and know that their sacrifices for the revolution were not being forgotten. Abu Malik, meanwhile, wanted to use his wall paintings to send out a message of his own: 'One of optimism rather than sadness, he said. 'Hope seemed a good theme. So I started thinking deeply about how I could best illustrate that.'

The people of Daraya were nothing if not resourceful. They wanted a library, and so they had set to work, retrieving thousands of titles from abandoned buildings and turning a dingy wreck of a basement into somewhere special. In just the same spirit, Abu Malik and his friend were not to be defeated by a lack of paint and paper. Majd, who was born and bred in Daraya, was on good terms with the owner of a shop that had sold art materials. While the shop itself had been badly damaged and was no longer open, the owner said they were welcome to use his surviving stocks of paint, pencils and paper. And even though Daraya had hardly any food, safe drinking water, electricity or medicine, Majd somehow managed to find nearly everything else they needed. The only element they lacked was a product to remove unwanted paint. Not to be defeated, Majd came up with a way of making this, gathering lots of plastic water bottles and other containers which, along with a few specially chosen chemicals, were thrown into a metal drum, before being melted down over a hot fire. The ugly looking liquid that resulted from it turned out to be a great paint-remover.

And Majd did much more than just providing materials. He would scrub the selected wall before Abu Malik started and then after the drawing was complete, he would help colour it in. When they had both finished, Majd would take a photo of the picture and post it on social media. Abu Malik told me that Majd soon became an invaluable assistant-cum-soulmate. 'We got on really well and worked together like this for quite a while. I really couldn't have done what I did without him.'

People told Abu Malik and Majd how deeply inspired they were by their artwork and encouraged them to do more. Some even asked if they would paint on the walls of their home. This uplifting response made the pair more ambitious than ever, and they put extra thought into the messages that accompanied the paintings. They chose a few basic themes to focus on – oppression, revolution and mistakes made during the revolution, as well as other topics suggested by locals. Sometimes they would base the pictures on special events. One mother's day, the pair thought of how mothers were suffering throughout the nation, and how Syria was everybody's mother country. A young mother swathed in black sits protectively embracing her newborn baby. Head on one hand, her face is grim and near despair. Behind her a helicopter circles over a town being blown apart. To the left is a large red heart with a gaping hole torn out of it. Next to that is the name Daraya.

They also did drawings to highlight the plight of those who had been arrested by the regime. Abu Malik told me: 'We wanted the people themselves, as well as their families, to know we were all thinking about them. We wanted to give them some hope.'

Just as the library was about much more than just passing the time reading books, so Abu Malik's paintings were not merely decorative. Both were forms of thoughtful resistance, aimed at raising awareness about what was happening in Daraya, while also encouraging people not to lose hope. The more paintings Abu Malik and Majd did, the more local people began to understand this. Now their art was being seen as a valid and important part of the uprising, helping to define the hopes and dreams of all those seeking to bring freedom of speech, democracy and civil rights to Syria. The two of them went on to do more than twenty different paintings around Daraya, each with its own message. Abu Malik had never felt happier. He had found his true vocation, as well as a friend for life.

Then tragedy struck: 'It was a bitterly cold winter's day in Daraya,' Abu Malik told me. 'I was at home preparing my paints. It was then that I heard the news. Majd was dead. He had been killed. It was terrible. I will never forget that day.' Well known as a brave and fearless photographer, Majd had been on the front line, taking photographs of the intense fighting that was raging around Daraya. Over recent months his photos of the fighting, rooftop snipers and barrel bombs had been seen around the world. He had taken huge risks to capture the scenes on his last mission. Despite the shrapnel flying all around him, he had carried on photographing the brutality of the war. He had done this often before, and had escaped with his life. This time he was not so lucky.

Abu Malik praised his friend, telling me: 'Majd was absolutely devoted to showing the world what was happening in Daraya. He was more successful in doing this than anyone else I know. He did so much for us all.'

Following Majd's death, Abu Malik considered giving up painting but the encouragement he got from local people persuaded him to carry on. They told him that this is what Majd would have wanted and it was what they wanted too. Some offered to introduce Abu Malik to other painters, photographers and illustrators who could fill Majd's shoes and help him with his murals. And it is testimony to Abu Malik's resilience that he took this help and carried on with his mission. After all, his most famous work of August 2014, the one mentioned earlier, was yet to come. 'The drawing I did of the little girl painting hope on the wall was the first one I did after Majd died,' he told me, his voice quavering. 'I am proud that I managed to do it alone, it was one of my favourites. But I missed him so very much.'

It is certainly one of my favourites too. So simple yet so powerful. According to the UK-based monitoring organisation, the Syrian Observatory for Human Rights, more than 3500 children were killed in Syria in 2014. By the end of that year that dreadful number rose still further as the overall death toll topped 200,000 – a shocking figure that was to more than double over the years to come. Yet the outside world was struggling to engage in what was becoming an ever more complicated conflict. And sadly, while Abu Malik's picture of the little girl helped simplify what was happening, in Daraya at least, it failed to generate much concrete help for the besieged town. This was tragic, for just as Daraya's extraordinary secret library gave people hope for the future, Abdul Malik's work aimed to win their support in the present. He was determined to show that there was more to Syria than war, hate and destruction. That amid all the brutality, there were decent people who yearned to live in peace, free from oppression.

Another of Abu Malik's much-admired murals was a painting of two teenage boys, best friends, who grew up together and later fought side-by-side in Daraya. When one of them was killed the other continued fighting, before he too died in battle. Both, Abu Malik told me, lived and died pursuing the same shared goals. So, in a way, not even death had separated them. It was a story that many in Daraya identified with strongly. Convinced that he would never get out of Daraya alive, Abu Malik clearly hoped that his work might also become a living memorial to his friendship with Majd.

Several months after Abu Malik's mural of the little girl appeared in Daraya, a wave of despair swept through the town. The siege was causing terrible hardship. Supplies of food and medicine had reached a new low and the number of dead and injured continued to rise. Abu Malik, whose visions of hope had helped persuade many not to give up, was back on the front line himself, involved in an intense and desperate battle. When the regime's soldiers bombarded the rebel-held town of Zabadani, just north of Damascus, the leader of Abu Malik's brigade decided to mount a fierce counter-attack. However, the operation did not go well for Abu Malik. He was in the first wave of rebel fighters that advanced towards the regime's positions. As he was running across open land towards the enemy, a bullet, fired from at least a hundred metres away, blew him off his feet. It was to be his last day as a fighter. 'It went clean through my chest and straight out my back,' he told me. 'By the time my comrades had dragged me to our first-aid post, I had lost a lot of blood.'

Abu Malik was badly injured and for the next four months he was unable to leave his bed. But this terrible experience did not dampen his enthusiasm for the cause. While recovering from his injuries, his mind turned again to art. He began sketching out plans for another mural, this time featuring a man with a red and white Santa Claus hat, lobbing a finely wrapped Christmas present in the direction of his enemy. He hoped to have it finished by Christmas, a time when its message might have maximum impact in the Western world. But when Abu Malik realised that, given the extent of his injuries, it was unlikely to be ready in time, he called on friends. With their help he managed to go outside and draw the main lines of the picture. Then, under his supervision, he left the others to colour it in, just like his friend Majd had done.

Fortunately, it was not long before Abu Malik was up and about, and painting again. 'Since recovering from my injuries,' he told me, 'I've done even more artwork than before. I'm not as fit as I was, so I've exchanged fighting for painting. All my energies are focused in that direction now.'

One of the murals Abu Malik did around this time shows a soldier sitting opposite a little girl who is pointing to a picture frame with a large red heart in it. As in his earlier 'hope' mural, he was depicting the image of a little girl as the face of innocence among the carnage. As we talked about it during one of our conversations, Abu Malik told me: 'The child is teaching a soldier the meaning of love. She warns him to avoid being manipulated by people during wars. I made sure that the soldier has no identity, he's just a guy in green, because I wasn't referring to any army in particular. Instead I want to get through to any soldier, anywhere, who is carrying a weapon. He needs to be clear why he is fighting and what he is fighting for. He should always be sure he is listening to his head as well as his heart.'

Abu Malik appeared to be well in tune with both. He had resisted armed rebellion until firmly convinced that the regime wasn't listening to peaceful protest. Yet his heart told him that violence could take the rebellion only so far. At some point talking, learning and planning would need to take over to seal the peace. It was this conviction that brought him regularly to the secret library. When not drawing on shattered walls or fighting on the front line, Abu Malik could often be found with his head buried in a book. Like so many other young Syrians, the war had brought his education to a sudden halt and he yearned for the day when he could resume his studies. 'The secret library,' he told me, 'is a great place for self-development. Each of us has our own separate role outside it, but as soon as we go through its doors, our objectives are the same. I have to confess that I never used to like reading much. It was coming to the library that changed that view and inspired my love of books.'

As we talked, I could see among the scattered pencils,

paints and brushes an assortment of books that Abu Malik had borrowed from the secret library. Some were about history, others dealt with human development and the rest were novels. Abu Malik treasured them all. 'Even after three years of living under siege in Daraya, I'm passionate about reading, I haven't lost my appetite for it at all. As I said, this is all thanks to the secret library. That's why we are all so determined to protect it.'

In a time of such awful death and destruction, this was to prove a difficult task. With Daraya plagued by daily airstrikes and shelling, the secret library was under constant threat. Although sited in an underground basement, a direct hit on the building above would probably wipe it out. Even a bomb landing next door might do the same. Yet I had the feeling that, even if the secret library were totally destroyed and Abu Malik's paintings too, it would not spell the end for the people of Daraya. It was far more likely that those who had created them would, somehow, start all over again. Buildings and paintings can be easily destroyed, but not the hope and inspiration they generated. The indomitable spirit of Daraya would be much harder to extinguish than that.

# Chapter Seven

As the siege wore on, getting food and medical supplies into Daraya became harder as government forces discovered more of the smuggling routes. The ongoing bombing was continuing to take its toll too, with few homes left undamaged. But none of this stopped, or even slowed activities at the town's secret library. Anas, Abdul Basit and their friends continued to rescue books, despite the attentions of ever-present pro-Assad snipers. Under cover of darkness they would discreetly ferry them into the library, where the books would sit in big piles until somebody could sift through them. The inside cover of each would be marked with the name and address of the place they had come from, and then they were given a reference number. After that they would be cleaned up, repaired if necessary and sorted according to author and subject matter.

Making contact with people in Daraya was often not only difficult but unnerving. What if I was to call one of the team when they were out collecting books under the noses of snipers? The last thing they would need as they tip-toed through rubble in the darkness, taking care not to talk or make any sound, was for one of their phones to light up and start ringing. Calling them at the secret library was less of a worry in that regard, although the Wi-Fi signal in the basement was very weak and getting through in the first place was enough of a challenge. This was particularly true when it came to Skype, which tended not to work when the signal was poor. This meant I often had to make do with audio calls and even just texts at times. But like all other users, I was always made to feel welcome when calling the library, even though my visits were via the airwaves rather than physical.

The library had been operating for a while now, and since its opening, it had also become everything from a meeting place, tea room, and education centre, to a lecture hall and a place of entertainment. I was told that as many as thirty people a day were now visiting it, which is quite impressive given that, because it was secret, people only knew where it was through word of mouth. In the course of trying to find out more about how this worked, I was told to speak with Saeed Sakka, a former pharmacy student in his early twenties. One of his tasks was to promote the library as much as possible without unduly risking its security. Saeed sent me more photos of it. One of the most interesting ones showed a kind of pinboard on the back wall with lots of notes stuck to it. Most were handwritten, enthusiastic-looking scrawls in Arabic. Given the poor light in the room, it was hard to make out either who had written them or what they referred to. I wondered at first if they might be the names and addresses of people who had failed to bring back their books on time. Was it, perhaps, Amjad's wall of shame? But going by the dates that appeared amid many hastily written messages, the notes seemed to be notices about upcoming events.

Saeed, a bright-eyed young man with the muscular build and steely air of a fighter, confirmed that many of the notes were, indeed, notices for an assortment of special classes held there. These seemed almost as numerous and varied as the books on the shelves. He told me: 'We are trying to provide support for just about everyone in Daraya, people of all ages and abilities. This means there are requests to teach and lecture on a wide variety of subjects.'

Saeed explained that over the course of time more and more locals had discovered the library and had come forward to offer their help and expertise. Now, rather than the ten or so young men who had set it up, there were more than eighty people involved in running the library, so it could offer more activities than ever. There was even a shift system in place to help keep it open for as long as possible each day, except for Fridays, when it was shut for prayers. He said they were always on the lookout for new ideas and new ways to promote the library locally without compromising its security. Sometimes, people would come up with great suggestions and if none of the secret library circle knew how to run the proposed event, they would seek help from outside. 'In the early days,' Saeed said, 'some of the people we asked to help us here hadn't even heard of the library because we have never advertised it. People still walk right past the library every day without ever knowing that it's here. But we also have to try and ensure that the regime never finds out where it is.'

Anas and his close friend Abdul Basit were the first people I had spoken to about the secret library. To me they both seemed such an integral part of it that I could not imagine it existing without them. Anas was keen to update me on what was happening and he confirmed that the library was fast becoming an education centre and lecture hall as well as a reading room. Classes were being held there, on everything from English, Maths and world history, to debates on literature and religion. These were usually followed by lively discussions. One of the most memorable and popular talks was on how the Japanese city of Hiroshima had been rebuilt after it was devastated by an atomic bomb in the Second World War.

Another lecture which fired people's imagination was on the London Blitz during the same conflict and how the city had survived near endless bombardments. One of the most recent talks had looked at what lessons could be learned from the brutal civil war in neighbouring Iraq – a subject the people of America and Britain, among other nations, have been grappling with ever since the Coalition's invasion in 2003.

The fact that the library was also fulfilling a vital social function was also confirmed to me by Rateb abo Fayez, the young fighter with the FSA. 'We all meet here to discuss Daraya's problems and how best to deal with them. We look for ways to get as many local intellectuals and experts of all types together here. With their help we can plan the best policies for the weeks, months and years ahead. We also talk about new ways to get our movement's aims across to the outside world and how we can go about attracting help.' At the moment, Rateb told me, the discussion groups were divided by age. He was part of the second group, comprised of around thirty young people born between 1992 and 1995. They tried to meet once a week, depending, of course, on the security situation. Somebody would agree to lead the session and give a talk. 'It was because of this project that I recently had to make my first public speech,' Rateb told me. 'I was very nervous.'

Such nerves were evidently a thing of the past, because Rateb told me that having done many talks since then, he now considered himself a bit of a pro. He had even held classes on *how* to give lectures, including the kind of research you should do first. 'When a person I have helped delivers a lecture well, I feel great satisfaction,' he said, 'It's almost as if I had delivered it myself. So when thirty people have given lectures to us in the library I feel I have succeeded thirty times!'

Not that Rateb and his colleagues were resting on their laurels. As soon as one session had finished, they were busy preparing the agenda for the next. And while all that was going on, someone else would be organising a committee to check what progress had been made on other projects. Rateb explained that this last measure was put in place because people tended to work better if they knew their achievements were being monitored. Here they were, half-starved, in one of the most dangerous countries on earth, yet organising such a host of different activities. I couldn't help thinking how impressive this was and how efficiently this group would be at running a library – or even a business – in the West.

While he had been a founding member of the secret library – and was now so clearly devoted to it – Rateb hadn't always been so keen on books. 'Before the revolution,' he said, 'me and my friends had little interest in reading. We only read books that we had to study for our university courses, but this completely changed after the secret library was created. And as we didn't have any TV or other ways to connect with the outside world, reading became our only window on life beyond Daraya. The library not only made us better informed on lots of subjects, it also let us escape to another world.'

Whenever he got a break from the front line, Rateb

would always make his way to the library. There he would read, recuperate, exchange stories and celebrate still being alive. But being a single man at the time, unlike men with families, he often had to stay at his post, or very near it, even when off duty. So he decided that if he could not go to the library, the library would come with him. 'I would take my library books with me to the front line, to the places where we would fight and often sleep for days. Most of the guys I was with did the same and we would swap books with each other. We obviously couldn't do this in the heat of battle, but it worked well when things were calm.'

Rateb's image conjured up a rather surreal picture in my mind: lines of men with guns, sitting reading in their trenches. But, as I was to find out from Rateb and some of his colleagues, life on the front line was not always how many of us would imagine it. There were long, quiet periods on both sides when little happened and life was sometimes more boring than frightening. There's nothing better to do at such moments, Rateb told me, than getting stuck into your favourite book.

One of Rateb's FSA colleagues, Omar Abu Anas, was a great fan of reading on the battlefield. He told me: 'When I sit there and the front line is quiet, it's a little like being at the library itself. I take out my bag of books, which I think of as my mini-library, and read bits of each of them. For half an hour I might read about economics, then half an hour later it might be history, literature or poetry.' Omar insisted that he and Rateb were far from being the only ones to do this. Many other fighters brought their book collections, or 'mini-libraries' as Omar had called them, to the front line. This meant that when one fighter had finished with a book he could simply swap it for another from somebody else's collection. And when there were prolonged quiet periods, fighters even got together and held what amounted to front-line book clubs in their foxholes. Given that they usually only had one copy of each book they couldn't all discuss the same one. Instead, each would give a talk about the one he had read and then take questions about it from his comrades. Discussions would range from queries about the plot line and quality of the writing to the moral issues raised in the story: 'On average there is an FSA front line point around every fifty metres. Each one of us has about four books or so, which we then swap and discuss. It's a wonderful way for us to exchange books and ideas when we can't get to the secret library.'

The secret library was now also home to a weekly book club. However, as it was more difficult to pass books around when readers were not sitting close to each other, and because, like in the frontline foxholes, there was mostly only one copy of each title in the library, those attending would talk about the one they had borrowed. It was, Rateb enthused, all about sharing knowledge and ideas. 'The atmosphere is wonderful. I really look forward to these sessions, even though I have a very long walk to get here. It allows me to meet with people that I would never otherwise see. These are cultivated people, intellectuals and good-natured souls, and we all look forward to getting together.'

Rateb revealed that, after the initial book club discussion, there would often be a presentation – by which he did not mean somebody just pulling out some scribbled notes, but a well-planned talk often involving the use of a slide projector. And such evenings did not end there. Following this, there would often be another discussion, which according to Rateb was usually a fun and very lively affair:

'We laugh and share anecdotes and sometimes we even run some small competitions. The atmosphere is wonderful. I feel so happy and comfortable spending time with these people, it makes me feel like I have everything I need and nothing is missing. We all forget that we are away from our parents, because in a way the secret library is our home. We are like a family here.'

When Rateb said this, I was in no doubt that he meant every word. He spoke with such warmth for those around him in the library. It was through Rateb that I had first met Homam al-Toun, another fighter with the FSA. Like just about all the men there, he had the obligatory dark beard, much fuller than Rateb's, and short thick hair. His face was rather thin but his eyes were bright and friendly. He was keen to tell me about sessions held at the library to help former students resume their education. He told me about a friend of his, who was studying to be an engineer, but who, like many others in war-torn Syria, had never been able to finish his training. The idea to help the many people in that position came about at a meeting in the library soon after it opened. Most of the people there were well educated but had younger siblings, friends and other relatives who had few, if any, qualifications. Some in the town were even worse off. Many had never even read a book and some could not read at all.

Homam recalled how at that meeting, one of the young men at the back became very emotional. He said how terrible it was that more educated people, like himself and the others gathered in the library, had ignored those who were much less fortunate. Such people look up to us, he had said, yet we have done nothing for them. Then, after moving to the front of the room, the man had added: 'Whatever

127

we are doing, we should be passing on our knowledge to others. We should be generous with what we know, as well as what we have. We must stop thinking only of ourselves.' Homam went on to tell me that the young man was in tears before he had finished speaking. He evidently cared so much for others and was one of the most ardent supporters of the secret library. This story did not have a happy ending: 'Sadly he was killed by a missile only a short time ago. He was just twenty-two years old,' Homam said. 'His death made me so very sad.'

Again, given the carnage happening night and day, I wondered how locals felt about these young men sitting around reading books. What did Anas, Abdul Basit and the others say to those who demanded that they pick up a gun and go out to help people like Rateb defend their town? When I asked him this, Anas listened patiently to my question and paused before replying. When the answer came his voice was steady.

'There's an old Arabic saying, "He who lacks knowledge will turn into a highway thief." I see no point in young men going to fight if they don't know what they're fighting for. We have to be educated. Also, when this war is over we will have a country that will desperately need rebuilding. We, the more educated ones, will be a big part of that. This is accepted here.' Anas added that many of those who used the library, such as Rateb's friend Omar, also spent some of their time fighting on the front line. At this point an old saying came into my mind. It was the old British one, about the pen being mightier than the sword. I asked Anas if he agreed with that sentiment. 'I don't think that even needs discussion,' he replied. 'My answer is yes, 100 per cent!'

Homam also strongly rejected the suggestion that reading

books was any less worthy or valuable than bearing arms against the regime. 'I was surrounded by people who had fought on the front line for years,' he said, 'and am a fighter myself, but most of us can only do that for a while. I really don't think that working at the library and fighting with weapons are two contradictory things. Some of us fight to save our beloved town of Daraya, while others concentrate on building this library and improving people's education. We all support the revolution and share the same goal.'

I knew, of course, that members of the FSA had helped set up the library. Many of their fighters were not professional soldiers, and had also been university students before the war. They held the library in high regard and were delighted it had been created. Omar had told me just how much he loved the peace and tranquillity there and how this basement home had offered him respite from the front line, the war and the baking heat above. Its calmness also freed his mind, and reading and discussing books had opened him up to new ideas. When I had talked to Omar, he had been sitting in the library with his rifle and dust-caked boots, looking very at home among the shelves of books. I'd mentioned this to him and he'd said: 'I'm not a career soldier and neither are many of the people I fight with. I was a second-year engineering student at university but I had to give up my education to protect Daraya. Most of those involved in the revolution didn't want to pick up weapons. But the brutality of the regime left us with no other choice.'

There were dissenters, however. It took a moment but then Homam admitted what I had long suspected. Namely, that there were those who believed that reading was a complete waste of time. In fact, he told me, some resented the library so much that they had threatened to destroy it. 'There were some FSA fighters who weren't educated and were totally against the library project,' he told me. 'They used to say, "Here we are, doing all this fighting and all you can think about is books." Things came to a head when we heard that some of them were threatening to blow up the library! I was utterly horrified.'

Homam went on to explain that most of those who made these threats had never appreciated libraries and books. Some even despised such things. The hotheads among them began saying the best thing to do with the library, which its organisers had initially called 'Dawn of the nation', was to have it bombed. Homam believes this decision may have been influenced by the name it was given. 'In Arabic the word dawn is very much like the word for a bomb, just a couple of letters different. I think this is what led them to suggest this form of destruction.'

Determined to keep their treasured library in one piece, Homam invited those who thought this way to visit it. They were reluctant until he pointed out that if they came they could listen to talks being given there by fellow fighters. That seemed to make a difference and Homam became optimistic that the detractors would come. All he needed, he believed, was to get them through the door. Once they saw what was really going on, they would change their minds and eventually come to love the place. 'Ignorance is always the enemy of humanity,' he said, passionately. 'The worst enemy facing a man is someone who knows nothing of what he speaks. When they had said that they didn't like what was happening in the library they actually had no idea what was going on there.'

Homam's efforts bore fruit. When the critics finally

accepted his invitation and came to visit the library, most were very impressed. They listened to speeches from FSA leaders with great interest, regularly erupting with rounds of applause. Homam added: 'It really helped to change their minds and inspired many of them educationally, personally and spiritually.' It then became clear why some of those who came had been so against books and libraries before. They were illiterate. Many had signed up there for classes in reading and writing, and began coming to the library regularly.

This was a library for everybody. On its polished shelves were books on just about every topic you could think of, each one either an education, an escape or entertainment for the reader, and often all three. They came in all different sizes, shapes and colours. From thin satin-covered poetry books embossed with delicate gold lettering, to sturdy encyclopaedias, richly embossed history books, sombre religious tomes and colourful works of literature. There was another category of titles that might easily have gone unnoticed by the casual eye. While often the plainest, least interesting-looking of all the books housed in the library, these were perhaps more valuable than any: specialist books on engineering, medicine, mathematics, chemistry, plumbing, law, teaching – all the subjects needed to keep society running. Such tomes were pored over by former university students, thirsty for the knowledge and tuition they had been deprived of by the war. Then there were visionaries such as Sara and Aysha who, in the absence of school books, used the library's resources to distil knowledge for their pupils. There was also the remarkable story of Ayham al-Sakka, who used the library's textbooks to continue his studies.

Ayham had been studying dentistry at Damascus University when the conflict brought a premature end to his education. In normal times, his failure to graduate with a certificate would have disqualified him from practising dentistry. But these were not normal times. All qualified dentists had left Daraya, along with the majority of other residents, when the terrible violence began. This meant that Ayham was the only one left with any idea of how to care for people's teeth. With the help of medical books from the secret library, he was able to step into the breach and provide a valuable service.

I was first introduced to Ayham, the dentist of Daraya, by Abdul Basit. 'Ayham is a very outgoing person. He is always smiling and has a very loud laugh. In fact, a smile hardly ever leaves his face. He is very good natured and liked by just about everyone he meets. One of the things I most love about Ayham is his wry sense of humour, and I mean that in a nice way. He's physically very tall and well built, but is saved from looking threatening by his childlike face.' The following day Abdul Basit texted me Ayham's WhatsApp number, along with several photos of him at work. There, deep in the bowels of what looked like some kind of clinic, was a man in a surprisingly crisp white medical coat. The walls surrounding him were covered in deep gouges and holes. In pride of place, bang in the centre of the room, was a rather antiquated-looking dentist chair in which lay a bearded young man in a check-shirt, pain etched all over his face. Bending over his open-mouthed patient was twenty-five-year-old Ayham.

When I managed to get through to the dentist of Daraya, the character I encountered was quite different to the one painted by Abdul Basit. He was not in any way unfriendly, but seemed rather reserved and a little intense. On being told how he had been described by his friend, a warmth came into his voice. He told me that Abdul Basit's words were very flattering, but he saw himself quite differently. 'I am quite a quiet person, a bit of a loner. Somebody who is often happier in his own company rather than going out so-cialising.' Ayham told me that he had time to talk because he had fewer patients in his surgery due to intensive bombing earlier in the day, although he said: 'Even if there is heavy shelling and people are scared to go out, this does not put everyone off. Some people have such severe toothache that not even bombs and snipers will stop them coming here for help. They'll risk anything to get treatment, including their lives.'

Ayham went on to explain that he could have left the country and finished his dental training abroad, but had decided to stay after hearing that he was the only person with dental training left in Daraya. The fact that he was not yet qualified for the job had been a worry at first but when the library opened, he quickly saw a solution. 'I realised that I could fill the gaps in my knowledge by borrowing medical books from the secret library,' he told me. These weren't specifically about dentistry; they were more general medical textbooks. But they had been a big help nonethe-less. 'I consult them a lot. I've also managed to download some specialist dental books from the Internet and these have been invaluable too.' He pointed out a bookshelf at the other end of the room, with a row of much-prized medical books, all borrowed from the secret library.

Ayham's tools of the trade were clearly far from cutting edge, though they looked better than I had expected. After all, this was a surgery that had been built up in the midst of a siege, where everything but courage was in short supply. Ayham, like many I had talked to in Daraya, was clearly resourceful. He explained that when he decided to set up a dental practice he had little in the way of specialist equipment. He went all over Daraya looking to buy some, but there was none for sale, as every dentist who had fled the town appeared to have taken their instruments with them. But then, Ayham told me, he had a stroke of luck. He came across a dentist who was just about to leave and persuaded the man to sell him his equipment. However, when he got it all home, he discovered that some of the instruments were badly damaged and would have to be replaced. That was when he decided it was time to start taking risks. 'On asking around,' he said quietly, 'I discovered that it was possible to buy most equipment I needed from people who had contacts in the government forces. This was a very difficult and dangerous thing to do. Some people I know have been arrested trying to get equipment and medicine in this way. I didn't like doing it, but there was such desperate need here and it is the only way now.'

It wasn't only a shortage of dental tools and equipment that Ayham was grappling with, he also lacked most drugs and other basic medical supplies. Many of the materials he had, especially the ones he used for fillings, were way past their sell-by date. This meant that there were many dental procedures that he could not perform. He was also short of sterilisation products, and the generators providing electricity for his surgery only worked for about an hour a day. 'As for anaesthesia,' he added, 'I don't have much of that. There's little I can do to ease the pain my patients suffer during some procedures.'

All these difficulties meant that Ayham had to prioritise

the patients he was best equipped to treat. I wondered whether, in a town stalked daily by unimaginable horrors, there would still be a fear of dentists. 'I think people in Daraya are just as anxious about going to the dentist as everybody else,' he said, smiling. 'It is normal. And I tell them they should see it as such. The fear of dentists is everywhere, regardless of war and shelling. One of my own fears is going to the doctor's. I don't know why I worry about that, particularly these days when we have anaesthetics. Not that I have any of those at the moment.'

Ayham was visibly upset when he talked about the children he treated: 'Many children come to visit me seeking help, but my lack of equipment means I often have to turn them away. I have to be very careful not to do anything that might leave them with a lifelong problem or an ugly smile. Tooth extraction is particularly challenging with children.' Due to Ayham's lack of anaesthetics, some of the children he operated on had to put up with a great deal of pain. But he said, his voice becoming low and angry, how could you explain to young children that the only reason they were suffering was because a dictator was blocking aid from entering their town? Ayham was clearly distressed about the hardships being suffered by children in Daraya. Some, he told me, had had to have limbs amputated, others would spend the rest of their lives paraplegic or quadriplegic. Many had lost their mothers, fathers, sisters and brothers, and were alone in the world. 'Although they physically still look like children,' he told me, 'their struggle for survival puts years on their lives.'

His words invoked photos I had seen of young girls and boys in Daraya, lugging carts full of branches for firewood or sitting in long, snaking queues, awaiting handouts of food for their families. Some just sat quietly staring down at the ground, as if the weight of the world was on their shoulders. War, Ayham said, had stolen their childhood. But he felt that at least he was doing something. 'Anyone who lives here needs to feel that they can help in some way. When you witness the constant shelling, the hunger, the lack of medicine and children dying in the streets, you can't just stand by and do nothing. Knowing you are helping even just a little, is the only way to keep sane.'

Later that day, Ayham was back at the secret library having heard that some more medical books had arrived that might be valuable for his dentistry work. Abdul Basit told me that his friend began poring over the two hefty volumes as soon as he arrived. He said that Ayham always seemed to get something useful from the medical books he read: 'He reads everything he can about medicine and dentistry and never stops learning. Every day he gets better at his job. He is an example to us all.'

To me, Ayham's determination to overcome his lack of training, the shortages of medicine and equipment, and the very siege itself, was extraordinary. Hungry, sleep-deprived, frightened and in constant risk of his life, he carried on – just like Daraya somehow did.

# Chapter Eight

As 2015 dawned, President Bashar al-Assad was feeling increasingly confident. So much so that he boasted that his army would win the war by the end of the year. His forces were fast encircling rebel-held Aleppo, Syria's most populous city, and threatening to sever the rebels' supply of arms from Turkey. But weeks later, his opponents fought back, capturing a strategic crossroads on a key route into Aleppo. Then came another blow for the Syrian leader. The large town of Idlib, in the far north-west of the country, fell to al-Qaeda-linked extremists, Jabhat al-Nusra (al-Nusra Front). This was the second biggest town to be captured by rebels since the start of the war four years earlier.

Daraya's beloved secret library had been born in a basement and the intense, ongoing bombing meant that more and more residents were spending much of their lives in one too. Now the battle for the rebel-held town was also going underground, as the conflict spread from the skies and the streets, to below people's feet. A maze of narrow tunnels snaked through the earth, man-sized wormholes, as soldiers burrowed their way under each other's lines. Those creeping along these dark, damp passageways hoped to spring a surprise on their unwary foes. Unlike the rebels who took many months to dig tunnels by hand with spades and pickaxes, pro-Assad forces had powerful machines that could speedily carve out the earth. But there was a drawback to this faster method: the machines made so much noise that rebel fighters could hear them from a long distance away, which gave them the chance to sabotage the operation while the tunnels were still under construction.

While those fighting in the tunnels were spared the destruction of street-level warfare, life down below was its own kind of hell. Most tunnels were little more than a foot-and-a-half wide and less than six feet high. Taller men struggled to walk upright, and breathing could also be a problem as the air became stuffier the further you were from the entrance. And with no lighting, fighters needed torches or had to use the glare of their phones to navigate. These cramped, subterranean passageways were no place for the claustrophobe.

Deep underground, there was no front line, no tell-tale markers to indicate where you were. Without landmarks, fighters needed maps. Misreading these, which was quite easily done in the grave-like gloom, might mean stumbling into the enemy or surfacing right by his guns. Noise travels easily underground. Talking on phones or radios, a sneeze or a cough could get you killed. Casual conversations, or the crunch of a boot, might alert the enemy to the location of a rival's tunnel. Sometimes one side, while making their way through the darkness, would discover the entrance to their enemy's passageway, and underground fire-fights would follow. On other occasions, death would come from carefully placed mines, which were hard to spot in the subterranean gloom.

This underground war was waged with various objectives in mind. Advancing rebel fighters might set up a base in a particular building, then by digging a tunnel beneath it, could escape if later outnumbered by pro-Assad forces. On other occasions they would burrow under their enemy's lines. A surprise attack could be followed by a quick descent back underground. Pro-Assad forces used different tactics. They often used tunnels to gain access to tall buildings on rebel-held land. Their snipers would then make their way up to the roofs of such structures and fire at the enemy below.

Above ground, the long battle for Daraya took a more traditional form, though even there the front line could be difficult to define. I studied Google Earth satellite pictures of the terrain, as well as photos sent to me by people on the ground. It was very hard to make out where the territory of one side ended and the other began. All I could see were ruins and rubble, one shattered, lifeless street crumbling into another. But to the trained local eye, a line did exist between the two, and survival depended on being able to spot it.

Rateb, one of the fighters with the FSA, told me more about the ground they fought on. Rebel posts, he said, marking military positions, varied according to the type of terrain, but the barricades used around them were all composed of barrels filled with soil and debris. These could absorb light shelling and machine gun fire. Rebel posts in open land were often connected by shallow trenches or deeper tunnels, so that fighters could move along their positions without being seen. This was harder to do in urban areas, where rebels had to use roads and paths, so these routes were protected with barricades, often draped with curtains and stuffed with soil and household furniture. The distance between the posts ranged from just a few metres to as much as 100 metres, according to the terrain and the concentration of enemy soldiers. Fighters at each post were split into three main categories. The most numerous were the watchmen, armed with light guns, whose role was to look for any signs of an enemy attack. Then there was a much smaller number of snipers who moved from one post to another, looking for the chance to target the regime's soldiers. Members of the third section, referred to as 'special forces', were tasked with coming to the aid of posts in danger of being overrun.

To get a better insight into what life was like on Daraya's front line I asked Anas and Abdul Basit if they could arrange for me to speak to any more of the FSA fighters they knew. The request was greeted with a big intake of breath. I was told that the FSA commanders would have to be consulted first – there was, after all, a war going on. I was reminded of the old Second World War slogan, 'careless talk costs lives', and reassured Anas and Abdul Basitt that I wasn't planning to ask any militarily sensitive questions.

Anas soon texted me to say that my request had been granted. The following day I arranged to talk to one of the fighters at the secret library via video link. It was another busy day there with Amjad bustling around in the background and people coming and going at regular intervals. Sat in an armchair next to the library's dining table was thirty-one-year-old Alaa Muaddamani. His neatly trimmed beard gave him a bit of a military look, though this was offset by his purple baseball cap and sky-blue T-shirt. Originally from Damascus, Alaa was drafted into the Syrian army's riot police just before the war began. For a year his job was to stop protests by people like Rateb, Anas and Abdul Basit, all of whom would later become his close friends. Disgusted with his job, he defected from the army and moved to rebel-held Daraya, where he was taken on by the town council. His initial role was to take care of civilians during attacks on the town. With bombs and shells raining down, that job was easier said than done. Angered, after witnessing the slaughter of several civilians, he enlisted with the FSA. From then on Alaa would be fighting the very force that he had only recently been a member of back in Damascus.

It soon became evident to me that Alaa was not the sort of man to boast or exaggerate. He began by making it clear that he hadn't had a clue what soldiering was all about when he first arrived in Daraya, having previously only been trained to suppress riots. But he told me that the FSA soon schooled him in military tactics and how to use a gun. Many of those he trained with knew no more than he did, and most had never fought in a battle before. The first thing he noticed was how basic the FSA's weapons were in comparison to those of the regime's forces. Their only high-tech weapons were grenade launchers or RPGs, though due to foreign funding they later got hold of some heavy rifles.

One thing that had long puzzled me was how the rebel forces had managed not to run out of ammunition. At this point they had been besieged for nearly four years, cut off from the outside world, yet they were still able to exchange fire with the well-equipped pro-Assad forces. How, I asked Alaa, were they managing to get hold of the zillions of bullets they needed to carry on defending their town? Alaa smiled at this question and slowly nodded his head. Then, scratching his full, dark beard, he pushed back his chair and sighed.

'This has been done by many different ways during

our four years of siege,' he replied finally. 'One of those ways,' he explained, 'was by smuggling ammunition and weapons in cars and trucks from the neighbouring town of al-Moadamyeh. This worked well for a while. Then government forces discovered what was happening and that route was blown. After that our best option was to try and get what we needed by smuggling it between the regime's checkpoints.' These, he said, were often several hundred metres apart, sometimes as much as a kilometre, so it was possible to do this without being spotted. 'People would come from outside with the weapons and ammunition and drop them at a previously agreed place. Then fighters from inside Daraya would go and pick the weapons up.'

After a while, Alaa went on, the government forces had rumbled this method too and the rebels had to come up with yet another plan. While they were working on that, an unexpected success on the battlefield gave them the chance to fortify their supplies. As the FSA forced government troops into a rapid retreat from a number of positions around Daraya, they were able to capture a large stock of guns and ammunition which their enemies had left behind as they fled. But it would never be enough, given the length and ferocity of the ongoing conflict and the siege they were living under. Unless they could find a way of getting hold of a constant supply of ammunition they would eventually run out of bullets and that would be the end of their defence of Daraya.

Just when things were looking very bleak, however, there was a breakthrough. It involved no ingenious new smuggling routes, nor fresh success on the battlefield. It all came down to regime officers and their thirst for money. 'Some of our people were able to do deals with corrupt officers who agreed to sell weapons to us, as well as ammunition. So, the same people we were fighting during the day would sell us weapons at night. A meeting place would be arranged and the corrupt officers would talk terms and then draw up a plan with FSA fighters. A drop-off point for the weapons would be agreed and then our fighters would come and pick them up.' I asked him if he was surprised that senior Syrian army officers were happy to sell weapons to their enemy, knowing that these same arms would later be used against their own soldiers. With a shrug Alaa replied: 'It might be surprising to you, but it wasn't really to us. We had become used to the lack of ethics and morality among some of these army officers. They put money above everything. Let me tell you, some of these officers did not only sell us the weapons, they actually delivered them to us themselves.'

I have heard many tales of corruption during wars but this really was extraordinary. However, given that the regime soon got wise to the various smuggling methods, I asked Alaa if the more ethical army officers had not eventually got wind of this too. 'I believe they knew, at least to some extent, about this sort of thing and tried to control it. But that is very hard to do. It is for this reason that the regime changes the soldiers on its checkpoints regularly.'

Alaa believed there was another reason why this corruption wasn't stopped. Some shipments of ammunition picked up by the rebels contained bullets that were booby-trapped, having being filled with TNT explosives. This meant that when the rifle was fired it would explode, killing or injuring the rebel fighter who had pulled the trigger. But, Alaa went on, the high command did seem to have managed to clamp down recently on corrupt officers and the local FSA's shortage of weapons had got worse again. The regime had also cleared large areas of land around Daraya, making it more difficult to go there without being spotted. As a result, more rebel fighters had died while trying to smuggle in rifles and ammunition. It was still one of the riskiest tasks they had to do.

One of the many things I was keen to find out more about was what it was like on the front line in Daraya. Alaa told me that a great deal depended on what type of terrain they were fighting on. In some areas fighters faced almost constant exchanges of fire, while other spots were much calmer. He reiterated that in rural areas the two sides might be separated by hundreds of metres, which would often be composed of a kind of no-man's-land between isolated farm buildings. Such areas would be constantly bombarded. 'In agricultural areas,' Alaa continued, 'we dig ditches and then make them into tunnels by covering them with wooden planks. That way we can move along our lines without being seen. We also use these shallow tunnels to get our munitions to other fighting points.'

However, regime forces had now discovered many of these, and had done their best to destroy them. 'They rolled their tanks over the tunnels and ditches and blocked them up so that they could not be used any more. In some cases, when they were being really thorough, they even got tractors to fill the ditches with sand.' They also spent time tracking the FSA's supply lines, cutting off weapons being taken from one area to another.

Sometimes the regime's forces would use their superiority in weaponry and numbers to advance very quickly after long periods of stalemate. Very often, though, they would then halt their advance to consolidate their new positions. This gave rebel forces the chance to reinforce their new lines. When time allowed, they would dig ditches about a metre and a half deep and place tall sand barriers, more than the height of a man, in front of them. Where there was time these would be reinforced with concrete, stones and anything else available. Such ceasefires would offer a brief pause from the carnage for soldiers and civilians alike but these could never be relied on. Alaa remembered one time when the regime had agreed to a temporary truce, but the day before it was due to come into effect, their forces began bombing rebel positions. 'On that day,' Alaa told me, 'I lost five of my closest friends. They were some of the finest fighters we had on the front. They had been terrific at motivating us all and we always felt stronger when fighting by their side. That was an extremely devastating day for me. In fact, it was a devastating day for all of us.' He went on to tell me that the rebels had lost more than the lives of their men that day. When, after the initial bombardment, regime forces advanced, the rebels were taken totally by surprise and had to abandon many of their hard-won positions. 'We were just praying for it to get dark,' Alaa said, 'which is when the battles usually calm down. Of all my time in the siege so far, that is the one day that I will never forget.'

All this death and suffering seemed so far from the comfortable leather chairs and neat rows of elegantly bound books of the secret library. It was as if all the mayhem was a world away, or taking place in a different country or time. While I had been talking to Alaa, Rateb had come into view and I could see him sitting patiently next to a pile of library books he was looking through. As somebody who had been through several intense battles, I was keen to draw him in.

Some of Rateb's most harrowing memories seemed to have been when the fighting was at close quarters. 'Sometimes both sides are in the same building, even on the same floor. In fact, I can remember one occasion when there was just one empty room between our forces. We each made holes in the wall on our own sides and fired into the room beyond, hoping our shots would go through the wall opposite. In the end there were so many bullet holes, these walls looked like sieves. There we were, sitting just a few metres away from each other, waiting either to kill or be killed.'

Rateb recalled how, in an effort to break the deadlock, some of the pro-regime soldiers had tried to sneak into the rebels' room in the dead of night. But having suspected this might happen, Rateb's comrades had set booby traps outside their door. 'When we heard sounds of footsteps approaching we retreated a little and let them walk into the trap. When we knew they had crossed the line we threw ourselves on the floor and detonated the explosives.'

It seemed callous, but as Rateb had pointed out, the enemy would have had no qualms about killing them. In addition to each other, another enemy facing both sides, especially the poorly equipped rebels, was the weather. Regularly outgunned, they were often forced to abandon their positions at short notice and take up new ones. This meant they could find themselves in some very inhospitable areas, often open spaces or bombed out-buildings which lacked roofs and sometimes walls. Such places were exposed to the baking sun in summer and the freezing winds and rain in the winter. Rateb told me that when it was cold, lighting fires to keep warm was out of the question as that would expose their position to enemy snipers. 'So to help fend off the cold we would wear as many clothes as possible,' he said. 'And when it was really hot we'd dig tunnels and ditches. These would offer a little shade. But surviving the hot and cold wasn't our biggest worry. That was simply staying alive.'

On 30 September 2015, Russian planes bombed targets in Syria for the first time. President Putin declared that this was part of a pre-emptive strike against Islamic State terrorists, aimed at hitting them before they hit Moscow. Yet, in reality there were few if any IS jihadists in the places targeted in these attacks. The rebel-held city of Homs, in western Syria, was a case in point. It was an FSA stronghold, rather than an IS one. It soon became increasingly clear that Russia's military campaign was really aimed at other rebel groups – some of them moderate, and partly armed by Washington – who opposed the rule of President Bashar al-Assad. Assad had become Putin's new ally in the Middle East, taking the place of Libya's Muammar Gaddafi, who had been set to spend billions of dollars on Russian arms before he was toppled by an uprising in 2011. After a string of defeats to both rebel and IS forces earlier that year, Assad needed such a powerful ally. Moscow was acting out of self-interest too. It had an eye on protecting its two military footholds in Syria: an airbase in the western province of Latakia, and a Russian naval base just to the south, in the port of Tartus. This intervention would go on to tip the balance of the war firmly in Assad's favour.

Those sitting quietly in their secret literary sanctuary, deep beneath the streets of Daraya, had some measure of protection from the continuing onslaught. Like all basements, it kept its occupants safe from flying debris and shrapnel, snipers' bullets and most mortar fire and small missiles. Its rows and rows of books offered mental respite too. A friend of Anas's, who for security reasons did not want to be named, summed it up like this: 'The books themselves help us forget all the troubles around us. When we are reading, the author takes us away to a different world. That's something we really need, it gives us peace of mind.'

But that peace of mind came close to being shattered early one winter's morning in December 2015. As Anas, Abdul Basit, Ayham and some friends rounded the corner of the small street that led to the library, they were faced with a scene of utter devastation. The entrance to the secret library had been badly damaged by a barrel bomb dropped the night before, and the house next to it was almost completely destroyed. It was hard to tell from where they stood whether their precious library had survived. Grabbing broken slabs of concrete and stone, they began pulling what rubble they could away from the door. But, as Ayham told me, it soon became clear that this was a hopeless task: 'There was so much debris that it completely blocked the entrance. The rubble was so heavy that we couldn't move it away from the door, or find any way through it. Our only option was to break into a shop in an adjoining building, and then try to make a hole in the wall. The hope was that we could then crawl through that into the library.'

Armed with whatever implements they could find, the group set about forcing their way into the abandoned shop next door to the library. Many hours later they finally succeeded in tunnelling through into their literary sanctuary. To their enormous relief, most of the books seemed to have survived the impact, though many lay scattered across the floor, some of the ruined shelves they had sat on beyond repair.

It is hard to imagine how they must have felt on rounding that corner, seeing the rubble and fearing that their beloved library, the lifeblood of their community, had been destroyed. Time and time again different members of the group had told me how devastated they would be if this ever happened. It would have been the end of so very much more than a basement and some books. Fortunately nobody had been inside the building at the time. Had young Amjad been buried under the rubble, I dread to think how they would have coped.

Later that day rumours began to spread that the secret library had been targeted by the Syrian air force after they were tipped off where it was. Though completely unsubstantiated, these reports caused widespread alarm. If the regime now knew where it was, surely they would bomb it again? There really was no way to know the truth, but everyone decided just to hope for the best.

# Chapter Nine

In the weeks after the near destruction of the secret library, Abdul Basit and his friends worked flat out to restore it to its former glory. First came the clear-up. Piles of books lay on the ground caked in dust and bits of masonry and all of them had to be cleaned up and sorted into the right categories again. Some shelves could be repaired but many new ones were needed. The wood had to be found, then cut and shaped, before being slotted into place. Repairs were also needed to the walls and ceiling of the library and heavy rubble cleared from its half-collapsed entrance.

Amazingly, when I called Abdul Basit at the secret library via Skype a few weeks after the near miss, all seemed back to normal. Tranquillity had returned, and the shelves looked as well stocked as ever. There was even a pile of newly rescued books stacked by Amjad's chair. Some of these, I was told, had been found in a gutted shop only a couple of streets away, while others had been brought to the library by a family nearby. I asked Abdul Basit about the titles that had been given in this way. Smiling, he got up from his chair and walked over to a section of books behind him, brushing his hand gently along the spines of a row of elegantly lettered titles on the middle shelf. 'All of these books were donated to the library by my grandfather,' he told me. 'This one here is one we used to read together.

I really enjoyed hearing my grandfather's thoughts on it. It talks about civilisation, and how this manifests itself around the world. It discusses its effect on humans across time, looking at such things as equality, religious tolerance and the ethics of war. God bless you, grandfather. I hope we will read together again soon and be happy once more, just like we used to be.'

Abdul Basit spoke so movingly and personally to his grandfather that I wondered for a moment if he was there in the library with him. He was not. This was clearly another Abdul Basit moment. He speaks in such a poetic way. When we first talked and he told me that his university education had been stopped by the war, I asked him what he had been studying. Having expected him to say something like philosophy or literature, I was surprised to be told that it was business and economics. He was obviously a man of many talents and it turned out that one of these was spotting the works of Shakespeare during his book-salvaging missions. On seeing one volume among a bag of freshly rescued volumes, he remembered that it had once been recommended to him by his uncle. The book in question was an Arabic version of Shakespeare's *Hamlet* – one of his favourite books of all time. A besotted Abdul Basit would often read it during spare moments. 'Shakespeare's style of writing is simply beautiful,' he told me. 'He describes every single scene so vividly that it's like I'm in a cinema watching a film. Among many other things, I adore his wonderful use of metaphors in this story. The play is amazing. It is such a deep and remarkable book that it should be read by everyone, everywhere. Once I started reading it, I just couldn't put the book down. In fact, I became so obsessed with it that I began reading it at the hospital where I work.

At first this only happened during quiet times, but then I began reading it at almost every opportunity. In the end I said to myself, Abdul Basit, this has to stop! I mean, it just wasn't fair on the patients.'

Hearing these words made me think of the saying that people around the world have far more in common than the things that set them apart. We may have different religions, languages, houses and clothes but many of our aspirations, hopes and fears are much the same. Our love of great stories, like *Hamlet*, that deal with human nature in all its forms, need no translation beyond the language they are told in. The joy Abdul Basit talked of when reading that particular book, rang so many bells with me. The fact that *Hamlet* was set so long ago in a country he had never seen did not in any way lessen his enjoyment of it.

Syria, or its antecedents, has also been home to many re-markable writers over the years. The year 64 BC marked the birth of Nicolaus of Damascus, who was to become a revered historian and author. Nicolaus became a close friend of Herod the Great and tutored the children of Mark Antony and Cleopatra. And when it came to putting pen to paper, few were more prolific than Nicolaus. Among his achievements was a history of the world in 144 volumes, several plays, as well as various biographies and works on subjects as diverse as philosophy and botany.

Over 800 years later, in AD 788, came the birth of the poet Abu Tammam. A Christian who later converted to Islam, he is best known for a ten-book anthology of Arabic poetry. It contains more than 800 poems which Saladin himself, the first Sultan of Egypt and Syria, is said to have learned by heart. Perhaps they were all very short. I am not sure if this book was on the shelves of the secret library, but if it was the founders might have taken exception to the following lines:

> The sword is more veracious than the book,
> Its cutting edge splits earnestness from sport.
> The white of the blade, not the black of the age,
> Its broadsides clarify uncertainty and doubt.[17]

When it comes to fascinating and controversial Arabic writers from this period, few can compete with Al-Ma'arri (973–1057), a blind poet and philosopher hailed as one of the greatest classical Arabic writers. His *Epistle of Forgiveness* is considered to be the precursor to *The Divine Comedy* by Dante. He had a rather irreligious world view and was as scathing about Muslims as he was about Christians and Jews, which has earned him enemies right up to this day. In 2013 the al-Qaeda-linked extremist group Jabhat Fatah al-Sham (previously known as Jabhat al-Nusra) beheaded a statue of him in his home town of Ma'arrat al-Nu'man in north-west Syria. I would imagine that today's pro-life lobby would not be too fond of him either. The great writer was an anti-natalist, who believed that children should not be born in order to spare them the pains of living. Al-Ma'arri, a rationalist who called for social justice, was also one of the world's first celebrity vegans, on ethical grounds. Here is one of his poems on the subject:

**I No Longer Steal from Nature**
Do not unjustly eat fish the water has given up,
And do not desire as food the flesh of slaughtered
   animals,

Or the white milk of mothers who intended its pure
    draught
for their young, not noble ladies.
And do not grieve the unsuspecting birds by taking
    eggs,
for injustice is the worst of crimes.
And spare the honey which the bees get industriously
from the flowers of fragrant plants;
For they did not store it that it might belong to
    others,
Nor did they gather it for bounty and gifts.
I washed my hands of all this; and wish that I
Perceived my way before my hair went grey![18]

Given the lack of almost anything to eat in Daraya in 2015, there would have been little to offend his vegan sensitivities there.

Still thinking about favourite authors I called Sara to find out what she liked to read after finishing a day teaching school children. The answer I got surprised me: 'I like a lot of different kinds of books and authors,' she told me, 'but I'm particularly keen on Agatha Christie. I love her writing. I think the book that I have enjoyed most by her is *The Body in the Library*.' I really did think she was joking at first. But no, that truly was one of her favourite books. Sara's English was so good that she had even read it in the original version. 'The way it's written is so compelling and I really relate to it,' she continued. 'Perhaps this is because of the circumstances I'm living in at the moment.'

It really touched me that Sara found Agatha Christie's writing so appealing and that she could get so much enjoyment from it. The old-fashioned style, never mind the subject matter, could not be further removed from bombed and besieged Daraya. Sara, who also loved books by George Bernard Shaw and John Stuart Mill, told me that she strongly identified with what she had read: 'I like the way Agatha Christie's books always carry a moral message,' she said. 'It's basically that crime and violence don't pay, they achieve nothing. I see the sense of that all around me here. And that's what I would love everyone to understand. Killing, fighting fire with fire, doesn't get anyone anywhere.'

Another of the library's books that Sara had very much enjoyed was *The Alchemist* by Brazilian novelist Paulo Coelho. The book tells the story of a young Spanish boy who has a dream about travelling from Spain to Egypt in search of treasure. On his way he keeps losing hope when encountering obstacles and difficulties, but he is told that eventually he will be sent a sign from the gods. This encourages him to continue. Sara initially thought the book sounded a little highbrow and dull when it was suggested to her by a friend but her view soon changed when she began turning the pages. 'As I started going through it,' she recalls, 'I began to forget everything around me, even the constant bombing went from my mind. This book always gives me great hope. Every time I feel that I can't take life any more, I repeat some of the words in this book to myself, and it lifts me up again. I have reread it so many times. It inspires me, especially since I'm an introverted person. I don't socialise much, so books are my friend. This book is a very good friend. My favourite passage shows that to be afraid of suffering is worse than actually suffering. And that it's impossible to suffer when in search of a dream, because every moment of the search is to meet with God. Any new pursuit requires entering uncharted territory – that's scary. But with any great risk comes great reward. The experiences you gain in pursuing your dream will make it all worthwhile.'

Reading, Sara explained, helped her make better sense of the trauma her country was going through. Then the room went quiet.

On another of my 'visits' to the library, Ayham and Rateb were sitting together reading on the large and rather comfortable-looking couch. When I asked them what their favourite books were, both smiled and nodded, as if each was about to reel off a long list of titles. Instead, what followed was a lot of scratching of heads and rubbing of chins. I did sympathise. It reminded me of times when I have been asked what my favourite piece of music is. There are just so many possibilities, many of them dependent on mood and genre. Finally Ayham piped up: 'I love being here. The trouble is that I've read so many fascinating books in this library that it's become hard to pin down which ones I like best. Having said that, one of my favourite authors is definitely, Ali al-Tantawi from Damascus. He is very famous in Syria. I have read so many of his books, memoirs and other publications. You ought to read his books too.'

Meanwhile, Rateb had managed to crystallise his thoughts: 'I still remember the first book I ever borrowed from the library,' he told me. 'It was by the Egyptian journalist Ahmed Mansour. I think the title was something like, *Under Fire in Afghanistan*. It was the story of a man during the war in Afghanistan. I definitely identified with the main character in the book, who was a news correspondent for Al Jazeera. There seemed to be so many similarities between the underground tunnels he talked about there and the way the war is fought here.'

By this time Homam had joined us. Unable to contain himself, he began reading out a long list of authors and books that he loved, most of which he and his lifelong friend, Omar Abu Anas, had shared. He admitted that some were challenging reads, but insisted that the effort was worth it in the end. Most of them were about religion. Among his favourites were *Religion* by Dr Abdallah Draz; *A Marxist Interpretation of Islam*; *An Introduction to Islam*; *The Story of Faith* by Nadim el Jisr and *History of Religions* by Muhammad Abu Zahra, which Homam described as 'a very important book to read'. Another of his favourites, which elicited an enthusiastic thump on the table, was *How to Reach Out to People* by Muhammad Qotob Abou. 'It is one of the best books you could ever read,' he said. And, from what he had been telling me, there had been many of those. 'I'm also very keen on titles about personal development,' he added. 'The author Stephen Covey has written several memorable books on this subject which I found in the library. The only subjects I can't find much on in our secret library is philosophy.'

Inspired by the enthusiasm for this wide range of subjects, I called in at an independent bookshop near where I live in London to see if I could buy some of them. Perhaps, I thought, I could then join one of their regular book clubs via Skype. *Hamlet* and Agatha Christie's *The Body in the Library* were obviously no problem, along with Paulo Coelho's *The Alchemist*, *Under Fire in Afghanistan* by Ahmed Mansour and *The Story of Faith* by Nadim el Jisr. But, when asking for a title such as *How to Reach Out to People* by Muhammad Qotob Abou, I was met with blank faces.

Some of the titles suggested to me by people in Daraya were available only in Arabic, a language I have yet to master. But reading the books I could get hold of, especially those by Syrian authors that I had never come across before, was a very rewarding experience.

Another author whose books adorned the shelves of the secret library was Ali Ahmad Said Esber. Better known by the pen name Adonis, he is regarded by many as the greatest living poet in the Arab world. Though yet to win a Nobel Prize for Literature, he has been nominated almost every year since 1988. Many compare Adonis to T. S. Eliot, due to the equivalent impact he has had on Arabic poetry. 'There is Arabic poetry before Adonis and there is Arabic poetry after Adonis,' said the poet Samuel John Hazo.

Adonis's legion of admirers praise him not just for the quality and artistry of his writing, but also for his creation of a whole new style of poetry. It is certainly fresh and compelling to me, even in the English translation. I only wish I could read Arabic properly, because to read his poems in the language he wrote them must take them to another dimension still. Adonis's poetry is rooted in classical verse yet encapsulates the many profound issues now facing the Arab world. Take his poem, 'A Time Between Ashes and Roses', which explores the utter devastation felt by many in Arab countries after the defeat of the forces of Egypt, Syria and Jordan by Israel in the Six Day War of 1967:

> A child stammers, the face of Jaffa is a child
> How can withered trees blossom?
> A time between ashes and roses is coming
> When everything shall be extinguished
> When everything shall begin[19]

Adonis is adored and respected by many, but never seems to court popularity. In fact, at various times in his life, his work has upset just about everyone. Recently, for example, he managed to anger both sides in his country's civil war. In the early days of the uprising, Adonis criticised both President Bashar al-Assad, warning him against trying to 'imprison an entire nation', and then the opposition, whom he accused of 'violent tendencies'. His questioning of the conservatism of some deep-seated traditions of Islam has also earned him death threats from some Islamic scholars, including calls for his books to be burned. Far from being shocked or cowed, Adonis said: 'I am not sad about burning my books, because this is an old phenomenon in our history. We are fighting to found a dialogue and a debate in a peaceful way. Founding differences in opinions is a wealth source. This counterfeiting humiliates Arabic.'

The indomitable Adonis has always carried on regardless, despite the wrath his work has engendered, though this has often had to be done at a distance from his homeland. In 1971 he travelled to the United States where he also courted controversy. In one of his best-known poems, 'A Grave for New York', he dwelt on what he saw as the city's desolation. The piece was roundly condemned as 'violently anti-American'.

In 1980 Adonis moved to Paris to become Professor of Literature and has lived there for many years, a Syrian author in exile – a fate forced on so many of his country-men who have dared to speak their mind.

Although I had heard of Adonis before, I knew little about his work until I talked to those who had built the secret library. Just about everyone mentioned him at one time or another, and suggested that I read his poetry. So while they were reading the works of authors such as Shakespeare and Agatha Christie in Arabic, I was busily making my way through books by Adonis in English. It was illuminating. I felt I was getting not only a kind of history lesson on Syria's recent past, but also an insight into the way some major events might be seen by many Syrians.

Until talking to Sara and the other members of the library, I was also unaware of the extent of the role played by Syrian women in literature and poetry. Given the country's patriarchal society, I had incorrectly assumed that their work would have struggled to be recognised. I soon discovered how wrong I was. As both Sara and Aysha told me, some of the finest wordsmiths from this region have been women, and their huge influence continues right up to this day. In former centuries, many were highly controversial and are now recognised as having been among the earliest feminists. Their works often focused on defying the expectations around women's subservient role in their society. One of the most prominent female Syrian writers today is Maram al-Masri. Born in 1962, she is a Sunni Muslim from Latakia on the country's north-west coast. In her early years, she adored listening to the popular music of the day, including foreign artists such as Bob Dylan and Joan Baez. Maram also had a great passion for poetry and began penning her own verse as a child. In later life, her poems on feminism and female sexuality were to make her name, but many believe some of her finest works are those concerning her country's ongoing civil war.

Maram's son joined rebel forces when the revolution began in Syria. No fan of President Bashar al-Assad, she later said: 'I was so happy. I would have felt so bad if he had said no.' Being a mother, however, she must constantly have feared for his safety and this may have inspired several poems she has written about children caught up in the conflict, including this powerful one that makes me think of Aysha and her son:

**Have You Seen Him?**

Have you seen him?

Carrying his infant in his arms
advancing with magisterial step
head up, back straight . . .

As if the infant should be happy and proud
to be carried like this in his father's arms . . .

If only he was alive.[20]

Syria's civil war is the subject of her latest book, *Elle va nue La Liberté*. Written in French, it looks at the conflict from several different perspectives. Some of her poems are very down to earth and concentrate on the stark realities of warfare. I found one of them, 'In a Small Suzuki Van', haunting because of the way it mixes the ordinary, almost mundane things in life – a Suzuki van and a bag of bread – with the stark reality of war. It reminded me of scenes I had witnessed when covering wars: people cradling loved ones, their treasured husbands, wives, sons or daughters, now lost for ever.

Any discussion about prominent female Syrian poets would be incomplete without mentioning perhaps the most controversial of them all. Ahlam al-Nasr is in almost every way the polar opposite to Maram al-Masri; about the only thing they have in common is their hatred of President Bashar al-Assad. Al-Nasr is a fully committed supporter of IS and has earned the moniker 'the poetess of the Islamic State'. I can only conclude that her books cannot have been very popular in Daraya because nobody I asked there had read any of them and it's thought none was in the Secret Library. Given how unpopular IS was among the founders of the library, this fact did not surprise me.

I first heard about Ahlam al-Nasr through a group of anti-IS activists in the Syrian city of Raqqa, which had become IS's caliphate capital in June 2014. One of them quoted to me, with utter contempt, an article she had written, praising the nobleness of the group's black-clad fighters. To people who had witnessed IS's appalling brutality, which included mounting the severed heads of those who had displeased them on fence posts, her words were preposterous. On reading up on her life I discovered that al-Nasr was born into a well-to-do, highly educated family. Her exact age is unknown but she was born in Damascus and is thought to be in her mid-twenties. She was encouraged to write poetry by her mother, a professor of law, who once proudly stated that her daughter 'was born with a dictionary in her mouth'. Al-Nasr began writing in her teens. Her favourite subject then was the plight of the Palestinians. Her maternal grandfather, an imam, was a firm supporter of President Bashar al-Assad, yet far from following in his footsteps, the young al-Nasr joined the street protests calling on Assad to step down. It's possible that her growing radicalism was fuelled by the brutal manner in which those demonstrations were crushed by the security forces.

In the autumn of 2014, al-Nasr fled first to the Gulf

before travelling on to Raqqa, Soon after arriving, al-Nasr began posting her thoughts online. In 2014 she published a collection of poems called *The Blaze of Truth*, in praise of the jihadi world around her. Unlike IS's gruesome videos of people being shot or beheaded, which were largely aimed at Westerners, her poems were targeted at other jihadists.

Al-Nasr went on to write a thirty-page defence of the barbaric burning to death of the Jordanian pilot Muath al-Kasasbeh in early January 2015. While much of the world viewed Raqqa as one of the most brutalised and fear-ridden places on earth, to al-Nasr it was a pristine and pious paradise: 'In the caliphate, I saw women wearing the veil, everyone treating each other with virtue, and people closing up their shops at prayer times . . . children played with sticks, pretending these were weapons they would use to fight heretics and unbelievers.'

Here was a great propaganda tool for IS. While they had plenty of young, tech-savvy video-making men, here was a female poet to proclaim their cause and woo more women to the caliphate.

One of the important roles of women in IS's self-proclaimed caliphate was marrying its jihadists. Al-Nasr was happy to fulfil this task too. On 11 October 2014, soon after her arrival, she married an Austrian fighter in the Raqqa courthouse. It was a second marriage for her new husband, Mohamed Mahmoud, who was born in Vienna in 1985. Mahmoud, who had earlier burned his Austrian passport, had previously been a propagandist for al-Qaeda. If there had been a jihadi equivalent of *Hello!* Magazine to cover their wedding, they would surely have been invited. For this was a celebrity event, announced on jihadi networks across the caliphate. But with IS's lands now lost,

Ahlam al-Nasr's future looks bleak. And it seems unlikely that other Syrian poets will be rushing to her rescue.

Neither, sadly, was there any realistic prospect of the outside world coming to rescue the people of Daraya. With the recent intervention of Russia on the regime's side, as well as ongoing military assistance from Iran and Lebanon's Hezbollah militia, the fortunes of President Bashar al-Assad were improving by the end of 2015. The once iconic FSA, though still strong in Daraya, was losing cohesion across the country as a whole, largely due to the growing influence of Islamist and other extremist rebel factions. Ever since its formation in 2011, the FSA had functioned as an umbrella group for different forces, but these were now becoming ever more numerous and disparate.

I was asked many times by people in Daraya why the international community, which had often spoken out strongly against Assad, failed to combine their words with action. I told them that fears were growing in the West that money and weapons given to the FSA might fall into the hands of extremist groups, such as IS or the al-Nusra Front. But we don't have groups like that in Daraya, they would tell me indignantly, outraged that the outside world did not understand this. Many were unaware of the growing influence of extremist groups elsewhere in Syria, marooned as they were in their besieged town.

Yet, despite all this, Daraya's secret library continued to generate hope. It also helped its people to feel connected with a world that seemed to have deserted them. Omar Abu Anas summed up what I am convinced were the inner thoughts of many of those around him. 'Books motivate us to keep on going. We read how in the past everyone turned their backs on a particular nation, yet they still made it in the end. So we can be like that too. They help us plan for life once Assad is gone. So we are in the process of planning what comes next. We can only do that through the books we are reading. We want so much more than Assad. We want to be a free nation. And hopefully, by reading, we can achieve this.'

# Chapter Ten

During a brief break from reporting the troubles of the Middle East, in January 2016, I was on a train hurtling through the frosty English countryside to see relatives in the West Country. It can't have been much after four in the afternoon, but the pale wintry light was already fading. The scene outside my window had a rather bleak, monochrome look. Could it really be that dark already, I wondered. Before I could come to any conclusion, my thoughts were interrupted by a voice to my right. 'It this seat free?' I was asked. It probably didn't look that way, given the pile of research notes covering it. When I had moved all the paperwork out of the way, a smartly dressed woman sat down beside me. 'I think this is yours,' she said, handing me my copy of *The Times*, open on an article on the Syrian civil war, which had slipped onto the floor by her feet. 'It's ghastly, isn't it,' she muttered, looking at the photo of the devastated urban landscape that dominated the page. I nodded in agreement, adding that there seemed no end in sight to the suffering of the population there. I mentioned the people I had been talking to by phone in Syria over recent months and the terrible scenes they had described. She sighed and said, 'I imagine it's different when you live in a country like Syria, isn't it, not like it would be for somebody like you or me. They must have got used to it by now.'

This was truly shocking to me. How could anyone, anywhere, ever, 'get used' to being bombed, shot at and starved? Yet this woman, who clearly meant no harm to anyone, appeared to think this was a rational idea. Perhaps, as I reflected later, it is just the courageous way people in war zones get on with their lives that might give that strange impression. And it was true to some extent – the resilience of people in Daraya, and so many others elsewhere in Syria, never ceased to amaze and humble me. Sometimes I would call Anas or Abdul Basit and all I could hear were explosions. Yet they rarely flinched, unless the explosions were so close that they could feel the heat of the blast. Even after having to step over bodies in the streets, breathe through the reek of chemical waste, or forage for food, life went on as it always did in Daraya. When the sun rose the next day and the day after that, its people just carried on. Nobody seemed to ask what they had left to live for. Not when death could come so quickly.

Yet I still wondered, how could such things ever be *normal*, however often they happened around you? Perhaps it was just that people simply became a little more able to cope with such horrors when they experienced them so frequently. But in a world where a kind of survival mode operated most of the time, what room would there be for other things in life? Chief among those must surely be romance. Many of the people I had got to know in Daraya, for instance, were young men in the prime of their lives. Yet so far none of them had even raised the subject of relationships or marriage. Might this, I wondered, be because in their often nightmarish existence there might be no time for such things? I found that hard to believe. We are, after all, dealing here with one of the strongest human motivations.

*

It took me quite some time to work up the courage to ask about this topic. First, this was a war zone and many women had left. Also, those I had come to know seemed tolerant and open-minded, but almost all were strongly religious. I feared some might view enquiries about their love life as frivolous and inappropriate. But given my belief that we human beings are all essentially the same at heart, I decided to go ahead anyway. Abdul Basit, who appeared to wear his heart on his sleeve, seemed like a good person to start with.

It turned out that I needn't have worried. True to form Abdul Basit was relaxed about the whole issue and happy to answer my questions. He told me that he was already engaged, though getting married was clearly going to be difficult. His bride-to-be, Zohour, lived only a couple of miles away, but it might as well have been a thousand. Her family home was in the neighbouring town of al-Moadamyeh, so close to Daraya that they could almost have waved to each other. But due to the siege they were now separated by a wall of steel. It was touching to hear the change in Abdul Basit's voice when he spoke about his fiancée. There was a softness, a warmth in his tone that had not been there before. I settled back to listen as he told me how their relationship had come about.

Abdul Basit's parents, who had been living with him in Daraya before the siege, had often talked of plans to find him a wife. But, perhaps because of the rapid descent into war, this had not been mentioned since. In fact, there had been such a long hiatus that Abdul Basit had almost forgotten about the subject. Then, out of the blue, he received a phone call from his sister. She was ten years older than him and had always been a bit like a second mother. This, he told me, is how the conversation went:

'"Tell me what sort of qualities you are looking for in the woman you would like to marry," she asked down the line in a matter-of-fact way. I didn't know what to say. I mean, it was all a bit sudden for me to just rattle off a wish list for the girl of my dreams. So I promised to get back to her. Later that afternoon I sat down with pen and paper.'

After much thought and crossings out, Abdul Basit finally assembled a list of desirable qualities for his perfect wife. Not, he quickly told me, that he ever expected to find one, should such a woman even exist. But he had done his best. Even if the future Mrs al-Ahmar had only a couple of the attributes he had asked for, she would still be quite a catch. So, long list in hand, he had called his sister back. That same evening his mobile rang. Had she struck gold already? Surely she could not have found anyone scoring so many ticks on his list that quickly. To his surprise it was his mother on the line. Abdul Basit told me that he was glad to be sitting down when he heard what she had to say.

'"We have found the woman you are looking for, no doubt about that at all." "This can't be possible," I said to her, "I've only just given my sister the list! I assume this must be somebody you already had in mind, but kept secret until you saw my wish list?" "No," my mother replied, "this woman is even better than what you asked for." At that moment I knew this was it, there would be no escape!'

Abdul Basit had the feeling that even if this chosen woman hadn't ticked any boxes on his list, she was now set to be his wife, come what may. Not that he really minded, as he had a feeling that he was going to like her. Yet he felt uneasy – she didn't live in Daraya, so how was he supposed to meet her? And what future could their relationship have when they were living in two different places? He didn't know it then, but his parents had already devised a plan. As a young man of fighting age he was unlikely to get through the regime's checkpoints without being arrested, but such a crossing should be less of a problem for middle-aged people like them: 'You see, Mike,' Abdul Basit told me, smiling, 'we Muslims have a different way of getting engaged than you in the West. To begin with, neither me nor my prospective fiancée played any direct part in what followed. Instead, my parents went to visit her parents and they proposed on my behalf.'

Not that it turned out to be quite that simple. Abdul Basit's fiancée, Zohour, was not as compliant with her parents as he had been with his, and while she did not actually turn down the proposal from his mother and father, she did insist on at least meeting their son. Thankfully, soon after his parent's visit, a ceasefire was agreed in neighbouring rebel-held al-Moadamyeh. This made getting Abdul Basit out of Daraya and into her town a little less difficult. On the second day of the truce, he managed to get through the checkpoints and was able to meet his prospective fiancée. 'We sat together for about an hour. I can honestly say that from our first moment together, my flustered brain stopped functioning,' he told me, before adding with his usual poetic flair, 'but this didn't really matter, because it was my heart that spoke the final word.'

Whatever that final word was, it evidently worked wonders on Zohour. Any reservations she might have had were swept away and the two agreed to get engaged a few weeks later. Several days after that, having again managed somehow to get out of besieged Daraya, Abdul Basit and

his family headed to al-Moadamyeh for the engagement
ceremony but, on arriving at a checkpoint just outside the
town, they were all refused entry. It was not clear why,
given that the ceasefire was still holding, but they dared
not argue with the soldiers and had to turn back. Not to
be completely defeated, Abdul Basit came up with a plan of
his own: 'I ordered a red flower and went to great trouble to
arrange to have it delivered to her door. I knew a man who
had a good relationship with the regime's soldiers on the
army checkpoint. So I gave him some money to bribe them,
so that they would let the flower through. Unfortunately
the soldier my contact knew best was not on duty that day.
The ones who were just ripped up the flower and threw it
back at him in pieces. It still upsets me to think of this.'

After telling me this story, Abdul Basit put his face in his
hands. When he looked back up his eyes were brimming
with tears: 'I miss my fiancée and my family so very much.
Being unable to see them is perhaps the most difficult thing
of all to deal with. It's very hard being separated for so long
from the people I love.'

Anas also had a fiancée. Asmaa was living with her family
in another part of the countryside outside Damascus.
Again, it was his parents who met her first, later describing
Asmaa to Anas. As each of them immediately liked what
they heard about the other, they began chatting over the
Internet. A flurry of texts and emails soon began to flow
and, within months, they, too, became engaged.

Since many families had fled from Daraya to al-
Moadamyeh during the massacre of August 2012, there
were many prospective brides and grooms cut off from
one another. But a string of ceasefires, negotiated with
the regime by rebels in al-Moadamyeh, provided a lifeline

for couples who longed to be married. During one of our WhatsApp calls, Muhammad Shihadeh – the former English teacher nicknamed 'The Professor' – told me about the first wedding to be held in al-Moadamyeh soon after the truces were signed there, in early 2014. He recalled how it created great excitement throughout the area, two young lives being joined in a ceremony that looked to the future rather than to the horrors of the past. The groom was a health worker at a field hospital in Daraya, just like Abdul Basit, and had been an activist since the beginning of the revolution. His fiancée had fled to al-Moadamyeh, so all they could do was dream of being together, while constantly fearing that a bomb or bullet might intervene before they had had the chance. And yet, here they were, their dream had come true. 'I vividly remember their tears of happiness,' Muhammad told me. 'Many of those watching were crying those same tears of joy, myself included. We cried out of happiness for our two friends, we cried at the sight of them both together at last, and we wept because of the joy we felt after so much sorrow. Many people are still separated in the same way they had been. They are engaged but can't get married. They just have to live in hope for the future. I look back on that wedding as an act of resilience as well as love, an act of determination to celebrate life over death.'

Sadly Muhammad's own wait to be reunited with his wife and children continued. For some months into the siege they had all stayed together, but when the shells and barrel bombs began falling in greater numbers, he became consumed with fear for their safety. Finally, when he was so worried that he could no longer sleep at night, he decided to try to get them out. Rebel-held al-Moadamyeh next door seemed the best destination. It was not being attacked as persistently or intensely as Daraya, so Muhammad made plans to get his family there. The trip to al-Moadamyeh was dangerous because the route between the two towns was regularly shelled, but finally they managed it.

At first Muhammad got to see his family quite regularly, by skirting regime checkpoints and braving shelling and sniper fire. But finally, about three months after his wife and children had settled in al-Moadamyeh, pro-regime forces tightened their control around the town. Daraya was now completely cut off. When he told me about this, Muhammad had yet to hold or even see his youngest child, who had not been born when he last saw his wife. 'My wife was seven months pregnant when the route between Daraya and al-Moadamyeh was cut,' Muhammad told me. 'She had no access to medical staff and had to give birth with just the help of her neighbour. She now has to raise our three children on her own. I haven't seen my newborn child. All I know is that he is a boy.'

Clearly not one for self-pity, Muhammad pointed out that he was far from alone in this regard. Scores of his friends were also in the same position, and many had not seen their wives and children for several years. He added mournfully that some of those who had left had not been heard from again. Suddenly the man widely known for his sense of calm looked distraught: 'I hope that I'll get to see my wife and children one day soon. I would love to hear their voices and at least be sure that they are OK. That would give me so much relief.'

Listening to Muhammad's agony made me think about Sara. Although she had her husband with her in Daraya, how, I wondered, could she ever get used to being separated from her beloved family? Like so many others, her parents and siblings had left the town when it became clear that the violence would only get worse. Several of them hadn't actually gone far from Daraya, but, given the siege, it might as well have been another country. Sara couldn't risk trying to go there and she couldn't even call them in case their phones were being monitored by the security services. Knowing that they would worry about her, Sara had come up with a pre-arranged signalling system: 'Each evening I change the photo on my Facebook page,' she told me. 'They know this is my coded message to verify that I am still alive. I don't know when I will see any of my family again.'

Sara's pain must have been all the worse for knowing how near her family was. Her husband was able to console her, though he too missed his own relatives. He felt compelled to stay in Daraya due to the work he was doing for the council, but his family had moved to a safer area. Sara appeared to take great comfort from the care and education she was able to give the children she taught, some of whom had been orphaned by the war. But at the same time she saw first-hand the grief they were enduring, watching their childhood being stolen by the war.

Sometimes, she told me, she took refuge in thoughts of her own younger days. 'I dream of the happy times back in my dear family's home in Daraya. I see myself there, sleeping in my old bed, waiting for my father to come and wake me up for breakfast. In a strange way it feels like it was only yesterday, yet I've been married for eight years now. To help me deal with these thoughts, I'm trying to make myself believe that I never had a family. It's just too painful thinking about them, I miss them all too much.'

*

By late February 2016, events on the ground had taken a further turn for the worse for the people of Daraya. Pro-Assad forces launched a new assault on the town and managed to seize more than twenty rebel-held buildings. A nationwide ceasefire should have prevented this happening, but because the government claimed that militants from the extremist al-Nusra Front, which had ties with al-Qaeda, were among those fighting in Daraya, the town was excluded from the deal.

Although many in Daraya had developed ways to calm their fears over bombing and snipers, being overrun by pro-Assad forces was an even more terrifying prospect. 'Right now Assad's forces are trying to invade Daraya,' Muhammad told me. 'In addition to shelling and missile bombardments they are using ground forces backed by tanks and armoured trucks. The latter are aiming to break through the FSA's defensive line. They are trying to capture the farmland on the western and southern edges of town. If they succeed in taking these farms, we'll really be in trouble. How, then, can we feed ourselves?'

Many families in Daraya were already asking themselves that same question. The one I asked myself repeatedly was, how had the people of Daraya managed to cope so far, both mentally as well as physically, when they had so little to eat each day? I heard that some mothers were giving their children virtually any food they had and then drinking large amounts of water themselves, which at least made them feel as if they had eaten. What, I constantly wondered, could they say to their starving children when they were crying with hunger and unable to sleep at night? Knowing what they needed, yet having to watch them suffer because they had nothing to give them.

The town's already dire shortages of food and medicine had been compounded by the pro-Assad forces' recapture of the road to nearby al-Moadamyeh, which until recently had been the way most urgent supplies had been brought in to Daraya. Now, even if people did have the ingredients to make watery soup, which was all that most had to eat, there was very little fuel of any sort left to cook it with.

One of the many attractions of the secret library was that reading books helped people forget about their hunger, as well as the war going on above their heads. Anyone who has missed even one meal knows how difficult it is to concentrate on anything when hunger is gnawing at your stomach. So it's hard to imagine what it must have been like to go for months, or even years, without a proper meal. In a conversation with Ayham he told me how mothers bringing their children to his dental surgery felt forced to lie to their desperately hungry children, telling them things like: 'Don't worry, your father will be back soon from the market with a bag full of food.' Or, when their father returned with nothing, 'There will be a big meal waiting for you tomorrow.' Such promises would, of course, be broken, the heartbreak only postponed.

Ayham told me that he had become obsessed with thoughts about food ever since the siege began: 'You will laugh a lot when I tell you what I dream about,' he said. 'I dream of drinking a large cup of tea with sugar in it. I dream of potato crisps; I dream of big pieces of chicken. We haven't eaten chicken for more than a year now. I confess that sometimes I stare at pictures of food. I stare at them for hours and hours, I really do. I try to convince myself that I've just eaten the food in the photos. I hope my mind will trick my body into thinking this is true.'

*

Despite the growing hunger and deprivation, many of those I talked to somehow managed to retain their sense of humour in those darkening days. Abdul Basit was certainly one of them. He told me how the previous month, he and his friends had managed to get hold of a small quantity of sheep's liver. Almost delirious with excitement, they had rushed home with their prized meal and carefully placed the delicious-looking meat in a frying pan, before cooking it slowly, savouring the wonderful smell. 'It smelt so good,' he told me, 'that we were finding it hard to resist pulling the liver out of the pan and eating it raw, there and then.' To avoid this temptation he and his fellow diners decided to leave the room for a few minutes while the meat continued to cook.

'When we came back just a few minutes later, we couldn't believe what we saw. There, sitting by the stove, was a cat. It had scooped the liver out of the pan and was happily chewing it. One of my friends, the one who had managed to buy us the meat, was so distressed that he burst into tears. I rushed over, pulled the cat away and saved what was left of our longed-for meal. We then shared it out and started gulping it down. All of us, that is, except one of my friends. He just stood there watching us without touching his share. He suffers from OCD and is very fussy about what he eats, even when we're all in danger of starving to death.'

Abdul Basit said his friend had lived in fear of catching some kind of infection from the things he was eating during the siege, despite there being so little food around. So he was unwilling to risk cat-chewed liver, however much of a delicacy the meat was. His friends could not help finding this funny, because earlier that very morning he had been complaining about how terribly hungry he was. But, Abdul Basit told me, this story seemed to have a positive ending, as far as his friend's OCD problem was concerned.

'Not long after the cat incident, we found him tucking into a strange-looking salad. It was made out of the leaves from a blackberry bush which he had drenched in salted water. He did not seem to be fussy any more! In the end the siege appears to have cured him of his OCD.'

Abdul Basit told me about another humorous incident, this time at the hospital where he worked. He was helping to treat an injured FSA fighter who kept shouting that his left leg was hurting. Blood stains covered the left leg of his trousers, so the staff got ready to take a look. Yet instead of gripping his leg he was tightly clutching his stomach. Abdul Basit and the doctor were rather confused. Why, they asked themselves, was he not holding his injured limb? Given that his stomach seemed to be causing the most distress, they ignored his leg and tried to examine his stomach. But the man would not let them. The more they tried, the tighter his hands gripped his belly. Unable to get any further they asked the fighter what was wrong with his stomach.

'But he ignored our question and kept telling us to forget his stomach and check his leg. We finally discovered what the problem was. There was nothing wrong with his stomach. It was just that he was hiding a kilo of dates in the hand that he had clasped to it! He didn't want us to see them in case we took them from him. When we looked at his leg we found he had some very worrying wounds, but he was still far more concerned about keeping hold of his dates!'

I sat there feeling terribly guilty as I listened to these stories, humorous though the last two were. I had just had a large lunch, half of which I had left untouched on the side of my plate. In a few hours' time, my wife and I were due to go to a friend's house for dinner. We would doubtless spend much of the evening eating, regardless of whether we were hungry or not.

From the start of the war, women across Syria had been flooding social media with protests about the lack of international help being given to people in Daraya and the other besieged towns. By early 2016, at least half a million people, though some believe it was double that figure, were living under siege conditions in fifteen different areas of the country. The majority were surrounded and being starved into submission by pro-Assad forces, though a few towns and villages were also besieged by rebel militia and IS jihadists. In early April 2016, forty-seven women in Daraya signed an open letter calling for the siege on their town to be lifted and aid allowed in. 'There is no food at all in Daraya,' they wrote. 'There are cases of malnutrition and we have resorted to cooking soups made purely of spices in order to stave off hunger. There are signatories to this letter who have not eaten for at least two days – some longer. There is no baby milk and no breast milk due to malnutrition. Even something as simple as dishwashing liquid is unavailable. There are no cleaning supplies in order for us to ensure hygiene and keep diseases away.'

To give their campaign visual impact the woman asked their children to stand in lines in the shape of the letters: S.O.S. In addition to highlighting how much children were suffering, they wanted to point out that the town was full of civilians and not terrorists as the government was claiming. One woman held up a protest message written on an IS-style black and white style flag as a sign that mocked the way the Western media only seemed to pay attention to stories that involved this extremist group.

For four years, the people of Daraya had pleaded for international food aid, yet still none had been allowed in. It had begun to look like the outside world had given up trying to help, so it came as a big surprise to many in Daraya when a fleet of white Land Cruisers, bearing the UN insignia, drove into the town on 16 April 2016. Elation soon turned to dejection, however, when it was discovered that the vehicles were carrying only UN officials, not food and medicine. The delegation, it was explained, had come to assess the needs of residents and listen to their requests. When I heard about this I couldn't help thinking that Daraya's needs were fairly obvious and wondered why this delegation had to drive there, empty-handed, just to find out what the town's people had been saying year after year. Whatever the case, the people of Daraya were pleased to see international officials walking through their shattered streets. Anas wrote about the visit in his diary: 'The delegation saw for themselves how the schools, mosques and churches had been destroyed. Local people told them about their suffering and explained how awful life is under the siege. The group then visited a field hospital before meeting some local children to hear about their pain. The delegation's leader, Khawla Mattar, asked a child what she wanted them to bring when they came back. I expected the little girl to ask for chocolate, biscuits or strawberries . . . but she requested rice, flour and bread instead. I don't think she could remember ever seeing the sort of things kids normally like.'

By the time the convoy of UN vehicles had left the town in their dusty wake, hopes were high. Perhaps, thought the people of Daraya, the outside world was finally listening and aid would soon come, and perhaps peace with it. But with no further break in the bombing and shelling, safety was clearly a problem for any relief convoy and yet more weeks went by without any sign of aid. There were widespread reports that food might be dropped from the sky, as it had been in some other besieged areas; but all Daraya got was more missiles and barrel bombs.

Then, on 12 May 2016, news reached the town that a Red Cross convoy was on its way. It was reported to be carrying formula milk for babies, vaccines and supplies for schools. Residents rushed out and scanned the horizon, and a collective surge of anticipation swept the ravaged streets. But that evening, bad news arrived: the Red Cross convoy had been turned around by the Syrian army's 4th Armoured Division, who had refused it permission to enter Daraya. For the first time in a long while the international community voiced its outrage. Heartrending photos and videos appeared on the world's media of near-starving children from Daraya and other besieged towns such as Madaya, Arbin and Zamalka. I remember covering this story myself at the time for the BBC and noticing how many people in Britain were shocked by the suffering in places like these. As the international outcry mounted, the UN and a variety of international NGOs stepped up their campaign against the Syrian government's siege tactics while also lobbying Assad's Russian allies.

Finally, just over a fortnight later, on a baking hot day

at the beginning of June, the same medical convoy rolled back into Daraya. This time though, there were no excited crowds to greet it. Quite apart from the years of frustration and disappointment at the lack of tangible aid, many feared that Syrian forces might bomb any large groups that formed on the streets. This was despite word that a forty-eight-hour truce, which most in Daraya didn't trust, had been agreed to allow the convoy in. It also soon became known that, once again, the trucks were not carrying any food, the one thing the people needed more than anything else. Instead, they brought medicines, though I was later told that many of these bore instructions saying that they should only be taken with food.

Then, just over a week later, on Thursday, 9 June, through the clouds of dust and late-afternoon heat-haze, came a nine-truck UN and Syrian Arab Red Crescent convoy. These trucks were laden with the first delivery of food aid since the siege of Daraya had begun in November 2012. On board were boxes of rice, lentils, chickpeas, beans, bulgur, oil, salt and sugar. Mothers with tears in their eyes, excited children, exhausted young men, all of them showing strain, gathered at a central distribution point organised by the local council. Food was given out in what UN officials described as 'family rations' – each enough, they said, to see a household through one month, though a council spokesman thought the supplies would only last for twenty days at best. The UN had based its estimate of rations per household on the assumption that Daraya's population was down to just 4,000 people, though in reality, the council insisted, it was nearly double that number. There was disappointment and concern that no fuel had been supplied by the UN to power water pumps and generators. But by the time all the food had been distributed, late the following morning, the town was a much happier, more hopeful place. The aid might not last long, but at least the world did seem to care after all.

# Chapter Eleven

High above the ochre-grey debris, the sound of a young girl's voice floated across the rubble. At times it was hushed, almost dreamy, then loud and excited.

'Once upon a time there was a dear little girl who was loved by everyone who looked at her, but most of all by her grandmother, and there was nothing that she would not have given to the child.'

Two head-scarfed figures could be seen through a cavernous gap in the shell-ravaged wall of their home, deep in concentration. One was an older woman, who listened intently, lost in the words her small companion was reading from an Arabic version of a famous children's story: They sat on richly embroidered, gilt chairs, complete in each other's company, seemingly oblivious to the desolation around them.

Twelve-year-old Islam loved books. She had helped teach her mother, Um Ismaeel, to read. She lived with her family in their small, half-demolished home on the outskirts of Daraya. So far it had avoided a direct hit from bombs and mortars, but near misses had demolished parts of the living room wall. Through the gaping hole in the masonry, rows of gutted buildings could be seen, scorched shells that had once been their neighbours' homes. But little Islam only had eyes for the words on her lap. Clearly shy of strangers, her small fingers carefully adjusted her leopard print headscarf as she continued to read aloud: 'The grandmother lived out in the wood, half a league from the village, and just as Little Red Riding Hood entered the wood, a wolf met her. Red Riding Hood did not know what a wicked creature he was, and was not at all afraid of him.' She paused and looked: 'It is very exciting,' she told me. 'I feel like I am Little Riding Hood myself when I read it. Even though it is a little scary, it takes me to another place, a better place. When I read a good book like that I forget how hungry I am.'

I had been introduced to Islam and her mother by Malik al-Rifaii, who was a friend of the family. Given that neither Islam nor Um Ismaeel owned a mobile phone for me to Skype them on, he brought them his. Islam spoke only a little English and her mother none, so Malik also translated for us. His warm and sensitive manner soon put them both at ease, though Islam still looked a little nervous at times. I asked her what she liked reading. In a quiet voice, she replied that she liked all kinds of books, everything from the Holy Quran to medieval fairy tales. As for her favourite one, well, that she told me, was definitely *Little Red Riding Hood*. She held up her copy for me to see, put it back on her lap for safety, then lovingly opened the pages and began reading again. As she read, her face was constantly changing expression, turning into one of wide-eyed fear whenever the wolf was mentioned.

Her joy in the book was palpable. The trouble was that many of her friends loved the book too, and were always asking to borrow it. As her initial shyness receded, Islam, who looked and sounded so much younger than twelve, revealed how difficult life now was for her family. The biggest problem, she told me, was how little they had to eat.

With a hand on her stomach, Islam said that they only had one meal a day, usually watery soup. Islam's way of coping, she said, was to read whatever books she had, often for the third or fourth time.

I asked Islam if she knew about the secret library. She said she did and would love to go there, but that it was too far away. The only books she had managed to read from the secret library had been lent to her by friends whose parents had been there. Looking a little sad, she asked me if I knew whether many other children went to the library. I told her that I wasn't sure about that but added that it was run by a fourteen-year-old boy called Amjad, and that he seemed to adore books as much as she did. Islam looked most surprised at this – so much so that I wondered if she thought I was making Amjad up. Then she smiled and said, 'I would love to go there.'

She told me that each day, when the light began to fade, she would play as energetically as she could around the house. This helped her forget the gnawing pains in her stomach, which often stopped her getting to sleep.

As Islam finished her sentence her mother, who had six children in all, put her arm protectively around her daughter's shoulders. As she spoke, Um Ismaeel's face reflected the anguish of her words. 'I feel pain all over my body when I hear her talk like this. Islam taught me to read and now I can't do anything for her. The other day I thought I was having a stroke because of the worry over my children. They're my life. I spend all my time now thinking where am I going to get their next meal from. I hardly eat anything any more. I give my portion to them. It is a truly terrible life.'

As her mother spoke, Islam buried her face in her book.

I got the feeling that by looking elsewhere she was trying to give her mother some kind of privacy. But her daughter's touching concern went unseen by Um Ismaeel. She was lost in despair. 'Until recently I wouldn't let the children leave the house because of the danger from bombs and mortars,' she continued. 'But that has changed now. I have two married daughters here in Daraya and I encourage my other children to go and visit them. It's really just to stop them saying, "Mummy I'm hungry, Mummy I'm hungry." I can't cope with that any more.'

Um Ismaeel said she even let her children play indoor football with their neighbour's children, something she would never have allowed before the siege. It would have made a mess of the home she was so proud of. Now such things were of little concern. 'Anyway,' she said, 'it is everywhere. How can you bother about your home being a mess when parts of its walls are missing?'

As she gestured around the room, Um Ismaeel suddenly stopped talking. In the background I made out the faint sounds of an engine. As it gradually faded away, a very relieved-looking Um Ismaeel, who had evidently thought this was an approaching plane, composed herself.

'When the bombs start falling,' she told me, 'we rush to a big shelter outside, which has enough room for us all. Sometimes we have to stay there for hours. When all is clear, I encourage the children to carry on playing in the shelter, anything to keep them from saying they're hungry.'

As if the world's media was listening to our conversation, what sounded like a news jingle boomed from a small radio next to Um Ismaeel's chair. Either Islam had just turned it on or Daraya was enjoying a brief respite from its almost permanent power cuts. In clipped tones came an announcement, which Malik translated, that a temporary ceasefire had been agreed. This news would be a huge relief to many. But not, it appeared, to Um Ismaeel. Instead, a weary scepticism swept across her face. 'Hearing this, I'd like to believe it is true and be happy,' she said. 'But I don't trust the Syrian government. They've constantly lied, over and over again. They have long been making statements like this. But it always ends the same way. What do they take us for, fools? This is what life has come to now. We keep being promised peace, but it never comes.'

Holding up a photo of her children, she demanded to know if the outside world cared about their lives, whether the deaths of such innocent youngsters, who had no role in this war, were of concern to anyone. 'Does the international community believe,' she continued, 'that Syrians have always lived like this, or that they deserve to have their homes and families destroyed? How would you feel?' she asked, angrily. 'Do *you* think this is really a life?'

The siege hadn't only stopped Islam from getting to the library, it had also ruined her education. Islam's school had been shut for many months due to intense bombing, but had recently reopened for a few hours a day. At first she was delighted, because she loved the few books they had there, but when she went back she discovered that there was not enough light in her basement classroom to read them. Islam told me that trying to read in such poor light was making her eyes ache. This, she said, made her want to visit the secret library more than ever. She had heard that there was usually plenty of light there, as well as numerous books to read. Um Ismaeel listened sympathetically to her daughter, and then explained again how it was unfortunately too difficult and dangerous to take Islam there. The library, she said, was always a big talking point in Daraya, and it was great that others were able to make such good use of it. 'I think the secret library is very good for all those who use it,' she told me. 'It's wonderful that they have a place like that to keep themselves occupied. It not only educates them; it also helps them escape for a while from the terrible world we're living in. Everyone is talking about how valuable education is for the future of our country and I wish more children could get to the library.'

Um Ismaeel told me how sad it was that so many young people had given up on their schooling because of the war. 'Most no longer even think about their studies because there are hardly any books to read,' she said. 'It's so hard for children to study properly now and I wonder if they are really learning anything. It makes me heartbroken. My daughter was one of the top students in her class, but now she is really struggling.' She told me that Islam had taken to memorising the few books she had by heart, just as a way to occupy her mind. She had even memorised passages of the Holy Quran.

And then came a harrowing revelation that brought tears to my eyes. A few months earlier, Islam had been injured when out looking for food with her mother. A rocket had landed near them in a field on the edge of Daraya, and Islam had been hit in the left arm and hand by flying shrapnel. Her arm had been broken and was covered with deep lacerations. Since then, she had feared going anywhere and rarely left her family's house. In fact, aside from walking to and from school, she never went out at all. The ongoing pain of her injuries, which had yet to fully heal, also made it difficult for her to sleep at night. While Um Ismaeel had managed to get some medicine for her, the drugs were way past their use-by date and were supposed to be taken with food, which they had so little of, three times a day.

But something other than her own injuries was clearly on Islam's mind. Now looking morose, she began telling me about her father and how much she and all the family loved him. Given that she was speaking about him in the past tense, I was prepared for what was coming next. 'My dad went to get us all food from al-Moadamyeh but he never came home. He was shot in the head by a sniper.'

Sensing that Islam was finding it hard to continue, Um Ismaeel took over. On the day it had happened, she had been sitting with her husband in the early hours of the morning, discussing how they would feed their children that day. They had no food of any type left in the house, so her husband said he would go out and look for anything edible. They both knew it would be a dangerous trip, as there had been a lot of mortar attacks in their area of Daraya that week, but they agreed there was no other choice. Without dwelling on this any longer, Um Ismaeel's husband had grabbed his bag and set off. 'By midday,' Um Ismaeel continued, 'there was no sign of him and I started to become concerned. The children were getting very worried and kept asking me, where's Dad, where's Dad? It was not like him to stay away so long.'

Finally, distraught with worry, Um Ismaeel phoned her brother-in-law to ask if he had seen her husband. He said he hadn't, but on hearing how long his brother had been gone, he set off immediately to look for him. 'A few hours later,' said Um Ismaeel, 'after searching all the places my husband usually went to find food, my brother-in-law found him and then brought me to the scene. He was dead, just lying there on the ground. I have been left with this horrible image. It is hard to get it out of my mind. My dear husband lying there alone, without a breath in his body. That sight has never left me. I would not wish such an awful vision on anybody.'

'He was very, very caring,' said Islam, taking over from her mother in a tearful but determined voice. 'I loved him, we all loved him. He was so caring that he would do everything he could to get us food. He hated seeing us going to bed hungry.' Um Ismaeel sighed deeply, tears welling in her eyes as she told me she couldn't think of a single happy moment since he died. It was not just the grief, she explained, but the stress of trying to feed and care for the children by herself. She worried about what would happen to them if she was killed when out looking for food for the family. What would happen if she survived, but came back with nothing to give them. She would never forgive herself, she told me, if they were hurt or killed while she was out. Before, she had taken Islam with her when she went to search for food, but after her daughter was injured, she had been afraid to do that. 'I go by myself now, but always tell her where I'm going and remind all my children that they must go down to the basement if the planes come. The airstrikes and shelling have destroyed everything. We used to have wheat, we used to have crops but they've left us with nothing.'

While Um Ismaeel was speaking, pictures of the war's various political and military leaders came to mind – middle-aged men making finger-jabbing threats, promising victory to come, while pledging to fight to the death. Meanwhile families like Um Ismaeel's were being torn apart. It is one of the saddest facts about most modern conflicts that civilians seem to suffer the most. Wars these days are rarely waged on faraway battlefields. Instead they come to the hearts of towns and cities. Homes, schools and hospitals mark the modern front lines. Women, children, the sick and the elderly all become casualties, 'collateral damage' in the push for victory. None are consulted, and many probably do not even know why the war is being fought, never mind why they are dying in it. I asked twelve-year-old Islam if she knew why people were fighting. 'I honestly don't know,' she told me. 'I mean, I'll be looking out of the window and seeing some place being shelled and I think, why are they bombing this place? Sometimes I hear that someone has died because of his injuries and I ask myself, why did he die, what did he do?'

In the past, Islam told me, her life was beautiful. Her family had lived such a happy life, but it had changed so much. Now she had nothing to eat, she went to bed being bombed and woke up to that too. Sometimes, she continued in a whisper, weeks would go by when there was no shelling or bombing but nobody would celebrate. They all knew, deep down, that it would not last and the bombs would come back. Islam and her family had lived with fear for a long time. Now there was anger in her eyes, as well as in her voice. She crossed her arms tightly, and shouted: 'Children are dying of hunger and being killed by bombs. I'm so sick of it.'

Islam, who had clearly been doing so well at school, who loved reading, loved stories, loved life, had been enjoying a happy childhood. Now her life was reduced to almost constant terror and alarm. Seeing the enormous potential in this young girl, with so much of her life yet to come, I desperately wanted to hear her talk of her hopes for the future. 'Islam,' I asked, 'When you grow up, and this terrible war is finally over, what would you like to be?'

She took a while to reply. 'I used to think about that, but not any more. I don't think I will get much older. I will probably die here.'

Of all the things that I had heard during this difficult conversation, this shocked me the most: 'Are you saying,' I asked her carefully, 'that you are not making plans for the future because you do not believe you have one?'

'Yes,' she replied.

Having found so much extraordinary hope in this beleaguered Syrian town, where many young people would rather read books than fight wars, I was utterly devastated by Islam's last words. The job of a journalist is to observe and report what you see happening, but I wanted to *do* something, somehow, to help.

Thinking of little Islam, as well as the secret library itself, I called a small charity based in Britain that had been helping to get relief into Syria. It might sound like an odd request, I said, but could they take books in? It clearly did seem like a strange request, until I told them about Daraya's secret library and the many children there who were deprived of almost anything to read. About three days later one of the charity's directors called me back. 'I would love to do this,' he said, 'but the Syrian government won't even allow much of the food and medicine we're trying to get into rebel areas, and I've been told that they would be very suspicious about books. Besides, it would be hard to justify carrying books over food and water.' I totally understood his point, but felt he had no idea just how important books were to people under siege. As Anas had said, 'Just like the body needs food, the soul needs books.'

\*

Shortly after my conversation with Islam and Um Ismaeel, in early July 2016, scores of children were killed by a ferocious barrel-bomb offensive on Daraya. Talking to Anas about this, I was struck by his growing concern for the prospects of the youngsters left in the town. 'They will have spent years living through chaos and destruction,' he told me, 'which is likely to blight their futures as well as their pasts.' Anas believed that despite the best efforts of those who were teaching them during the siege, their education had been badly damaged. To Anas they were a lost generation. Yet these were the leaders of tomorrow, the ones whose job it would be to rebuild this traumatised nation. 'It makes me feel so sad,' he told me. 'This revolution was supposed to benefit them. Yet they are the ones who are suffering the most.'

Given how intensive the fighting had become following the Syrian army's latest offensive, I wondered why parents in Daraya continued to send their children to classes at all. Why not keep them at home and worry about their schooling later? The answer, I was told, was that school basements were still safer than most homes.

As if Islam's testimony wasn't enough to articulate the damage done by this siege, there was no doubt in Sara's mind that the carnage on the streets was taking its toll on the nerves of her young pupils. In a recent exercise, she had asked the children to close their eyes while she described her vision of heaven to them, a place where rivers were made of honey and chocolate, and there were flowers everywhere. She then asked them to visualise their own image of heaven, and after ten minutes asked several children to describe what they had imagined to the class. One little girl, Yana, was asked to speak first. Keeping her eyes tightly shut, Sara expected to hear about a calm and magical world, far removed from the one her pupils were living in. But when the little girl began to speak, Sara was shocked. Little Yana merely described her father standing over her family's broken electric generator. He kept telling her that he had been trying to fix it but did not know how. Sara thanked Yana and turned to eight-year-old Amir. Looking nervous and shaking slightly, Amir talked of a plane coming towards him out of the sky. It was diving faster and faster and screeching as it came. He and his family were all running to their basement. They looked up and saw a bomb falling towards them. No matter how hard they ran, they made no progress, but the bomb was getting closer and closer. The boy became so terribly upset that he was unable to finish his story. 'I can't relieve their stress,' Sara said, trying to keep her voice even. 'I can't help them live for even a moment in an imaginary heaven. They simply can't seem to visualise such a place. They clearly can't imagine that somewhere like heaven exists.'

Part of the children's nightmare appeared to be down to the long-running lack of food. 'Lessons require concentration and it is hard to have that if you are constantly hungry, and your mind thinking of nothing but food,' said Sara. Yet despite this, there were moments when such deprivation brought out the very best in them, such as when Sara decided it was time to give out the biscuits that Sawsan, the head teacher, had hidden away for emergencies. Handing one to every second child, she told those with biscuits to break theirs in two and give one half to the child sitting next to them. Her hope was that this tiny bit of food would bring them at least a few moments of happiness. And it certainly did that. When Sara looked around the classroom, it was as though the children had treasure in their hands. They were concentrating hard, taking tiny little bites, in an attempt to savour the taste and make their meagre half biscuit last as long as possible.

Then Sara noticed that one of the children, a boy called Joram, had not given half to the girl next to him. After telling him off for being greedy, she made Joram give the girl her share. One of Sara's colleagues told her later that she had watched Joram put his half of the biscuit in his bag without eating it. The next day Sara was told by the boy's mother that he had given that half to his little sister when he got home. Their father had been killed just two days before and now he clearly felt responsible for looking after her.

As she recounted this incident, tears come flooding back into Sara's eyes: 'I was upset for a whole week after this. But I know I can't show my feelings to the children. I mustn't ever cry in front of them. They need to feel that the adults are coping, to help them believe that they can cope too, though I must admit that in a way, children like Joram are teaching me. They are helping me to see the world differently.'

With the recent onslaughts, Sara had noticed a real shift in the children's ability to cope and it seemed to her that since the day of the biscuits, their resilience had slowly begun to ebb away. She didn't quite know what had caused this, as they had already endured so many years of danger and hardship. But perhaps, she wondered, they had simply reached the limits of their tolerance of hunger, death and destruction. They might also have picked up on the growing fear felt by adults, as the military situation worsened.

By mid-July 2016 nearly all of the town's farmland had

been overrun by pro-government forces and food supplies were running shorter than ever. So too was space. The remaining rebel-controlled area of Daraya was now a fraction of what it had been before. More families had been forced to flee their homes and join others in whatever overcrowded and bomb-damaged buildings were left standing. 'Life is now quite miserable,' Sara told me. 'The children have begun to lose their motivation and enthusiasm. It's terrible to see because these were things we'd always admired in them. They're finding it really hard to cope. They have no energy. Even when we hold sports events to help bring back their enthusiasm, it doesn't work. This has really shaken me. It's left me very drained. They are my hope.'

In an effort to raise the children's spirits and help take their minds off the siege, Sara had managed to get to the secret library and borrowed some books for her school. But, she told me: 'It didn't work. They seem to hate books altogether now and don't want to have anything to do with them. This makes me feel terribly sad. I truly think it's because they are so very hungry all the time, some are actually suffering from malnutrition and they just can't concentrate any more.'

Sara was determined not to give up and despite the children's reaction, she continued her visits to the secret library. Her hope was that she might yet find books that would help rekindle her pupils' fading love of learning and their interest in life. Each visit involved great personal risk and she told me she had nearly been killed trying to get there on several occasions. She often asked her husband to go with her, so that if either of them were injured or killed the other might be able to call for help, or bring news to the family. Sometimes one of Sara's closest friends, Najah, who was also a teacher at her school, would accompany her. Najah's house was halfway to the library from Sara's home, so they would often meet there and continue on together, discussing the books they were reading, though sometimes they were too scared to talk. Like Sara, Najah loved books, often reading four a month, on a wide range of subjects including religion, education and literature.

On one occasion they arrived at the library to find that some children had had to sleep there overnight as it had been too perilous for them to try and go home the afternoon before. At other times, they would go through all the risks of getting to the library, only to find that it was closed. As the military situation on the ground worsened this became more common, now that the library staff often couldn't make it there themselves. So Sara began calling ahead, to check if the library was open before setting out on her perilous journey. But even Sara's love for the secret library had its limits. When we spoke a few days later, in the third week of July, she told me that the bombing had reached such an intensity that it was impossible to go out at all. The last time she had made it to the library, she said, the only person there was Amjad, who was busily dusting the books and shelves in his loving and cheerful way. None of the adults who had created the library was anywhere to be seen. 'Seeing the secret library so empty has had a really strange effect on me,' Sara told me. 'I don't quite know how to describe it, but it felt as if the walls themselves were crying. That must sound crazy, but that is really how it seemed. In a way it makes me think of the film *Titanic*. People back then couldn't believe that such a great ship could end up sinking. That is the same as the secret library for me. It is the best thing in my life and we have all worked so hard building and maintaining it. Yet now, it's as if it has died.'

After that conversation, returning to my own life in safe, affluent London was not easy. I felt very uncomfortable. Even though we were separated by thousands of miles, Sara, Abdul Basit, Anas, Omar and their friends had let me into their frightening world, seemingly holding nothing back. They had shared their pain, grief and loss as well as their jokes, hopes and occasional moments of triumph. At times it often felt as if I was really there with them, inside their besieged city, exposed to the same awful dangers, hardships and horrors. Yet, of course, I was not. I remember one particular Friday evening, when this situation really played on my mind. I had just been talking to Muhammad in Daraya, and hearing explosions all around. Then, at the end of the call, I set off home to spend the weekend with my family. All the way there a voice kept telling me that Muhammad, Sara and everyone in Daraya would not be going anywhere. While I relaxed in front of my TV, or dined in a nice restaurant, they were being shelled, bombed and starved. I'd had this horrible feeling several times before over the months and years I had been talking to people there. The stark contrast in our two, so very different worlds, left me feeling like some kind of journalistic voyeur. Despite the knowledge that I was bringing their plight to the outside world, that feeling continued to haunt me.

It was becoming clear to most in Daraya that their long resistance against Assad's forces was nearing its end. Government forces had captured all of the remaining rebel-held farms around Daraya, so this was now a town with no access to crops. From here on, its people had nothing to eat other than the few vegetables they could grow on rooftops and balconies. As if that was not bad enough, the bombing and shelling were growing more intense by the day. Around this time the residents of Daraya watched in horror as rebel-held Eastern Aleppo became completely surrounded by pro-Assad forces. On 16 July the regime tightened its siege by cutting off the Castello Road, nicknamed the 'road of death'. This dusty two-lane highway, littered with bombed buildings and burnt-out vehicles, had been the last route in and out of Eastern Aleppo. Its 250,000 people were now under siege, just like their counterparts in rebel-held Daraya.

On 24 July an artillery and rocket bombardment against rebel positions was followed by a ferocious offensive. This was beaten back by the rebels, who claimed to have destroyed a Russian minesweeper and killed nine Syrian government soldiers. Around this time, I managed to speak again to Omar Abu Anas, who was still fighting on the front line with the FSA. Sadly, he told me, the deteriorating situation meant he had little opportunity to read any more. He also had little time for talking on the phone, and I only managed to speak to him briefly. Initially, Omar steadfastly claimed to be optimistic, insisting that because President Assad's family had been in power for many decades, the rebels could not expect to defeat him overnight. But when I pointed out that time appeared to be something that the rebel forces in Daraya now had precious little of, Omar's mood darkened. After a deep intake of breath, he replied: 'To be honest, things are getting much worse. Too many people are being martyred and it's not just Daraya – it's the whole revolution. In Daraya, my friends are dying every day. One day I see them alive, and the next they are dead.'

Despite this, and the fact that his life was now in more

danger than ever, Omar's main concern was for Daraya's beloved library. 'I swear the library holds a very special place in all our hearts,' he told me. 'Every time there is bombing and shelling nearby, we pray for it. In the past the library has nearly been hit several times and we've come close to losing all of its books. That would be terrible. It is so treasured by us all.'

In order to help protect the secret library, Omar and his friends had recently placed more sandbags around it, after becoming increasingly convinced that the regime's forces had found out its location and would soon send their planes to bomb it. 'What dictator,' he asked me, 'would stand by and watch the people he is fighting educate themselves with books, some of which his regime has banned? There is no doubt,' he continued, 'that Assad would want to destroy the secret library.'

It seemed strange that, with the whole town apparently on the verge of falling to government forces, Omar was still so concerned about preserving the secret library. I began to wonder whether he was unaware, or perhaps in denial, of the military situation around him. But from what he had already told me, that was evidently not the case. Omar clearly saw the library, and its contents, as something indivisible from the revolution itself. A part of the very soul of those fighting for it.

Four days later, on 28 July, shelling and artillery fire came raining down again, pounding central areas of Daraya. It was the beginning of yet another offensive by government forces, aimed at winning full control of the town. The regime's helicopters hovered above, dropping their barrel bombs. In his audio diary, Abdul Basit recording his terror: 'A helicopter is over us now . . . I can hear the noise of its rotor blades. Listening to that sound is making my heart beat fast. Now I can see it, I think it is loaded with barrel bombs . . . it is falling fast . . . shrapnel is everywhere . . . the flames. All our nights are like this now. We go to bed with this, we wake up with this.' Trapped in the carnage below, civilians posted videos of napalm attacks on residential areas. Reports came in of mounting injuries among rebel fighters defending the town. Later that day the Syrian army's 4th Armoured Division broke through rebel lines, taking a 300-metre-long strip of territory in Western Daraya. Among those killed in the battle, was the key rebel leader, Abu Aref Alayyan.

Sadly, he was not the only casualty.

# Chapter Twelve

On Thursday, 28 July 2016, the result of my many months of interviews with the people of Daraya was broadcast on BBC Radio 4. A slightly shorter version was also transmitted on the BBC's World Service, giving the story of this beleaguered town and its inspirational secret library a worldwide audience. The half-hour documentary generated a tremendous reaction from listeners, both in Britain and across the globe. They were both moved and inspired by this extraordinary community who were celebrating books and learning amid all the killing and hatred. Many listeners wanted to donate books, though that was almost impossible to organise given the intense fighting and iron siege around the town. One of the comments I liked most was, 'Syria doesn't feel like a distant land any more', a tweet that echoed the effect these candid and courageous testimonies had had on me, that whatever our country, belief system or culture there is more that unites us than sets us apart. A tweet I mentioned earlier from an American lecturer on International Affairs in Washington DC read: 'I have been researching and teaching about Syria since 1993. When I awoke this a.m. and listened to your programme, I felt a glimmer of hope for the future of Syria for the first time in a long time.' Abdul Basit, Anas, Amjad and their friends had clearly touched many lives beyond those in their beleaguered town.

Perhaps even more important was the response that came from those I had talked with for so long in Daraya. 'Mike, I have just heard our radio documentary! It was wonderful to hear our story finally told to other countries. Everyone [is] much excited. We feel alone no more.' That text came from Malik. Without his enormous help and enthusiasm it would have been hard to have made the programme. I had sent him a link to the broadcast from the BBC website. Part of me dreaded what he and others in Daraya might think. No criticism would have been more devastating than one that came from them. After all, it is their story, not mine. But Malik, as well as others from Daraya, couldn't have given the programme a warmer response. At least they had now been heard. Year after year of almost unremitting siege and bombardment had left many there feeling abandoned, convinced that the world didn't care. Some wondered if much of the international community had even heard of their troubles, such was the apparent lack of interest in their fate. Now, at what looked like their twilight hour, recognition had come at last. But, sadly, this came too late for one person I was beginning to get to know.

The following Monday felt like a very normal summer afternoon in the leafy north London suburb of East Finchley. It was warm and sunny. Traffic was light and the mood on the suburban streets relaxed. Except, that was, for the shouts of a passing motorist. Leaning out of his window he cursed a pizza delivery driver whose moped had pulled out in front of him. I was in the small terraced house of an old friend, deep in discussion about an art project she was planning. As we talked, music from a car parked nearby drifted through her open sitting-room window. U2's 'Sunday

Bloody Sunday', a song lamenting the horrors of the troubles in Northern Ireland, briefly jolted me back to the terrors of Syria. As I tried to refocus on what my host was saying, a shrill bleep from my mobile phone signalled the arrival of a text. Concerned that fumbling for my phone might look rude mid-conversation, I ignored it. Then, around twenty minutes later, when my friend got up to make some tea, I finally took a look at the message. Three words glared out from the screen.

*Omar is dead*

I stared at the text, struggling to absorb what it said, before scrolling down to see if there were any more details. Any explanation, any verification, any account of how this had happened. There was nothing else. It seemed inconceivable that these three short words, these ten letters, spelled the end of a man as vibrant, warm and positive as Omar Abu Anas. He was twenty-four years old.

I tried to reach his many friends, including Anas, Saeed, Homam, and Rateb to find out what had happened to Omar. But the town seemed, yet again, to have lost all Internet connections. I turned to Facebook where, after some searching, I finally came across a heartfelt dedication, posted in Arabic by Homam, one of Omar's closest friends:

### Letter to Omar

By losing you, I have lost my soul and my heart is darkened. Without you, life is meaningless. You were my hope in the midst of sorrow. You gave me peace when my mind was full of worries. You brought life to me when death was around us.

It is with you that I spent the best moments of my life. By your side, I learned about dedication, because you were a good and determined man. By your side, I learned about the purity of friendship, because you were an honest friend. You taught me about brotherhood. Our fellow obedience to God, our goodwill and our love for education made us closer. You were a tutor, a confidant and a genuine companion, who helped me sow my future. But now, now that we are no longer together, I worry about what is coming next.

We came together to this world and now you are leaving me with a heart full of sorrow. I look forward to meeting you again. You were a role model to me. I learned so much from you. You were always polite, with exemplary ethical behaviour. You were generous, you were compassionate and you were always present during the hardest times. You never hated or held on to bitterness.

I saw you crying during emotional moments. I always admired your ability to express your feelings. Your kindness is a blessing that shows how great your soul is and how strong your relationship to God. You taught me about conscience and a sense of duty.

I eventually managed to make contact with Homam, who was clearly traumatised. His depth of feeling for a friend he loved and clearly looked up to in every way really moved me. 'Omar was everything to me,' he told me, 'we spent so much time together during the last two or three years. We were born on the same day in the same year. His death was the most painful event in my life. We used to always sit together, eat together and read the same books together. I think of our time together so very often. I even see him in my dreams, and every time I think of the library, I think of him.'

*

The details of how Omar died were sketchy. He had been one of a group of rebel fighters who had become surrounded by advancing government forces and was being shelled repeatedly. They held out for some time, but eventually, a direct hit had finally killed them all. This had happened just a couple of hours after the broadcast of my BBC documentary, which had, so poignantly, ended on Omar's optimistic and inspirational words: 'Right now we are in the process of planning what comes next. We can only do that through the books we are reading. We want a free nation. We want something better than Assad, and hopefully, through reading, we can achieve this.' Those words had stuck in my mind for days after my interview with Omar. Here was a man who had become a fighter, seen many lifelong friends killed beside him and only narrowly escaped death many times himself. Yet he knew that although guns, tanks and bombs might win wars, they don't win peace. Peace takes research, planning and reconstruction, the secrets to which can be found in books. The very fact that he could comprehend this while embroiled in a brutal civil war astonished me. He didn't want to replace President Assad with another ruthless, bloodthirsty tyrant, knowing that history would then soon repeat itself. He wanted something more, something better, something longer-lasting that could help heal this broken nation.

In another tribute to Omar on Facebook, Homam wrote:

He wasn't keen on being in the spotlight and he didn't ask for that. He never expressed borrowed opinions. His thoughts were his own. He was a free thinker. He used to research, read and discuss. He constantly sought justice. He was balanced, self-confident, patient, ambitious and working wisely towards achieving his goals. He was a loving, caring man. Today, I find myself alone, unable to see you again Omar. You left my heart riddled with sadness. But as much as I am sad to see that you're no longer by my side, I am happy you were chosen by God.

Only a few days before his death, Omar had told me of his grief at watching his friends die each day: 'One day I see them alive, and the next they are dead.' Now he was gone too. Yet another death to add to the hundreds of thousands in Syria. I could only hope that his optimism during this time of war, his wish to achieve a free nation, based on a foundation of books and learning, would not die with him.

Although, sadly, many hundreds of people had been killed in Daraya by this point in the siege, Omar was the first person I knew there who had died. I shouldn't need any reminders of the grim realities of war, having covered so many, yet I struggled to come to terms with his death. How awful it must be, I thought, for his family and friends. I have sometimes tried to imagine daily life as I know it after I have died, yet always struggle to visualise that, even though the world would obviously carry on just as before. But that was not true of Daraya after Omar's death. As the casualties mounted, the town's very survival hung in the balance. During the first week of August 2016, pro-Assad forces continued their advance into Daraya, taking control of a square kilometre of the town. Two days later they seized three more blocks. During the intense fighting, Ahmad Abu al-Majd, the rebels' commander, was killed, but in the early hours of Monday, 15 August, his forces fought back.

Using a secret tunnel, they launched a surprise counter-attack on government forces and recaptured several of their positions in West Daraya. This victory was short-lived, however, for that same evening the Republican Guard, an elite mechanized division also known as the Presidential Guard, launched a counter-strike and took both areas back again. I dread to think of the lives lost in vain on both sides during all this.

As had often been the case throughout Daraya's long years under siege, the eyes of the world were mostly looking elsewhere – the opening of the 2016 Summer Olympics in Brazil; the worsening Zika epidemic; the death of hundreds in an Italian earthquake, and floods in the American state of Louisiana which had left thousands in need of rescue. But then a harrowing photo emerged taken far to the north of Daraya, in besieged, rebel-held Eastern Aleppo. It showed a bloodied and dust-covered little boy, sitting forlornly on a bright-orange chair, the suffering of so many of the shattered nation's most innocent and vulnerable, embodied in this staring, frightened figure. The child's face was soon staring out from television screens and the front pages of newspapers around the world. It put the international media's attention back to the horrors of Syria. Political leaders demanded action against Assad, aid agencies pleaded for more convoys to be allowed in, and the United Nations insisted that the atrocities stop.

Shortly after midnight on 19 August, government forces barrel-bombed the rebel's last functioning hospital in Daraya. Videos posted on YouTube appear to show that incendiary weapons such as napalm were used in this attack, despite an international agreement forbidding this in areas with a significant civilian presence. As many as eight thousand people, the majority of whom were civilians, now had no access to medical care. Later that same day, rebel defences in southern Daraya partially collapsed as pro-regime troops captured the town's railway crossing. Another twenty-four commercial and residential blocks then fell as the invading soldiers swept into the town's Christian district. Over the next few days, the advance continued. After nearly four years of siege, rebel forces now faced total defeat. On the morning of Thursday, 25 August, I received a text from Sara Matar: 'I was sitting at home planning what I would be teaching the children over the coming week when my husband stormed in. He told me we are leaving Daraya. I am absolutely shocked!'

The end had finally come. Rebel leaders had reached a deal with the government, which promised everyone safe passage out of Daraya. Early the following morning, aid convoys sent by the medical charity, Syrian Arab Red Crescent, drove into the town. All rebel fighters were to be evacuated to rebel-held Idlib province in north-west Syria, while thousands of men, women and children would be taken to reception centres and then transferred either to Idlib or Western Damascus.

Given the fear, loss, deprivation and horror that everyone had been through for so long, I expected there to be some joy or relief at this news. Yet there was little sign of that in the next message Sara sent me: 'I've spent the last few hours thinking of my life here over the years and how precious it has been. But now there is just a very eerie silence. The guns have stopped firing and there are no bombs or planes in the sky. I have no children of my own to worry about, but many others here have young families to care for. Where,

I wonder, are they going to go? What will they do? I really worry about them.'

Government forces were giving civilians two options. They could either go north to the rebel-held province of Idlib, which was often bombed, or west to the government-controlled area of Kiswe abutting Damascus. But the latter was only on offer for those willing to testify to the security forces that they did not support the revolution. To do so, locals told me, they needed to make official statements verifying that they accepted the authority of the regime, had never been 'terrorists', and were against the uprising in Daraya. I can only imagine how conflicted many of those who had braved years of siege and hardship in order to support their rebellious community must have felt. Although testifying that they were against the rebellion would have been a betrayal of all they had stood for, it would mean they could get their children to comparative safety.

Having been corralled into a tiny area of the town and cut off from any reinforcements and food reserves, it must have been obvious for many that fighting on was no longer a viable option. Among those stunned by the sudden turn of events was Abdul Basit. Hearing what he was saying amid the chaos was difficult, but we both did our best over a series of interrupted calls.

'I was in the hospital when I heard about the agreement between our leaders and the regime,' he told me. 'I had been wondering if something big was about to happen because in the hours before this news there was no bombing at all. For two whole hours there was silence. Previously we'd been bombed around the clock, almost every minute. The silence felt really odd. A little earlier I'd gone upstairs to my room to see if my laptop could get online. It was then that I saw the announcement that our leaders had agreed to everyone being evacuated by the regime.'

Although that announcement was a surprise, Abdul Basit knew that life in Daraya had become impossible. He accepted that by this point the choice facing rebel leaders had been a stark one. Either they agreed to leave or everyone might die. With so many women and children among them, there was really only one option. Then, as if talking to himself as much to me, Abdul Basit added that no one should feel defeated. They had resisted the regime for nearly four whole years, held its forces at bay all that time.

I asked him if, deep down, he felt conflicted by the deal, which meant abandoning the town he had been born in, the place he loved, which so many of his friends had died trying to cling on to. Shaking his head, Abdul Basit brushed the question aside but admitted that it was hard to put his feelings into words. He saw no other realistic alternative to the decision made by his leaders, even though it meant the end of everything he'd known. To make matters worse, somebody loyal to the regime would probably be given his family's house. The pain of it all was contorting his usually kind and pensive face. 'I just can't describe how all this leaves me feeling. It some ways it would have been easier if I'd been killed and buried in the ground. At least then I would be at rest.'

Abdul Basit drifted into silence, the weight of current events clearly too much to come to terms with so quickly. After a while he took a deep breath, sighed and began describing how on hearing about the evacuation, he had gone to the town's cemetery to say goodbye to the many friends he had lost. Then he went to say farewell to the places that had meant the most to him over the years: first his family home, then his school, followed by parks and picnic spots where he had laughed, talked and reminisced with friends. Then came the most special place of all, the one he was saving until last. The place that had been the source of so much solace throughout the long and frightening siege. He began, he said, by standing outside the secret library, just staring at the damaged but much-loved entrance. He remembered the excitement and danger of collecting so many books, of finding chairs and tables and filling the shelves and then, on the day it opened, walking down the stairs and entering a completely different world. A peaceful underground sanctuary of reading, learning, friendship and hope. 'When I tell you what I did next please don't think that I am crazy or shell-shocked or something. But this is what happened. Knowing this might be the last time I would ever see the library, I walked over to the shelves and hugged the books. I hugged as many as I could. While I did this I cried. I cried a lot. Then I walked around reading the titles on the spines out loud, and flicking through the pages of some of them. I so wished I could take all the books with me, all of them. I feared they would be burned or destroyed in some other way. I'm sure this will happen. It would be so terrible. I believe in the books, and I believe in our secret library.'

Slowly, Abdul Basit reiterated that, in his view, no society could rebuild itself or truly grow without first being educated. For that, he insisted, you needed books and you needed a library: 'Principles are planted in a library, and they grow into ideas,' he told me. 'It is a factory for thoughts and solutions. So in order for us to be educated and be more aware, we had to have a library. Libraries are the fuel of life.' Abdul Basit admitted that even he had questioned his decision to make the library the site of his final and most important farewell, but it had become clear that this was the right thing to do. 'I realise now,' he said, 'that I did this so that I could leave part of my soul there. This way I have something to go back to.'

In contrast to Abdul Basit, Muhammad wasn't surprised by news of the evacuation deal with the government. In fact he had acknowledged the possibility of this happening as early as May that year. Back then, he had still harboured hopes that it could be avoided, but the lack of any action by the UN or foreign governments had made him see that it would only be a matter of time. From then on, he told me, he viewed every day that rebel forces were able to cling on in Daraya as a miracle. But the situation had become steadily more perilous, with civilians being pushed into an increasingly small area of the town, forcing some to sleep on the streets. Even though this had failed to break the spirit of local people, its teachers, hospital workers, farmers and fighters, there was clearly little that could be done to save the town.

As head of the council's civil administration, Muhammad had become involved in discussions over the evacuation deal. He and his colleagues had tried to get government negotiators to allow those who wanted to stay in Daraya to remain behind, but this request was flatly rejected. Government forces did agree, though, to let rebel fighters leave with their light weapons, which, as Muhammad told me, was crucial because none of them completely trusted the army's offer of a safe passage to Idlib.

Listening to Muhammad's exhausted voice, which I could only just make out, I could tell he was under huge pressure. I had had trouble contacting him over recent

ABOVE: Shells fired by Syrian government forces hit Daraya
BELOW: Living and dying under siege in Daraya

LEFT: Daraya: a town without walls and windows

BELOW LEFT: Books rescued for the secret library from bombed and abandoned buildings

BELOW: More books are found for the secret library

30-3-2014

ABOVE: Fourteen-year-old Amjad tends the bookshelves of the secret library

RIGHT: No fuel, no road, no produce, but life goes on in Daraya

Chief Librarian Amjad enjoying a quick read during a break in his duties . . .

RIGHT: Sifting through the rubble during a break in the bombing, Daraya

BELOW: Twenty-four-year-old Saeed refuses to leave what is left of his home

ABOVE: Abdul Basit relaxes
with a book in the sanctuary
of the secret library

ABOVE: Anas Habib in the secret library
BELOW: Books and bullets: Omar Abu Anas reading on the front line

In Abu Malik al-Shami's graffiti a little girl teaches a soldier the meaning of love

This picture by Abu Malik al-Shami, drawn on a wall amid the ruins of Daraya, inspired people around the world

RIGHT: Twelve-year-old Islam reads
with her mother in a home missing walls

BELOW: Getting together at the secret library

BELOW RIGHT: Omar giving a lecture

Daraya's women and children call on the world for help

Books from the secret library being looted by men in uniform

The ransacked secret library, with once treasured books littering the floor

Malik al-Rifaii prepares books for the mobile library (below), Idlib

Amjad lovingly cleans books in the secret library

Some of the secret library team

days, even when the Internet there had been good, and I asked whether the strain of events lay behind his decision not to take my calls. 'Yes,' he replied, 'the challenge was getting harder and harder and our response had to be right, so the pressure was growing on me and those I worked with. Everyone was very disappointed, tired and frustrated. I felt I needed to put on a happy face to reassure them, give them hope, and try to hide the turmoil and sadness I felt inside. At other times I shut myself off from the world. I told people, if it's an absolute emergency you can call me on my phone, but otherwise, please do not contact me.'

I can imagine just how many people must have tried to contact Muhammad. Not only those wanting practical guidance due to his role with Daraya's council, but the many who would have turned to him for personal advice. This indomitable 'Professor', as he was known, was everyone's wise and responsible uncle, the sort of person who always seems rational and calm when everyone else is in turmoil. Having to constantly be this strong, supportive pillar of the community throughout such desperate times, must have been very demanding, but I sensed that amid the bitter disappointment that pulsed through his veins, lay a sense of relief. His job was nearly over. Much work needed to be done over the next couple of days, but after that all he had to do was pack his bags and board the buses, just like everyone else.

On the day I spoke to him, there was a two-day window for people to leave Daraya. Muhammad had had a busy morning, making arrangements for the evacuation, telling everyone what to do next and where to go. Even the ever-organised Muhammad wasn't sure of all the details, but knowing that the regime's soldiers would search their bags, he advised people to only take the things they absolutely needed or were most precious to them. Deciding what fell into the latter bracket after what for some had been a lifetime in the house they were leaving, would not be easy. Though for those whose homes had been badly damaged or destroyed there were fewer choices to make. After making a special pilgrimage to the town's cemetery to say farewell to the many friends buried there during the long siege, Muhammad headed for the evacuation point. He would be boarding a bus bound for Idlib, where the fighters and their families were going, rather than joining most civilians in the west Damascus countryside. Although not a fighter in a military sense, he wished to continue his non-violent battle against the Assad regime from the country's last remaining rebel-held province. Besides, he believed that if he set foot in a government-controlled area, he would probably be arrested because of his outspoken support for the uprising.

One thing that lifted the heavy hearts of all in Daraya, was the absence of bombs, shells and sniper fire. For the first time in many months there were no explosions, cracks of rifle shots, no hovering helicopters, no screams as barrel bombs fell from the skies. The guns had fallen silent forty-eight hours before the evacuation process got underway, in order to allow government negotiators to come into what was left of the rebel-held town and discuss terms.

Anas was amongst the crowds, doing his best to find out more about the details of the evacuation agreement, and what he and others would be able to take with them. With help from Muhammad, I managed to get hold of him. Though outwardly calm, Anas was clearly struggling to come to terms with the speed of events. 'Forty-eight hours is very little time to pack up and leave somewhere you have lived all your life. I found it almost impossible to decide what to put in my suitcase. Everything held memories of my twenty-eight years in the town. It was very difficult.

'All those memories are so precious,' Anas continued, 'it is almost impossible to decide which things are more valuable than others. Should I prioritise souvenirs from my childhood, those with my family or the ones with my friends?' He concluded, sounding increasingly bereft, 'I will just have to carry most of my memories in my head. That way nobody can take them from me or destroy them.'

Anas seemed in a complete state of shock. A few minutes later, having recovered his composure, he told me that negotiators had advised residents to take only personal items with them in a maximum of two bags. After much deliberation Anas had decided to include a clean set of clothes that he could change into as soon as he got to Idlib. He also packed a few of the treasured mementos he had agonised over, some other valuables and his identity papers. Earlier that morning, he had been talking to friends who were also frantically packing. After four years of chaos, which had often involved moving from one bomb-damaged house to another, people were finding it hard to locate their ID papers, without which there might be big problems with officials later. Some of his friends, Anas told me, fearing that the regime's soldiers would steal belongings that had been left behind, had decided to destroy what they couldn't take with them, such as personal photos and even some very expensive things. Anas was advised not to take any books because these would probably be taken from him before boarding the bus. Though, somewhat alarmingly, just like the shell-shocked, half-starved children at Sara's school, he had somehow lost his once insatiable appetite for reading and books. 'To be honest with you, and I do want to be honest,' he told me, 'given all that's been happening over the last few days, the sudden end of the siege and the need to get packed up and leave Daraya so quickly, I had almost forgotten about the secret library. I never believed this could happen. I love it so much. It must be the continuous lack of food, the constant barrel bombs and the round-the-clock effort to stay alive. My mind can no longer concentrate on reading any more.'

In the circumstances, that seemed far from surprising, yet Anas was riddled with guilt. He clearly felt as though his brief neglect of the library was some kind of mortal sin, like failing to turn up at a place of worship on the holiest day of the year. Perhaps this was because the library had offered him and his friends such a refuge, a peaceful shelter from the storm, yet they were now abandoning it.

There was, however, one person who I thought would find it harder than anyone to stay away from the place he adored so much, even when facing the trauma of imminent evacuation. Sara had told me that on each of her last visits there, Chief Librarian Amjad had been hard at work in the library, lovingly dusting and shelving the books he adored. Given that his family had found a basement to live in, almost next door to the library, getting there, even in these chaotic last days, would clearly not be a problem for him. I tried his number. Each time a recorded message told me that the number was either out of range or switched off. I wondered if Amjad and his family had somehow already left Daraya. But with pro-Assad forces advancing through the city over the last few days, that would surely have been almost impossible. I kept trying, but still the same message. Eventually I gave up. Then, around half-an-hour later, a text pinged on my phone. It said simply: 'Yes.' It was Amjad.

I called his number once more, this time with success. It was great to hear Amjad's cheerful young voice again, so full of life and enthusiasm. He seemed the same bright-eyed little charmer that I had first talked to so long ago. After we had exchanged hellos, I asked where he was and what he was doing. He replied that he was with his parents packing up their possessions. He, too, was struggling to work out what to take with him, though his job had been made easier, he said, by a bomb that had badly damaged his family's former home. They had lost most of their possessions, so deciding what to bring with him didn't take long. What about your time, I asked him, how have you been spending that over the last few days? What felt like an endless pause followed, though it was probably no more than a few seconds. When Amjad finally answered, the smile in his voice had gone. 'I have spent a lot of my time sitting in the secret library, not really doing anything. I haven't been able to take in what is happening. I kept being told that the regime's soldiers were getting nearer and nearer. People said the end was coming. I would look at the books and think to myself, How am I going to leave them all if we have to flee? I felt very sad. But I kept on working there. I never left the library.'

Amjad told me that for a while the secret library had become really quiet. Very few people came any more and it was pretty deserted. Then, over the last day or two, it suddenly got quite crowded again. Many people came back wanting to return the books they had borrowed in case they were forced to leave Daraya. They were worried about what might happen to the books if Assad's soldiers came to their homes. They knew that all the books belonged to people who treasured them and might want them back one day. Many had come over the last twenty-four hours thanks to the ceasefire agreement: the lack of bombing and snipers had made it possible to get to the library safely. 'It meant that I was very busy,' Amjad continued. 'I thanked the people returning the books and told them that I would make sure they would be stacked in the correct categories and that none would be discarded or left on the floor.'

Amjad went on to tell me that some people had become very concerned about the books. They told him how valuable they were, clearly worried that they might be stolen or destroyed when everyone left. Amjad shared their fears, but said there was nothing anyone could do. They were in God's hands, he told them. I tried to imagine the scene. At that stage nobody knew for sure exactly what was going to happen next. They wondered if the evacuation deal would go ahead as promised, or if instead they might be arrested or even butchered by Assad's soldiers. And even if they were evacuated safely, as promised, what would happen to them when they arrived at their destination? Where would they sleep, what would they eat? There were so many unanswered questions hanging in the air. Yet back at the library, despite facing such fearful unknowns, people actually seemed more worried about the welfare of their library books. This was astonishing to me. In Britain, many of us sit by and watch our long-serving libraries being shut down in their hundreds by cash-strapped councils, sometimes without as much as a murmur. Yet these dutiful individuals in Daraya, uprooted from their homes and heading into the complete unknown, still made sure they returned their library books.

Not that Amjad appeared to think there was anything strange about this. Although his future was also hanging in the balance, he didn't just throw the returned books in a box and run for the door. Instead, he dutifully signed all of them in, before carefully placing each one on the shelves according to subject, author and title. I was struck by his absolute love and dedication, not just for the books them-selves, but for the library they were housed in. It seemed to me as if it was almost a place of worship, a temple of lit-erature and Amjad's description of his last few hours there seemed to bear that out: 'I walked round and round the library asking myself, How am I going to leave this place? Each step I took, I stared all about me, trying to memorise all I saw. It was almost as if I was seeing the library for the first time. I was terribly sad. When I looked across the room at my little desk, I felt even more upset. I cried. I couldn't stop myself. I had sat there so many times and learned so much in that very spot.'

I remembered Sara telling me how often she had seen Amjad sitting at that little desk, eagerly trying to catch up on the school work he had missed. How she had told him to just keep at it and he would get there in the end. Like so many children and young adults, the war had sabotaged his education. When Amjad arrived there he had found it hard to concentrate but that changed over the following weeks. He had discovered a sanctuary within whose tranquil walls he could read books on all kinds of complex subjects and learn about his country and the world beyond.

As our conversation drew to a close, I asked the Chief Librarian what plans he had for the future, and whether he had any particular career in mind. A long silence followed. Thinking he may not have heard me properly, I asked the question again. But Amjad's mind was still in the secret library: 'I'll never forget my last hours at the library,' he told me. 'It was such a sad day, knowing I would be leaving it behind. The night before I just couldn't sleep. I had always believed that I would never do that, that I would always work there and look after it. But I have no option. I console myself with the fact that I have some books to take with me. Most are to help me with my education. I also have a story book and another about praying. I am really lucky to be able to take these. My parents have told me that we can only bring two or three suitcases for the whole family, so I do hope there will be room for my books.'

By midday on Friday, 26 August, buses accompanied by ambulances from the Syrian Arab Red Crescent had begun massing in the centre of Daraya. Thousands of people stood waiting for whatever might come next. Anxious mothers, hands clasped protectively around their children, next to frail old men with crooked sticks and weary, wrinkled faces. From afar they might appear to have massed on some kind of far-flung, hostile planet. A stark, grey world of rubble-filled craters and burnt-out buildings. The vibrant colours of normal life muted by summer dust and the debris of war. Daraya was now a crumbling urban desert, a mangled, broken wreck of what once was a town. That so much life still existed here amid the wreckage was a miracle of its own. Yet fleets of buses would soon begin draining the blood from its veins.

Gathered in small groups under the scorching sun, young men engaged in intense conversation. Defiance mingled with despair in their half-closed, sleep-deprived eyes. To many of those huddled in the scorching summer heat, this was no peace deal. It was a humiliating surrender. Though at least their long-lasting ordeal by siege was nearly over. The question on many minds, both young and old, fighters and civilians, was: What next? At least Daraya, despite all its bombs, hunger and devastation, was home. Tomorrow, or the next day, brought the unknown. Life should be safer, at least for a while, and food more plentiful, but they would all be strangers in a faraway place. Where would they sleep, what would they eat and when could they come home again? If, that is, they ever could. Questions were many, but answers few.

For the first time in four years, Syrian government soldiers walked through the streets of Daraya, rifles at the ready. Their faces showed no trace of uncertainty or fear. They had won. Some strutted past the lines of weary, encumbered civilians, their backs straight and heads held high. A victor's walk. Yet, while the world watched on, the scene remained surprisingly calm. The UN had insisted that civilians should not be evacuated against their will. Though quite what the organisation could do if this was ignored remained unclear. Many pro-government Syrians elsewhere viewed the scene on television. They would have had little sympathy for the bedraggled lines of shell-shocked civilians, waiting forlornly to leave. Such people had long been depicted on state TV as terrorists, violent extremists bent on destroying everything ordinary Syrians held dear, a description the regime applied to all who opposed it with guns. An image that couldn't be further removed from the inspiring souls who built the secret library, remarkable people who I had come to know well, lovers of literature, poetry and science who had long campaigned for tolerance and democracy.

Finally, the first bus, packed with women, children and the elderly wended its way through Daraya's rubble-strewn streets. Over the next two days many more buses followed, each ferrying exhausted and traumatised people out of the town they had clung to for so long. Front-line areas where few had dared move for years became scenes of frantic activity. But the same could not be said for the shell of a town they had left behind. Daraya, famous for its fine grapes, peaceful protests and love of learning, was dying.

Unnoticed by most of those lugging their lives in bags towards the buses, a group of young men were dashing backwards and forwards around an inconspicuous basement entrance, carrying sacks of dirt and rubble. Like scurrying ants, they busied themselves, emptying their cargo over what remained of the door. They paid no heed to passers-by, nor the sweat that dripped down their faces and soaked their clothes. The young men entombing Daraya's treasured secret library hoped to ensure that it stayed secret, hidden from those who might do it harm. One day, the burial team hoped to return, and bring it back to life.

# Chapter Thirteen

In the weeks following the evacuation, I worried about the people I had come to know so well. Desperate for news, I tried calling and sending texts, but received no answer. Some of my attempts seemed to connect after a series of strange bleeps and whirring sounds, but there was never a human voice at the other end. Others led to nothing but silence, before the line cut out altogether. Where were they all now? Had they reached their destinations safely? For the moment, I had no answers at all.

I couldn't help worrying whether they were okay, but reminded myself that there were many practical reasons why I might be unable to reach them. Aside from a lack of Internet access, they could have had their phones and laptops taken from them by Syrian government forces when leaving Daraya. If so, it might be a while before they could get new ones in Idlib. Yet I kept remembering how few had trusted the regime to keep its word and allow them to leave the town safely. After all, President Bashar al-Assad had labelled all rebel opponents like them as terrorists. And this was a regime that, according to the human rights group Amnesty International, had hanged large numbers of its political prisoners, up to an estimated 13,000 detainees at the notorious Saydnaya military prison near Damascus.[21] Amnesty also claimed it had found evidence that more than thirty different methods of torture had been used by the regime since the early 1980s and that such abuses had contributed to the deaths of a further 17,000 people held in detention facilities across Syria since 2011.[22] When considering terrifying statistics like these, the last of which were published just a week before the evacuation of Daraya, it was hard to feel confident that all would be well. Did Syrian forces really just stand by and let thousands of their declared enemies simply walk away? Well, that is exactly what they had done three months earlier, after the besieged, rebel-held city of Homs fell to pro-Assad soldiers and around 1,000 fighters and some civilians were allowed to leave for Idlib. I could only hope that this would again be the case, and it was mildly reassuring to see news footage showing numerous buses packed full of people heading in the direction of the same rebel-held province.

My enquiries there had also been encouraging. People told me that several buses had arrived safely from Daraya soon after the evacuation. So far nobody had recognised any of the names and descriptions I had given them, but all had promised to keep looking.

Idlib is one of fourteen provinces in Syria. It lies in the far north-west of the country, where its upper region borders Turkey. Its capital is the city of Idlib, situated about 500 metres above sea level, and sixty kilometres south-west of Syria's second city, Aleppo. In 2010 the city, which is home to a museum containing 17,000 clay tablets from the ancient city of Elba, had a population of 165,000. This had increased hugely since then, due to the arrival of hundreds of thousands of people from formerly rebel-held areas of Syria. Many more were to follow in the months and years to come as other besieged, rebel-held towns fell to government forces. All this put growing pressure on local food supplies, health services and housing, though the largely anti-Assad community had so far accepted the new arrivals generously and without complaint.

Those arriving from Daraya would find it a very different kind of place to the one they had left behind. To begin with there was no secret library, nor any public libraries at all, from what I had been told. Books were available, but only for those with the money to buy them, something most people from Daraya did not have. Even more significantly, much of Idlib was under the control of extremist Islamist groups whose idea of the revolution had little in common with those from Daraya.

One of the most powerful of these extremist groups was the al-Nusra Front. After joining other Islamist militia groups, it took over large swathes of north-western Syria in early 2015. Al-Nusra was officially linked to al-Qaeda until the summer of 2016, when it claimed to have cut these ties, changing its name to Jabhat Fatah al-Sham or JFS. Despite this change of name and alleged break from al-Qaeda, many believed this was a largely cosmetic exercise aimed at placating locals, many of whom distrusted foreign-dominated groups such as al-Qaeda. Few of JFS's leaders were Syrian and while the group's aim of deposing President Assad was shared by most in Daraya, its views on what should replace him were very different. Like IS, it wanted to create a state run under sharia law, and had no truck with democracy, freedom of speech and human rights. Though unlike IS, JFS focused on creating an Is- lamic state within Syria, rather than seeking global jihad. Also, the group had largely rejected IS's practice of publicly beheading opponents and sometimes held back on enforcing sharia law in areas where local people did not want it. Nonetheless, the organisation continued to be viewed as a terrorist organisation by the UN, the United States and many other countries.

As the weeks passed by there was still no word from Abdul Basit, Sara, Anas, Amjad and all the others since their evacuation from Daraya. I began to fear that they had either been arrested by Syrian security forces or fallen foul of extremist groups in Idlib, but took comfort from the strong possibility that their silence was instead down to their inability to get online. Either that or the demands of surviving in a strange new city meant they simply lacked the time to get in touch. After all, with no home, few local contacts and no way of getting money to buy food, survival might have become their sole concern.

On the morning of Monday, 12 September 2016, President Bashar al-Assad marked the public holiday of Eid al-Adha by joining prayers at a mosque. Nothing remarkable about that, you might think, except that this particular mosque was in the heart of Daraya. Little more than two weeks after the town's besieged population had been evacuated, the Syrian leader was making his presence felt. In a video aired on Syrian state TV, Assad drove himself to Daraya's Saad Ibn Muaz Mosque. This highly choreographed move aimed to highlight that his forces were in total control of the town, a place that until so very recently had been an iconic symbol of rebel resistance to his rule. The defiant president did not stop there. Just hours before a forty-eight-hour national ceasefire took effect, he used the occasion to make a vow. His forces, he said, would retake every inch of

Syria from the 'terrorists' who opposed him. This threat did not bode well for evacuees from Daraya, who were starting new lives in rebel-held Idlib.

That same week a text arrived on my phone. It read: *Mike, it is Abdul Basit. I am in Idlib now I am safe.*

I read this several times. Then read it again. Abdul Basit had made it. The warm and sensitive young man that I had come to think of as 'the poet' of Daraya, because of his imaginative descriptions of life around him, had survived. Ever since the recent death of his friend Omar, I had feared the worst. Although Abdul Basit was a civilian, not a front-line fighter like Omar, I had become pessimistic. The sudden loss of this idealistic and optimistic young man had left me fearing for all his circle. I enthusiastically tapped out a response. How was he, and what news did he have about everyone else from Daraya? But when I tried to send my message, Abdul Basit was no longer online.

Three days later I finally managed to speak to him over the phone. He sounded tired and a little depressed, but gradually brightened as our conversation went on. I asked a flurry of questions. What had his journey been like? How was Idlib? What had happened to Anas, Sara, Amjad, Muhammad, Ayham and the rest? Clearly a little overwhelmed by my verbal barrage, the line went quiet for a few seconds. Then Abdul Basit replied that he had only seen a few of them but there was no reason to worry about the others because he was sure that they were all OK. This was wonderful news. And it was about to get better. I could hear somebody talking to Abdul Basit in the background and theirs was a voice I knew well. It was Muhammad! I shouted at the phone. My greeting was met swiftly by a bright *Hello, Mike!* I soon learned that Abdul Basit had also seen Anas, who was safe and well, and he promised to text me his new number.

While I digested this wonderful news, Abdul Basit began describing his momentous journey out of shattered Daraya, on 27 August 2016. 'When I got on the bus I held my head high. I looked out of the window at all the supporters of Assad. They were standing there looking at us with smug faces, as if we were dirt. Yet I felt victorious, because it seemed to me that they were the ones who were weak, not us. We had been outnumbered, starved and bombed for four years, yet it took them all that time to make us leave. Over those years we had achieved so much together. We had carried on learning in our secret library, carried on resisting, carried on striving for a better world. Yes, freedom and democracy had lost out for now, but they would triumph eventually. I was certain of that.'

Muhammad, now sitting right next to his friend, nodded in recognition at what he had said. He told me how, on looking out of the bus's window, he had been amazed at the size and power of the troops he saw. All held at bay, for so long, by Daraya's comparatively small rebel force. 'We drove past all these really heavy fortifications. Three lines of defence, sandbags, with trenches filled with water so that nobody could get under them. Our defenders numbered just a few hundred people yet here was the whole Syrian army ranged against us. We must have terrified them.'

Abdul Basit described how much inner strength this had given him at an otherwise sad and desperate time. He had stared intently at the scenery as the bus drove away. He wanted, he told me, to remember every sight and every sound, just in case he could never come home again. The convoy went around the outskirts of Daraya and on through the old quarter of Damascus. Familiar landmarks flashed by: favourite shops and museums, and a bakery that Muhammad had loved as a student. An ocean of memories sailing past. After a while Mezzeh military airbase, which is just outside the town, came into view. That was where most of the planes that had bombed Daraya took off from, and it was the launch site for many of the rockets and shells that had bombarded the area, killing and maiming men, women and children. Abdul Basit said he had glared at the base, eyeballing the soldiers who patrolled outside. Anger had welled up in his stomach. Outside of his home town for the first time in years, he remembered being shocked by what he saw: 'I only discovered the true scale of the devastation when I left Daraya,' he told me. 'As we drove along the motorway, which has a view of the town, I was staggered by the destruction. My town was almost completely destroyed.'

Abdul Basit revealed how the pride he felt in his community's achievements began dissolving into bitterness when he thought of what their stand had cost. Though it had been a battle, he thought, that had been lost by humanity and not the people of Daraya alone. As the journey continued, his mood had darkened further. They had been failed, he insisted, by almost everyone. 'Instead of helping to evacuate us from our beloved town, why didn't the Red Cross and UN stop this ethnic cleansing? I felt so angry at that moment. I thought of everyone outside Daraya as traitors. I really felt that deeply. It seemed to me that every single person who said they sympathised with us was a liar, because they just stood by and let this happen.'

As the coach drove on, Abdul Basit's mood had failed to improve. He remembered feeling that without the town he loved, the town that now lay in ruins, life did not seem worth living any more.

As the buses drew up at the military checkpoints along the way, government soldiers would stop the convoy and raise their guns at those on board. It seemed to Muhammad that they were trying to provoke the FSA fighters travelling with them and carrying their light weapons. They would be sitting ducks if a firefight started. At one of these stops, Abdul Basit told me that the level of intimidation reached a whole new level. Guns were aimed at each of the evacuees as they were asked to confirm their identity. Some were shouted at and pushed around and although both UN and Syrian Arab Red Crescent officials were there, they stayed in the background, not saying a word. It was thought that the soldiers were taking revenge for being stopped – by international officials overseeing the evacuation – from getting people's fingerprints before the buses left Daraya. In the end, after being questioned for five hours, the convoy was finally allowed to move on. Each of the buses was separated by a gap of around a hundred metres, and the convoy was escorted by cars and helicopters bristling with weapons. This journey into the unknown was a frightening experience for all on board, especially the women and children.

Abdul Basit told me how his spirits rose a little on seeing how weak the once mighty Assad regime appeared to have become. It certainly could not claim to run all of the country now. Before the war, he told me, the journey from Daraya to Hama would have taken no more than three hours, yet it took their coach more than twelve. The reason for this, aside from the checkpoints, was that pro-Assad forces did not control much of the road. Both the FSA and

IS had taken over long stretches of it, and in these areas government forces did not dare to show their faces. Even though Abdul Basit said he despised IS, and their presence on the road made his journey much longer, he felt oddly elated. While travelling on roads controlled by the regime's soldiers, Abdul Basit felt void and empty, but whenever they crossed into rebel areas, the atmosphere improved so much. Heart-warming celebrations greeted his bus, rice and flowers were thrown at the windows as their convoy passed by. 'This made us feel so welcome, so happy, even though we had left behind all I knew in Daraya.'

The first time this happened, a grinning Muhammad told me, a child at the back of the bus asked why the people were doing this, saying all that rice would have made a wonderful soup. But one of his fondest memories was when they reached a checkpoint in a rebel-held area. Lots of people greeted the evacuees in a wide variety of cars and small trucks. There were even some military vehicles, with anti-aircraft guns, amongst them. It was, he told me with a smile, a heart-warming and inspiring scene: 'Lots of people were firing their guns into the air as a kind of salute to us. The amount of bullets they used could almost have saved Daraya, because we had virtually run out by the end. But amazingly, here in the north, they had plenty of ammunition. It was a great show of support. But I couldn't help seeing all this as a bit of a paradox. Here were all these guns and bullets in rebel hands, yet none of them had been used to save Daraya.'

Muhammad said that his memories of the journey faded at that point because he had fallen asleep. It was, after all, late at night, and he was very tired after such a stressful and exhausting few days. Abdul Basit, on the other hand, stayed wide awake throughout the journey, but said he felt like closing his eyes on seeing the terrible devastation outside his window. He was deeply saddened to see so many schools, mosques, factories and farms in utter ruins. Lifeless, structural corpses, lying in broken heaps. All further evidence, he said, if any was needed, of how much damage the regime had done. Much of the destruction, he believed, had been in revenge, spiteful acts against any area that had opposed the dictatorial regime. It was all, he said, a callous demonstration from Assad that this is what will happen to all who stand in his way. Abdul Basit then opened his mouth to speak, before shaking his head and turning away, having clearly decided that some thoughts or memories are best left unsaid. He told me later: 'As the bus drove on other dark thoughts poured into my mind, but I cannot describe them now. There are some things in the heart that can't be spoken. It is perhaps better that they are left buried where they are.'

With those words Abdul Basit went quiet, his thoughts saved from further questions by a faltering Internet connection, which crackled and squawked before finally dropping out altogether. When I managed to reach him again a little later, he seemed revived. He told me, with great enthusiasm, about the warm reception he and others from Daraya had received on their arrival in Idlib. They had been met by swarms of well-meaning locals, clutching blankets, pots, pans and all sorts of food. Instead of the newcomers having to plead for help, those welcoming them almost fought for the privilege of looking after them. Some of those offering assistance, Abdul Basit explained, were visibly upset when others beat them to it.

Within hours, he was given an apartment to live in. Its

owner had moved out to stay with relatives, in order to make his home available. Abdul Basit said he was deeply moved by this extraordinary hospitality towards strangers, from people who had so little themselves. Yet he continued to miss the company of others from Daraya, some of whom, he heard, had gone to live in camps outside the city.

Before long, perhaps inevitably, our conversation turned to the subject of books. Which ones, I asked him, had he managed to take with him from Daraya's secret library? 'Sadly,' he told me, 'we weren't allowed to take any books, may God ruin Assad! He is the enemy of knowledge, the enemy of education, the enemy of humanity. His soldiers didn't allow us to take a single book. All we could put in our backpacks were a few spare clothes. If I could, I would have taken nothing but books, and left the clothes behind. In fact, I would have taken the whole secret library with me. I promise you, I really would.'

I asked Abdul Basit, who was still visibly angry about this, what books he would have most liked to have taken with him, had he been able to. He replied that one of the many titles he would have liked to bring was *This is What Life Taught Me* by Mustafa al-Siba'i, a former Dean of the Faculty of Theology at Damascus University, which had been a gift from his father after Abdul Basit had passed his university entrance exams. He sighed and smiled gently. Another that would definitely have been on the list, was his old favourite: '*Hamlet* is an extraordinary book, such a wonderful piece of literature. Every time I read it I am taken to a different world. It has given me such deep and powerful memories.'

Yet another contender, the title of which Abdul Basit could not quite recall, was a kind of self-help book about how to overcome difficulties and take your life in a positive direction. He had passed it on to a close friend, whose whole outlook on life had been changed by what he read: 'My friend was a total hash addict,' Abdul Basit said, 'who sat around doing nothing but smoking the stuff all day. His life was going nowhere. Then, after reading the book, he gave up smoking the drug and got involved with all kinds of good and creative things in the community.' Abdul Basit clearly took great joy in being the one who had passed this life-changing book on. And there are many others, he told me with boyish excitement, that he would love to have brought with him. 'Those are just the books I have read that I love so much. There are also thousands of others that I have not read yet and am aching to discover. I would like to have taken those too.'

Having managed to make contact with both Abdul Basit and Muhammad, my hopes of finding others from Daraya were growing by the day. This tight-knit community seemed to have stayed that way, despite all being parted in the evacuation. Proof of that arrived on a chilly autumn morning in London. It took the form of a brief WhatsApp message from Abdul Basit. Beneath a polite enquiry about my well-being was a contact number for his close friend and co-founder of the secret library, Anas Habib. I was told that he was well and keen to talk to me again. This was very cheering news and I wasted no time in dialling his number. After several attempts a voice emerged through the crackles and bleeps. It was Anas. We hadn't talked or exchanged texts since news of the evacuation, yet here he was on the line. I began by asking him if he was in Idlib: 'Yes, Mike, thanks be to God, I am in Idlib, near the Turkish border. It is far from home but conditions here are so much better than in Daraya. Thankfully we are no longer under siege or being shelled and shot at. There is food here, whatever you can think of, I have found somewhere to sleep and local people are very kind.'

Anas told me that the people he missed the most from Daraya, were those he had become close to during the siege. Friendships forged during such traumatic times of shared pain and suffering tend to endure better than most. After all, if you can get along well during harrowing periods like those, ordinary life should be a comparative walk in the park. Anas had come to love this unity and regretted that it was harder to find in Idlib. Also, he told me, some people there held very different views about the aims of the revolution to the evacuees from Daraya. They wanted sharia law not democracy and civil rights. For Anas, this was definitely troubling: 'It's a new world that is not pure in the way Daraya was. I'm not comfortable here, within myself. I'm not at peace any more.'

One thing that I knew would have consoled Anas in these challenging times was books. I wondered if he had somehow managed to smuggle out a couple of his favourites from the library before leaving Daraya. Shaking his head, Anas told me that he didn't even think about doing that. He had heard rumours that others who had done this had come to regret it. He later discovered that the regime's soldiers searched everyone's bags very thoroughly, and would have found anything he had hidden. That would have meant that the books, which didn't belong to him anyway, would have been lost for ever. He hoped that, in leaving them all behind in Daraya, they would at least still be there when he managed to go back. But this topic got Anas thinking about one book above all others that he would love to have packed. 'It is a collection of poems that I adore,' he told me. 'It's called *The Tears of Men* by Faisal bin Mohamad Alhaj. I would have given so much to have this with me now because it so closely reflects my mood.'

**The Tears of Men**
Never dead are those who left the world to the tombs,
If what they died for is preserved in our will and
    carried in our hearts.[23]

Anas said that as soon as he had mentioned *The Tears of Men*, other treasured books flooded into his mind. It was not just being able to read and hold the ones he cherished most, he told me, but the memory of having all of them around him. 'I miss so many books, but most of all, I miss the secret library itself, the place I read them all in. We were truly blessed to have had that throughout those terrible, dark times. In some ways I love it now even more than ever. I suppose it's human nature to only truly miss what you have when it's gone.'

I asked Anas if he had managed to buy or borrow any books in Idlib. He sighed, as if defeated by the question. There were, he told me, several bookshops there that sold a wide variety of titles, but he could not afford to buy them. As for libraries, he added, he had yet to come across one. Sometimes it was possible to get hold of some children's stories and school textbooks, but there was little else available unless you had money. To get around this problem, many of Anas's friends from Daraya had been reading online PDF copies of publications, which they could also share with others.

The line went quiet for a while. In the silence I could

hear the sound of a motorbike followed by a deep boom that sounded like an explosion. I asked Anas what was happening and whether he was all right. He laughed, before reassuring me that it was only people next door doing some rebuilding work. That, he said, was the sound of creation, not destruction, a welcome change in a land that seemed to have forgotten what peace was like. As I was thinking about this I heard Anas rummaging around in the background. 'I'm currently reading a great book that is helping me feel better,' he told me. 'It was written in 2012 by a man from Daraya. He was hit in his spine by shrapnel during an air raid and became paralysed.' This did not, on the face of it, sound like the kind of book that would cheer anybody up. Anas told me that he had met the author briefly at the hospital where he worked as a volunteer. Doctors there had not been able to do much for the man, as they had few medicines and little in the way of the advanced equipment needed to care for him. It was clear that he would never be able to walk again, and perhaps not even manage to sit upright. His prospects seemed awful but, fortunately some of the man's friends managed to get him smuggled out of Daraya so that he could get the medical treatment he needed. Now, living in Jordan, he had written a book. 'Amazingly, given the fact that he was paralysed, this book is not about despair, it's all about hope,' said Anas. 'In fact it's called *Mountains of Hope*. The chapters have titles like: Don't Be Sad, Don't Give Up, Never Stop Smiling and so on, it's very positive. On its front page are the words: "The lanterns of hope. If we lose hope we lose life." His book is an inspiration to me.'

I made a mental note to find out more about this man and his story. Meanwhile, I wanted to ask Anas more about living in an area that contained so many different extremist groups, some of which had links with al-Qaeda. 'Of course, it is completely different here,' he said, 'but I have had no trouble so far. There is great symbolism attached to Daraya because of its long fight against the regime, so anyone from there is usually held in high regard in Idlib. Even the more extreme fighters tend to want to help rather than harass us.'

Anas added that he and others from Daraya had also been doing their best to integrate with the local community. They had arranged to meet members of Idlib's council, and were already developing a good relationship with some of them. Also, he said, there were many others in the area who, like people from Daraya, wanted President Bashar al-Assad's ruthless regime replaced by a democratically elected government that promoted civil rights and freedom of speech. Anas sounded very tired but otherwise seemed to be bearing up well considering all he had been through since we last spoke. He warned me that Internet access in Idlib wasn't much better than in Daraya, but we cheerfully agreed to speak again, technology permitting, in a few days' time.

On 3 October 2016, a text arrived from Sara Matar. It had been more than a month since I had last heard from her. I had tried to make contact on many occasions but the line would never connect. So I gave up on trying to call her and texted her a long list of questions in the hope she might be able to reply to those when she next got online. 'Dear Mike,' she wrote back. 'Life here has made me forget many of my dreams. I have even begun to forget that I am a woman, with a past and memories and a family. Life here makes me feel that I am just a doll with no feelings. Your questions brought life to me again.'

Like Anas, Abdul Basit and Muhammad, Sara was also in Idlib province, but deep in the countryside away from their base in the main town. She had settled in a camp near the Turkish border reserved for people from rebel-held places like Daraya. Bombing there by government planes was less common than in Idlib's towns, but the area was still far from safe. In some ways, she wrote, living there was even more frightening than in bombed and besieged Daraya: 'Here we live in fear of militant groups who often fight each other. We constantly worry about being caught in the crossfire or kidnapped.'

To help me visualise the camp, Sara sent me a photo she had taken of it on her mobile phone. A sea of speckled canvas, thousands of sky-blue and white tents stretched to the hilly horizon. There were no trees, bushes or grass, just acres of reddish-brown stony soil that turned to dust in summer and got everywhere. It covered the washed clothes slung over makeshift washing lines, hung in the air like clouds of inanimate mosquitoes, and clung to the faces of little children. In winter, she told me, pools of water would litter the ground and the wind, with nothing to stand in its way, would whip across the barren landscape.

There was comparative safety there, though, and some food and water, but this could never be a home, it was even colder and less comfortable than her bomb-damaged house in Daraya. 'I still haven't adjusted to life in Idlib,' she wrote. 'Sometimes, in my worst moments, I feel we are living the life of the dead here. I try to gather my strength, live in the present and understand the people around me. But inside of me, there is an emptiness. I hope this feeling will go away soon.'

Sara went on to describe the fear she felt in her new and

alien home. Before, although at constant risk from bombing and shelling, she at least had the company of people she knew and loved. They all shared the same goals, the same deprivation and the same hopes for the future. But here, in this rural exile, there was little such camaraderie or sense of purpose and she actually missed life in besieged Daraya. But it was the young children she had taught that she missed the most: 'We would all sit together, sometimes night and day, while the bombs fell outside. I never felt afraid when I was caring for them. I even enjoyed it. We were so close. It saddens me deeply that most of the children I taught, and the colleagues I worked with, have been displaced by the war. I wish we were together again.'

Like other evacuees I had spoken to, Sara talked of the rousing reception local people had given her convoy on arrival in Idlib. Everybody seemed to want to help. People offered to show her to her new home and offered her food and water, but Sara made it clear that she had more of an appetite for something to read. This, it seems, did not go down well: 'When I asked the people who met us if they would give me books instead of food,' she wrote, 'they looked utterly shocked. I explained that I hoped to set up a small library, so that we could feed our brains as well as our bodies. They just stared at me. I remember one man saying: "How on earth can you ask for books when you're a refugee with nothing? Come on, be serious now!"'

Like Anas, Sara said she had been looking everywhere for a library, but had not yet found one and had resorted to trying to download PDF books from the Internet. This, she said, had proved hard, given the great difficulty of getting online, and even when she managed this she struggled to cope with the small print. Years of trying to read books in a dimly lit basement had, she believed, damaged her eyesight. All this was clearly not helping her state of mind. There was no secret library to escape to in Idlib, and there were few people she knew to talk to. Most of the children she had taught and longed to see again had been sent to different camps, far from hers. Like her friends, she ached to see her family again, after nearly four years apart. Most of all, she said, she longed to hug her mother. 'Sometimes,' she wrote, 'I wake in the night with a happy, warm feeling and can't think why. Then I remember. I had dreamed that my mother was here with me.'

That same evening in early October, a cool autumnal breeze jostled the late summer leaves, an early warning of darker nights to come in London. As rain began to fall I hugged the lapels of my jacket, chin on chest, walking faster. All around, the heavy rush-hour traffic fumed and honked, as weary London commuters struggled home. Just after I had crossed a busy road, a middle-aged man clutching a large carrier bag charged past me, shouting excitedly. Dropping the bag he threw out his arms as a grey-haired woman in front turned towards him. Screeches of delight followed as both hugged like long-lost lovers. After narrowly avoiding tripping over the abandoned bag, I stumbled into the cuddling couple. Both seemed oblivious to the collision, just as they were to the gusting wind and the driving rain. On regaining my balance I automatically mumbled a few words of apology, despite harbouring a grumble that it wasn't actually my fault. Yet I felt strangely happy to be some part, albeit accidental and unnoticed, of this evidently heartfelt reunion. As I walked on home, I thought again of all those from Daraya, now refugees, who were desperate to be reunited with the ones they loved. The recent words of Abdul Basit were the first to come to mind: 'The only member of my family that I've seen since the siege began four years ago,' he told me, 'is my little sister. She is five years younger than me and got married and went to live in Turkey. She came here to Idlib briefly for a few days soon after I arrived here. It was so wonderful. Yet this brief pleasure made me miss the rest of my family more than ever.'

During the four years of siege in Daraya, Abdul Basit had been separated from his large and close family, but took comfort from still being in his home town, the place where he grew up with them all. Since being evacuated from Daraya, that link was gone, and he clearly felt the separation even more strongly than before. 'I feel I hardly know who I am today, it's as if I don't have a past any more. I'm in exile from my own life, not only my home.'

Like Sara's parents, Abdul Basit's mother and father were living in an area of Syria controlled by the Syrian government. Also like her, he feared that because he had stayed in a besieged rebel-held town and spoken openly of his hatred of the government, this would make him a 'terrorist' in the eyes of security services. He feared they were monitoring his family's phones, so dared not call his parents in case this made them 'terrorist' suspects too. He sensed that his mother and father were proud of him, and comforted himself by remembering the understanding looks on their faces when he had told them he wanted stay in Daraya, as the regime began tightening the siege. There was pride in their eyes amid the tears and the fear. He told me how he missed them both, as well as his brothers and sisters, every minute of every day and prayed they would be reunited soon. Abdul Basit's voice began to quaver with emotion. For the next

minute or so he was unable to talk at all. Finally, he asked if
we could leave the raw subject of his family to another time,
before adding softly: 'I hope this never happens to you, that
you have to live without your sisters, brothers and parents.
To know they are there, yet you can't see them, you can't
even talk to them. It is so painful.'

Keen to change the subject, I asked him if he had been
able to buy any books since the last time we spoke. He told
me he had acquired a copy of the Holy Quran and a book
entitled *Historical Men*, both of which, he hoped, would
help him further his education. This, he announced, was
just the start. He was now scouring the streets for others.
Books on history, business and economics were top of his
shopping list, partly because he hoped to be able to finish
his university degree. Though it seemed that Abdul Basit's
love of the lighter side of life, which first showed itself in
his love of comics as a child, was as alive as ever. 'Since I'm
being open and honest with you,' he said, 'I must admit
that I also like reading less serious material, too. For instance, good comedy books help take my mind off the hard
life that I'm living in Idlib now. I love to laugh.'

One of Abdul Basit's favourite writers, he told me, is Aziz
Nesin, a Turkish author who wrote satirical books about
everyday life. Nesin also wrote amusing novels, but these
tended to be too expensive for him to afford. Or at least,
he then clarified, to cost more than he was willing to pay.
There had been a sudden change in Abdul Basit's voice,
tinged with an air of excitement that had been missing
before. For some time, he confided, he had been saving any
money he could get his hands on for a very special purpose.
Just for once, this did not involve books: 'I can't spend the
little I have entirely on books, because I need to save up

for a very big event in my life. Mike, I'm planning to get married. Everyone tells me that I'll need money to do that, especially here. Unlike in Daraya, I don't have relatives living nearby, so I can't rely on help from anybody else. I'm hoping that my fiancée will soon be able to come to Idlib. Though I do worry about her safety. Getting here can be very dangerous.'

So, that long-ago marital wish list Abdul Basit had drawn up, and those dangerous trips to visit his fiancée, had all been worth it. The young woman so specially selected for him by his mum and big sister, was hopefully to become his wife. That is, of course, if he could find a way of getting her safely to Idlib. An image came to mind of the rose he had tried to send her from besieged Daraya, which government soldiers had cut into pieces at a checkpoint. If his bride-to-be could find a safe passage to Idlib, it seemed certain that no checkpoint or siege would separate them again. But with the war tilting ever further in favour of President Bashar al-Assad's regime, the odds were lengthening against such a fairy tale ending.

# Chapter Fourteen

Having managed to trace many of those I'd come to know in Daraya, I was now intent on discovering what had happened to their beloved secret library. The omens did not look good. From what I gleaned from various sources, Daraya was now completely abandoned. All who lived there had been evacuated and only Syrian army soldiers were said to walk the streets. But, I wondered, had the soldiers discovered the secret library yet? In the hope of finding that out for myself, I applied to the Syrian authorities for a visa, along with permission to go to Daraya.

Several weeks passed without any response and then, one bright and sunny day in early October 2016, my phone pinged. The text wasn't from the Syrian government, which seemed determined to ignore my visa request, but Malik al-Rifaii. Now in Idlib, he had a very pertinent question for me. It read: 'Have you heard what has happened to the library?'

Ever since the evacuation I hadn't heard any news about the fate of Daraya, never mind the secret library itself. Given that the only people likely to have access to it by this point were Syrian troops, any news seemed unlikely to be favourable. No, I told Malik, feeling distinctly uneasy, I hadn't heard anything about the library. Had he? While I waited for his reply, which could take hours as he appeared to have gone offline, I typed the words 'library' and 'Daraya' into Google and hit return.

The following CNN headline, dated 6 October 2016, immediately appeared: 'Uncovering a secret underground library in Syria'. Could this, I wondered, be merely a late follow-up of my documentary on the library a few months before, or had something big just happened to it? I clicked on the video next to the brief description of the story and, after a short wait, it became clear that this was, indeed, an update. Film of bombs exploding in rubble-strewn streets was followed by what looked like very recent shots of a desolate city landscape, devoid of almost any signs of life. Then came scenes that appeared to be *inside* the secret library. At this point, CNN Senior International Correspondent Frederik Pleitgen revealed how his TV crew had been one of the first to be granted access to Daraya since the evacuation. He went on to say that as he was driving through the deserted town, he spotted men in uniforms carrying piles of books out of a basement. The camera followed their path into a dark, unlit room. Hundreds if not thousands of books came into view. Some still sat neatly on long wooden shelves, but others lay in messy piles on the floor. Outside, a pick-up truck laden with books was shown driving away, doubtless soon to return for more literary loot. Shocked and saddened, my eyes stayed glued to the screen. I was in no doubt about what I was looking at. The location of the treasured secret library was clearly secret no longer, and it had evidently been looted and destroyed. Once-adored books, some soiled by footprints, lay face-down and discarded on the floor, others were stacked in crates like two-a-penny trinkets at a car boot sale. This extraordinary collection of poetry and prose, saved from numerous bombed buildings under sniper fire, was being carted away. Built up over years with love and devotion, destroyed in hours, by a couple of squaddies with a pick-up truck.

The sacking of Daraya's secret library seemed not only heartless, but also made no obvious sense. While it may have earned those behind the looting a few dollars, what harm could this large collection of books have done to Assad's regime? Many were textbooks, their contents instructive, rather than ideological or political, and those who created the library had been looking for ways to rebuild their nation, not destroy it. Not only that but they were gone anyway, and even if they managed to get back some day, it would surely be better from the regime's point of view to have their opponents spending their time reading books, rather than picking up weapons.

Eager to know more about what had happened, I called CNN's head office and asked to speak to Frederik Pleitgen. I must confess to having had mixed emotions at this point. Firstly, I was frustrated that my request for a Syrian visa and access to Daraya had been completely ignored while CNN's had been waved through. Also, due to a kind of journalistic pride, I have always felt uncomfortable asking other reporters for information on stories they had covered, but this was different. This was all about a place that the people I had become so fond of treasured more than any other. Added to all this was the concern that as a journalist from a rival news organisation I might not get much co-operation anyway. In the event, I need not have worried.

Frederik and his senior producer, Claudia Otto, could not have been more helpful and Claudia had been fascinated by the secret library ever since first hearing my documentary. Like me they had become determined to discover its fate following the evacuation of Daraya: 'I had heard your radio programme about the secret library on the BBC,' Claudia told me, 'and it made me very curious. I really wanted to know what had happened to it. I investigated a little bit further and then decided to try and go to Daraya with Frederik to find out.'

Like me, Claudia had not found this easy at first. Getting into Daraya while it was under siege was next to impossible. But she and Frederik, who had been reporting from the Syrian government's side of the front line, were allowed in around five weeks after the evacuation of the by-then wreck of a town. Determined to find the secret library they got in touch with a contact who had lived in Daraya during part of the siege and was able to give them some directions. Though they first had had to promise him that they wouldn't take anyone else with them and would be careful to avoid being followed there by soldiers. The directions they got were rather vague, a factor made worse by the destruction of most of the landmarks their contact had given them: 'We were told about the little side street it was in,' Frederik said. 'But it was very difficult navigating in that area because a lot of those small roads had debris all over them. Most of the houses had been bombed to rubble, and so even when we drove down that street we had problems finding the library. The only reason we eventually succeeded in finding it was because we spotted the little pick-up truck parked outside. We saw the guys carrying out lots of books – that's how we knew we were at the library. All we could see otherwise was a small side entrance that went straight into a basement. We may never have found it at all if they hadn't been there at that very point, loading all those books onto their truck.'

Frederik suspected that the soldiers stumbled across it accidentally when doing house-to-house searches. Claudia was convinced that the uniformed men they saw were either Syrian government soldiers or allied militia men. She told me how the soldiers carrying the books out had left very quickly when they spotted the TV camera. Going by the shots I saw from Frederik and Claudia's video, their activities amounted to vandalism and blatant daylight robbery, so their camera-shy reaction was hardly surprising. Although conquering armies have done this sort of thing throughout history, they did not have an international audience watching at the time. Claudia was clearly still outraged by what she had seen: 'It was complete destruction. There was nothing left there. Finding the library would have been a big opportunity for them. Not only that, but they were going through everything elsewhere too. We even saw them ripping cables out of houses.'

Claudia's description made me feel for those who had been forced to leave behind almost everything they owned. Many desperately wanted to return as soon as possible, but given what I had just been told, I asked Claudia, would they find anything left if they did? 'No, no, nothing,' she replied. 'Definitely not. It's a complete ghost town.'

Frederik, a senior international correspondent who must have seen many awful things in the course of his work, was equally appalled. Not just about what was done to the library, but the state of Daraya itself. 'There were basically no homes left untouched. Some were just shells. When we got there, it was about three weeks after the fighting had ended and quite a few houses were still on fire, or at least smouldering. There was just utter destruction, you could barely move through the streets because of the debris everywhere.'

He told me that he felt really sad, seeing people's possessions being picked over. Small groups of men, presumably with the permission of the army, were sorting through the debris and carting away whatever they liked. It was, he told me, the kind of chilling mayhem you often see when an occupying army moves into a conquered zone.

'It was definitely an odd feeling,' he continued. 'It was eerie too. It brought the fighting that much closer. I mean, when we were in Damascus before, we obviously heard a lot of the artillery fire coming down on Daraya. But you really can't envision what people there went through until you actually go through this place and see the destruction.'

Frederik then talked of the other nightmare that leaves no evidence behind. The years of terrible hunger that had stalked the streets day and night and left children unable to sleep and adults struggling to carry on. The silent, invisible, relentless pain of siege. But the debris from the bombs and bullets was almost everywhere. The only places Frederik and Claudia found that seemed to have escaped the devastation, were the myriad tunnels and basements beneath the streets. The most cherished of all these subterranean hideouts was the basement that housed the secret library, though by the time they got there it was far from the calm and peaceful refuge it once had been. With no lights of any kind they had entered a desolate world of darkness and potential danger. 'When we walked in,' Claudia told me, 'we had to think about the possibility that booby traps might have been left in the library, perhaps as revenge on the soldiers who had taken over their town. It really was quite worrying. So we entered the building very cautiously. But once we were inside, it felt so quiet, so peaceful.'

Listening to Claudia I could well understand her fear of booby traps. They are the first hazard anyone working in a war zone is warned to watch out for, especially in situations where territory has just changed hands. Yet I couldn't image those who had loved their library so much planting bombs in it. Their biggest wish was that it would still be there for them when they got the chance to come home. Taking revenge on soldiers in that way would surely have made little sense, nor compensated for the loss of their fondest treasure, the place that brought comfort to their past and hope for their future.

As I was reflecting on that, Frederik's attention had moved on to the dimensions of the secret library. Given its huge importance to the long-besieged community, he had imagined it would be so much bigger.

'It looked and felt a lot smaller than the photos,' Frederik told me. 'It was basically just one room and it looked quite dilapidated. There were headings saying religious books, science books, physics books, things like that, but it was hard to see much of it. There was no light in the place. It was very dark, quite spooky.'

Claudia told me that despite all the looting and dilapidated state of the library, there seemed to be no structural damage inside. The basement looked quite intact. There were still cushions in the reading corner where people had sat with their books, she said, and much else looked pretty much like it must have done before the evacuation. This helped Claudia picture the warm and peaceful atmosphere she had heard people talk about in my documentary. Now, she herself was standing in their treasured secret library: 'It was very exciting to actually find this place. We were both really excited. I kept thinking about how all those people had been there in this secret location. I mean, it was still so very quiet inside. It must have been a place where you couldn't hear all the bombs and the shelling that was going on outside. That was the first thing we felt. It was such a peaceful place.'

They had both wondered at the time what had happened to all those people. 'We were delighted that we managed to find Amjad,' she told me. 'He is alive and well. Before we went to the library we were told that some people from Daraya were taken to a refugee camp near Damascus. We found Amjad living there with his parents. It was quite magical really.'

This was wonderful. Until now nobody I had spoken to had had any idea what had happened to that delightful young boy, who had perhaps loved the secret library more than anyone. Seeing how overjoyed I was at this news, Claudia and Frederik said they would dig out his new phone number for me, so that I could get back in touch with him. I was greatly looking forward to hearing how he was and how he had coped with the dramatic run of events. But while I was pondering on that coming encounter, Claudia told me that I was not the only person interested in Amjad. She and Frederik had mentioned their meeting with him to the Syrian government's Information Minister, though without giving his name and where exactly they met him. When she told the minister how much the former Chief Librarian missed the secret library and its books, he came up with a rather unbelievable pledge: 'We told the minister that after finding the library we had met Amjad, and what an interesting, intelligent kid he was. We then mentioned how very sad he was when he saw the pictures we had taken of the military looting all the books. So we asked the minister to let us take those books to Amjad ourselves. But he said, no, I can do this all myself, I will bring them for them and take care of everything.'

It was not hard to detect the sceptical tone in Claudia's voice when she relayed this unlikely sounding pledge, especially given that, for Amjad's safety, they hadn't told the minister where to find him and his family. 'I think both of us feel utterly the same way about that little kid,' Frederik continued. 'Amjad is such an interesting boy. I have no doubt that being in the library so much, and reading so many books there, did an incredible amount for him. I think that really transformed him from being just a small kid in Daraya, into a very critical and analytical thinker. This is particularly amazing given the impression we got that both his parents, who are living in the refugee camp with him, are illiterate.'

Amjad's parents had both seemed concerned about Claudia and Frederik's visit because the heads of the refugee camp came with them, and the occasion had drawn a large crowd. Their worry was that word of Amjad's role in what the security services would see as the 'rebel library', might get back to the authorities. Not, Claudia added, that Amjad himself appeared bothered about that at the time. On the contrary, Frederik told me, he seemed uninhibited and voiced some very strong opinions. He kept telling them how much he loved the secret library and what a big difference it had made to his life. 'The library had clearly changed his life in many ways,' Frederik said. 'It seemed to have reformed and strengthened his personality. You could see that within his family setting. He has now taken on a leadership role. All this sprung from the fact that he had managed to educate himself by reading all these books and taking on the responsibility of running the library.'

While all this was enormously heart-warming and impressive, I was concerned that Amjad had been so quick to speak his mind. Might the combination of his new-found authority and youthful exuberance bring him unwise attention in such a dangerous country? Frederik seemed to share my fears: 'Amjad is now a public figure and that's not something that will make life easy for him. That has been emphasised by both your work and ours. These articles and broadcasts are watched and read by very powerful people, and these are the ones who can get him into trouble.'

I could only hope that Amjad, who always wore his heart on his sleeve, would learn to be more careful what he told people sometimes.

Over the following days, as news of the looting of the secret library spread, I received a stream of messages, many expressing anger as well as distress. Some came from people who had heard my radio documentary a couple of months before; others were from those I had come to know in Daraya. Anas, Sara, Rateb and Ayham all told me how shocked and heartbroken they were and Abdul Basit, who was one of the first to be told the news by Malik, wrote: 'This is what I always dreaded, our beloved library being desecrated in this way. I am so sad to hear this news that I can't take it in, I can't find the words to express my deep sadness.' I pictured his description of how he had lain across the books in the secret library and cried before being evacuated, how this cherished literary sanctuary had inspired him to carry on during the darkest days of the siege and how he dreamed that one day he would return to it. Yet now it was gone. I just didn't know what to write back to him. It took me ages to compose a short, rather inadequate text, saying how I felt that even though the regime's soldiers had looted the library, they couldn't destroy the spirit of those who built it.

One of the most poignant dedications to the library came from the former pharmacy student and FSA fighter Homam al-Toun, who had written so movingly of his life-long friend Omar Abu Anas. He posted his thoughts on Facebook:

**Thoughts about the Library (9 October 2016)**
I knew I was gonna cry on a day like this and I remember telling my brother Omar Abu Anas that if Daraya falls, the destruction of the library will go down as our most painful loss. I always thought of this possibility. But I used to avoid imagining what it would be like to see it demolished. Barrel bombs were sometimes dropped near the library and I used to pray asking God to protect it.

After seeing this Facebook post I managed to make contact with Homam, who was also now living in Idlib. When our conversation turned to the looting of the secret library, I could hear the pain in his voice: 'It was a really awful thing to read about as there was nothing we could do to stop it. The revolution inspired the building of the secret library, because before then we were prevented from reading many books. Some of the ones we had there were banned by the government. Yet now all who came to the library could read them. Our secret library was not just a nice place to read books, it was a crucial part of our revolution.'

It was now clearer than ever just how important the

library had been to the people of Daraya. Not just as a treasured secret reading room and place to escape the bombs
and bullets, but as an icon of their uprising. A fact that
explains why it was unlikely to be left in one piece when
discovered by the Syrian army.

There was also a financial aspect to this, too, that had
helped determine its fate. Some of the books in the library
were apparently quite valuable; even the more ordinary ones
were worth a few Syrian pounds if traded on the streets
of Damascus. I had seen no evidence of the books being
sold since the CNN crew filmed them being taken away,
but a few days after talking to Frederik and Claudia, Anas
texted: 'We have confirmation that books stolen from the
library have been found on sale on the streets of Damascus.
The reason I know this is that we referenced every book
using our own coding system. Inside we always wrote who
each one belonged to and where the owner lived. Since the
looting of the library, books with these markings on have
been found on sale.'

Still visibly angry and upset, Anas told me that this il-
lustrated how the regime put no value on knowledge. The
books, he continued, had been sold for whatever they could
get, which appeared to have been very little. He wished that
the looters had left them behind and taken the furniture
and everything else instead. But he had not lost hope despite
what had happened: 'I think books are like rain. Wherever
rain falls things grow. So hopefully wherever our books
land, the person who reads them will gain knowledge, and
his or her mind will grow. This in turn will help humanity
grow. We will always be proud of our secret library and I'm
sure that good things will continue to flow from it.'

*

The young voice that answered the phone did not sound like the one I remembered. It was nervous, suspicious and wary. When I checked that I was speaking to Amjad, the reply was simply, yes. There was fear in that word, not the warm, endearing enthusiasm of old. When I explained who I was and what I wanted to talk about, the bubbly boy I had known suddenly returned. He let out a raucous welcome. Where was I, he asked, had I come to Syria? I explained that I was in London but longing to find out how his life was going since leaving Daraya and its secret library. Suddenly, on my mention of the library, his tone cooled again. I got the feeling that young Amjad, who I had learned was now fifteen, had finally been told to watch what he said. This was probably just as well. I remembered thinking only a short while before how necessary such caution was, in a country as dangerous as Syria, especially for somebody as naturally open-hearted as Amjad, though it certainly didn't help our conversation flow. When I asked if he had seen anybody from Daraya since arriving in his new home, he answered curtly: 'I'm sorry, it is not possible to answer that.'

Was somebody with him, I wondered, warning him not to say anything about the formerly rebel-held town or anyone from it? Or perhaps he was in a public place and worried that anything he said might be overheard by the wrong people. It seemed possible that his nervousness might be connected to the visit by Frederik and Claudia from CNN when Amjad and his family were living in a centre for displaced people near Damascus. I remembered Frederik telling me that crowds had gathered, and wondered whether that might have led to them all being questioned by the security forces. That would obviously cause problems. Unlike in parts of Idlib, there was no bombing or fighting there, which must have been a huge relief. But the downside was that, in government-controlled areas like that one, anyone from formerly rebel-held towns like Daraya, was never free of suspicion. I had been told that the population in such places was monitored closely by the security services. All of which might explain Amjad's nervous behaviour.

Determined to help ensure that nothing I said would get him or his family into any trouble, I ran through a list of questions I wanted to ask him and told him to check with his parents if it was all right to answer them. And when I called Amjad back the following morning, he seemed much happier, far more like the open, zesty and trusting boy I had found so endearing. He told me that his school work had come on quite a lot and that his family were eating proper meals again. When I reminded him how he had told me during the siege of his dreams of eating eggs, he giggled and told me that those dreams had now become reality. It was only when we started talking about the secret library that Amjad's tone changed. 'I am very, very sad about this because the library was my life. I read so many books there and spent so much of my time in that wonderful, quiet and friendly place. I always liked to think of it still being there, untouched, waiting for us to go back. The loss of the library is what saddens me most, more even than anything else that happened to our town.'

Amjad sounded quite emotional and there was a pause before he seemed ready to continue our conversation. His thoughts then turned to what might have happened to all the books that were looted from the library. He wondered, somewhat optimistically, whether some of their owners might have seen them on sale and demanded them back.

After all, he pointed out, their names and addresses were written inside the covers. I doubted if he truly believed that might happen. But there again, Amjad is clearly an optimistic boy who believes anything is possible: 'If the secret library is rebuilt,' he told me, 'I can tell you I will be the first person in line to go in. I would love my old job back! I would soon have the library just like it was before. It would be looking good and organised in no time, I promise you.'

When I asked young Amjad what plans he had for the future, he simply replied: 'I haven't yet given it much thought.' It struck me, somewhat sadly, that he was more focused on reliving the past than planning his future. I could only hope that with so much of his life still to come he would soon find another project or cause to pour his boundless energy and enthusiasm into. As a voice in the background began calling his name, Amjad made me promise to come and see him when I was next in Syria, before hurriedly saying goodbye.

A fortnight later, near the beginning of November 2016, I got a text from Sara telling me that she had managed to find a place near her displacement camp, where she could get online more easily than before and was happy to talk if I would like to call her. Delighted to hear this, I replied immediately, saying that I would try and ring her that afternoon. The first thing I noticed on hearing Sara's voice was how much happier she seemed than the last time we spoke. And before I had even asked any questions about her family, she told me: 'I got to see my mother at last! She came and visited me, here at the camp. I still can't quite believe that it happened.' After Sara had been evacuated to Idlib province, her mother promised to find a way to come and see her there. Sara wasn't sure how serious this pledge was, or whether it was even feasible for her mother to make this long journey, but she had lived in hope. 'It was like living in a different world when she finally arrived here in Idlib. I was so happy, so very, very happy. Throughout the seven days she was here I kept shouting out, Mother, Mother, Mother! I repeated that word again and again while I looked at her. It was me trying to get used to the idea that my dear mother was actually here, in person, with me.'

It was marvellous to hear Sara sounding so happy. What an unbelievable transformation this was. Sara described how she had been in phone contact with the driver of her mother's car throughout her long journey from Damascus. It took them twenty-four hours to get to Idlib because there were so many military checkpoints on the way. She told me that every time she heard that her mother's car was approaching one of these, her heart would start thumping and her mouth would go dry. At any point she might be arrested or turned around. There was danger, too, in between these posts. By this point in the war, numerous militia groups roamed the countryside, many of them little more than bandits, intent on kidnapping or robbery. Even at this stage, Sara found it hard to imagine her mother actually arriving. 'I had come to wonder whether I still really had a mother,' she said. 'You see, I hadn't seen her for so long or heard her voice. It had been years since we hugged or even talked on the phone.'

Every time Sara was reassured by the driver that they had got through one checkpoint, she simply transferred her worries to the next one they would meet. As the time of her mother's expected arrival neared, she waited patiently, listening for her phone to ring or for a knock on the door. Then, when the light began to fade, her fears grew. Driving in wartime Syria was often scary enough in broad daylight, but far more dangerous after dark. Finally, just when she had become convinced that something terrible had happened, Sara saw her mother's car pull up outside her home: 'It was completely dark when she got here. There was no light anywhere. So when I opened the door of the minivan cab I couldn't see her at all. But that didn't matter. I just followed the sweet smell of the scent she always wears. I was so overcome with emotion that I couldn't think of anything to say. All I could do was touch her face, over and over again. I became very, very emotional. We both did. We could have drowned in each other's tears, we cried so much. All night long I would wake up and touch her face. I had to be sure that it wasn't a dream, that she really was here with me.'

The following morning, Sara continued, she looked at her mother and thought how much older she seemed since she had last seen her. Gently stroking her face she told her how much her features seemed to have changed. With tears welling in her eyes, her mother replied that their long separation was the cause of that, it had aged her so much. Over the next few days they did their best to make up for lost time by talking, walking and just being together.

Finally, the time came for her mother to return to Damascus: 'I knew she had to go,' Sara said, 'but I was terribly sad. When her car drove away I felt I was in shock. I found it really hard to handle my emotions.'

As her mother's car drove off on the long journey back to Damascus, Sara said she kept staring at it, trying to imprint the image on her mind. She could then conjure it up whenever she doubted that the visit had actually happened. I sensed the smile on Sara's face fade away, just like the disappearing car her mother had been in. Memories of being separated all over again had brought her close to tears.

Despite Sara's anguish and grief, there was no evident self-pity, just a lingering, stoic sadness and a determination to carry on, come what may. I wondered if her situation was made worse by the fact that this devoted teacher no longer had young pupils to care for. It seemed that calming their fears had helped soothe hers too. Then a smile returned to her voice. Sara told me how a small number of children she had taught in Daraya had recently arrived in Idlib with their families. Although they had been dispersed in different camps, some quite a distance from hers, it had, nonetheless, greatly lifted her spirits. 'I don't get to see them often. But when I do it makes me so happy. I'm filled with hope again. At the same time, I do feel sorry for them. We can't give them the many things that we could in Daraya. This is because the community here is quite divided. Not everyone thinks the same way as we did back home. But there isn't much we can do about this. We are migrants now, we are refugees.'

By late 2016, Sara was one of more than six million people inside Syria displaced by the war, a number swollen by the tens of thousands evacuated from besieged Eastern Aleppo, after it fell to government forces in December that year. A further five million Syrians had fled the country and become refugees abroad.

These are mind-boggling numbers, so big that it is hard to visualise the human beings involved. While much is made in the West of the huge number of refugees who have fled their country, I find it even more incredible that the six million people displaced inside Syria decided to stay. People like Sara, Abdul Basit, Anas and their friends, who somehow retain hope that one day they will be able to go home.

After Daraya was evacuated I feared I might never again hear from those I had become so close to. People who had trustingly shared their darkest thoughts and brightest dreams with a faraway stranger they had never actually met. Yet, rather amazingly, I had managed to get back in touch with just about everybody. All had been deeply saddened to leave behind their treasured secret library and then to hear of its destruction. Yet as we talked it became clear that even though their adored library was gone, the spirit that created it and the inspiration it brought clearly lived on inside them all.

# Chapter Fifteen

Over the next months, I would get random texts from Anas, Abdul Basit, Sara and others telling me about what was happening where they were, as well as birthdays and all kinds of other personal news. One of the most moving and happy of these messages had come from Abdul Basit in late November 2016, though unfortunately I didn't see it until nearly two months after he sent it. The problem was that he had both changed his number and sent it via the Telegram app, which I rarely monitored, instead of the usual WhatsApp. He had written simply: 'Mike, my fiancée finally made it to Idlib and we plan to get married.' Feeling absolutely delighted, I sent him what was by now, a very belated text congratulating them both. Far from taking offence at my slow response Abdul Basit immediately texted back a string of emojis, from thumbs up and big red hearts to beaming faces and flowers. I loved the way he and his friends were so affectionate and supportive of each other, as this must have been enormously valuable for them all on arrival in alien Idlib. And without their close-knit network I probably wouldn't have been able to keep in contact with the group for so long, or found them all again after the somewhat chaotic evacuation of Daraya.

One illustration of this was being reunited with Abu Malik al-Shami, Daraya's very own 'Banksy', who was among those evacuated to Idlib. His arrival was relayed to me by Malik who had asked him to contact me. That same afternoon I received a photo of one of his pictures. Emblazoned on a crumbling white wall, near the town of Jisr al-Shughur, deep in the Idlib countryside, was a large tree. Its trunk was shaped like a rifle, with a subtly drawn trigger halfway up. Every leaf that sprouted from its twisting branches bore a one-word message such as 'hope', 'love', 'honesty', 'ethics', 'charity' and 'justice', and beneath the tree, in dark-blue letters fringed in white, was the word 'Daraya'. Abu Malik had clearly lost no time in getting down to work in his new home and once more his artistic skills were being used to both raise local morale and oppose President Bashar al-Assad's regime. But, as he told me over the phone the next day, some in his new home town did not appreciate his work, or the views of his friends: 'Achieving our goals here is proving more difficult than we had imagined. Not just because of the ongoing war but also because of the numerous armed groups in this city. Many of them don't share our vision of the revolution and often fight among themselves.'

In Abu Malik's view most of these armed groups had little interest in what was happening, or had happened, elsewhere in Syria. Their sole concern seemed to be to keep control of as much of Idlib as possible. But Abu Malik insisted that he was not letting this hold him back. He was making plans to further the revolution by doing more street art all over the province. As in Daraya, some people in Idlib who had heard about his work, had invited him to paint his murals on their walls and buildings. Most lived in areas where there had been intensive bombing and believed the drawings would help generate hope, just as they had in Daraya. Abu Malik was also in the process of teaming up with artists elsewhere in the country: 'I recently got in touch with some illustrators in other areas of Syria,' he told me, 'and we now have a project aimed at creating more projects like mine. We want to encourage others elsewhere to do the kind of drawings I did in Daraya. There will also be a mixture of slogans, big banners, writings and paintings reflecting the revolution. My work will be inspired by daily life here in Idlib.'

Abu Malik was also making plans for the city of Idlib itself, where he was preparing to launch a big project, with some local artists, aimed at bringing a whole new look to the town. 'I can't wait to get started,' he said, the excitement in his voice palpable. 'What we want to do is change the image that people have of Idlib. We want to show the world that it's not just a place full of Islamist extremists. There are many other very energetic people here, with lots of good things to say on many different subjects. Idlib isn't only about Islamism, it really isn't. We're going to site the project right in the centre of Idlib in a very sensitive area.'

Abu Malik was clearly not looking for a quiet life. The area he referred to was home to a large number of the Islamist militia who neither liked his art nor shared his views on free speech, democracy and human rights. 'We know that we'll be facing opposition from these Islamist extremists, but this is not going to stop us going ahead with the project.' His enthusiasm overflowed as he outlined his plans, even though he knew they would almost certainly lead to direct confrontation with the Islamists he mentioned. This surprised me. After all, Abu Malik had only just escaped besieged and bombarded Daraya, a place where sudden, violent death could strike at any moment. Now he was risking more of the same. Why, I asked him, was he carrying on with a project that was endangering those he worked with as well as himself? 'If we go about this randomly, without planning everything very carefully, then, yes, it could well be very dangerous for us all,' he replied. 'That is why we are now talking to members of the Free Syrian Army here to see if they will agree to protect us. We are also having discussions with the local administration. So, in answer to your question, yes, it is risky, but I think it's a risk well worth taking.'

Abu Malik's defiance was not to last. When I spoke to him a few weeks later he told me that he had been forced to suspend his planned graffiti project because of the deteriorating security situation in Idlib. The al-Qaeda-linked Islamist extremists he had defied so bravely before had become more threatening and warned that he could be arrested, or worse, if he set up his planned exhibition without their consent. For the moment at least, Abu Malik had decided not to push things any further, but many in Idlib continued to resist the diktats of armed groups like these, with some even staging street protests against their hard-line policies. Although the FSA broadly backed such demonstrations, nobody knew if they were strong enough to take on the increasingly powerful extremists. Abu Malik told me: 'It is still unclear who is in charge of Idlib city and violence continues to be a big worry. The FSA is very supportive of the people involved but I don't think they want street battles with al-Nusra.'

Sometimes news from the exiled Daraya community would reach me at the most unexpected times. One Saturday evening in mid-March 2017, I was at a club in central London, listening to a band. The six-strong ensemble were managed by a neighbour of mine and a bunch of us, middle-aged wannabe hipsters, were 'dancing' away at the front. Fortified by glasses of wine, fine music and good company, I had forgotten the world outside, until I felt my phone vibrate in my pocket. When the song finished I pulled it out to discover that I had a WhatsApp voice message. I pressed play, more out of habit than curiosity and retreated to a corner away from the crowd to hear what it said. It was Anas. 'Hi, Mike. I got married on Tuesday!'

As the crowd around me danced I stared at the screen of my phone and a feeling I can only describe as elation washed through me. For so many years in Daraya, Anas had waited for his fiancée, not knowing from one day to the next if she was alive, risking his life daily to run the library and help at the hospital. And now, in Idlib, they were finally united. I felt very touched that he had chosen to tell me. Here I was, a person he had never met, thousands of miles away from his troubled land, and yet he'd chosen to include me in such happy, intimate news.

I listened to those seven words again and again and as I did so, tears rolled down my face. Seeing this my wife Jane rushed over, suspecting I had received some terrible news; as she wrapped her arms around my shoulders and asked what had happened, I smiled and told her what the message said. That's wonderful, she shouted, having heard me talk about Anas several times before. I suddenly needed to tell her more about him, more about Abdul Basit and Sara and Ayham and Muhammad and Amjad and Abu Malik and Omar, and more about the secret library. I suddenly wanted to celebrate them, to give voice to their courage and their tenacity, so I pulled Jane through the throng and out through the nearest fire exit. And there, in the cool night air, it all poured out of me. I was still going strong some time later, when the door behind us opened, and people spilled out into the cool night air. Then I felt my phone vibrate again. It was another WhatsApp voice message, this time from Anas's fiancée herself: 'Hi, Mike, my name is Asmaa. I am very happy because I have got married to Anas. I am so proud of his work on the secret library . . .' The rest of her words were drowned out by street noise, but hearing that short, sweet message, was truly uplifting. I texted them both back, saying 'CONGRATU-LATIONS!' in capital letters and wished them every possible happiness.

My euphoria was not to last long. Just after dawn on Tuesday, 4 April 2017, when many were still asleep in their beds, planes appeared over the town of Khan Shaykhun, just over forty miles south of Idlib city. Moments later a huge explosion shook the town. This was no ordinary bomb. A sinister-looking yellow mushroom cloud billowed skywards and hung like a poisonous shroud over the area. What some later described as a 'winter fog' swirled through the streets. People's eyes began to sting, their pupils dilated and they struggled to breathe. Then they died. Rescue workers arriving at the scene, many of whom fell victim to the same symptoms, found people lying on the floor unable to move. Their face and skin had turned blue, foam oozing from their mouths. In all, more than eighty people died in what was later confirmed as a chemical attack on the town by pro-government forces.

The world was outraged and retribution pledged, but

there had been talk before of punishment for President Bashar al-Assad if such 'red lines' were crossed and little had happened then. In August 2013, President Obama had hinted at launching a military strike against his forces after a chemical attack on the Ghouta area near Damascus left more than 1400 people dead. Yet even though a UN chemical weapons team confirmed that the nerve agent sarin had been used, retaliation never came. However, Obama's successor, Donald Trump, did take action four years later after the chemical attack on Khan Shaykhun in Idlib. On Thursday, 6 April 2017, he ordered a missile strike against an airbase used by Syrian forces to launch the sarin nerve agent attack. At least fourteen people were killed, most of them Syrian soldiers and Shia militia, but coming events were to show that the move did little to deter Assad from using chemicals weapons.

Meanwhile, infighting among allied rebel groups in Idlib had reached new heights. In what seems a somewhat trivial dispute in a time of war, they were rowing over what flag they should fly. One local faction, Harakat Ahrar al-Sham insisted on raising the revolution flag, widely used by anti-Assad protesters, but this angered the al-Qaeda-linked HTS coalition (Hay'at Tahrir al-Sham), who insisted that only the black Islamic flag, bearing the Muslim profession of faith, should be flown. The open warfare that followed, which often involved firefights in the streets, made life even more precarious for Idlib's already blighted civilians. It also meant that pro-Assad forces could keep their powder dry in Idlib, and simply watch on as their rebel opponents killed each other.

While internecine war raged in Syria's north-west, the regime used the opportunity to step up security in areas under its control. And as Sara told me, this very much threatened plans for another much-hoped-for reunion with her mother. She texted me to say that her mum's visit had now been postponed: 'The government is tightening control on the streets and arresting people travelling to and from Damascus. It is no longer safe for my mother to travel here. I only wish I could go to Damascus myself. It would enable me to live again. In this dirty place it is difficult to think about the future, or to imagine a better life.'

Talking to Sara again reminded me of others from Daraya who I had not heard from in a while. One was former English teacher Muhammad Shihadeh, who was also now in Idlib. I wondered how he was getting on. The voice that answered the phone was as calm and welcoming as ever, not that I should have been surprised, for this was a man who sounded just the same back in Daraya when bombs were exploding all around him, some of which were so loud that they had distorted the speakers in my BBC studio. When I had suggested to him that we should stop our conversation until he had found somewhere safer, he had softly replied: 'There are no safe places in Daraya, Mike. Just carry on.' I'm sure that Muhammad had his worries just like everyone else, but he certainly managed to hide them better than most. He admitted that infighting among rebel groups in Idlib was making life there tougher than ever. This, he feared, would weaken rebel defences and might tempt pro-government forces to attack this last rebel-held province. Then, his voice dropping to a whisper: 'I hope it doesn't get much worse but I have to say I'm worried that it might.'

Those few words were chilling. After all the people of

Daraya had endured, to face yet another full-scale onslaught would be terrible. I glanced through my window
in London at the frost covering the ground outside. Winter
was on its way, a season that brought freezing temperatures
to Syria too. Yet they did not live in centrally heated homes
with hot water and three good meals a day, and with the
Turkish border closed, civilians would have nowhere to run
to if an offensive began. But Muhammad, as usual, was not
going to sit around worrying about something he could do
little to change. Instead he was spending his time trying to
help his community cope with the psychological traumas
they had endured in the past and the threats they faced in
the future. To do this he and some colleagues had decided
to learn what they could from others who had experienced
such traumas before. With this in mind they had contacted
the renowned American journalist Janine di Giovanni,
author of the powerful book, *The Morning They Came
for Us: Dispatches from Syria*. They asked if she could put
them in contact with people in Bosnia who had survived
the war there. The hope was that those who had suffered
like them, but come through what must have seemed an
endless darkness, could help the people of Daraya do the
same. Janine had been happy to bring them together and
Muhammad told me that it had been a big success: 'We
were hoping they could help us on a personal level. We
talked to them in detail about our situation and the secret
library and they spoke of their memories. How they had
survived the terrible events in Bosnia and then moved on
with their lives after the war. Hearing all this and forming
these human relationships helped all of us a lot. Hopefully
it will continue to help us get through what is to come.'

Life was clearly still very difficult for all those I knew

from Daraya following their evacuation to Idlib, but at least all but poor Omar had survived. When you think of the terrible dangers and hardships they had lived through, that in itself was remarkable. Abdul Basit, Anas, Ayham, Malik, Rateb and Muhammad were all still close and living in Idlib city. And though clearly homesick and missing the secret library, they were still very positive about life. Abdul Basit and Anas were happily married and Amjad was at last away from the fighting. Worryingly I still had no news about what had happened to twelve-year-old Islam and her mother, but Malik promised he would try to find out. Abu Malik was carrying on painting his pro-revolution murals around Idlib, despite demands for him to stop by Islamic extremists. Sadly, though, I learned that his painting of the tree with its rifle-shaped trunk and its leaves bearing symbols of hope and peace had been destroyed, not by jihadists, but by Russian bomber planes.

Although they were now in a comparatively safe area, I did worry about their future. Part of my unease grew from the worry that with their secret library gone, this close network of friends might slowly fracture and lose touch, not just with each other, but with the inspiring ideals that spawned it. But it seems I should have had more faith, because far from sitting around lamenting their losses, the foundations were being laid for another remarkable project.

One summer day, in a small village in the Idlib countryside, a mirage appeared through the heat haze. It took the form of a brightly painted van with fluorescent lime-green sides and a pillar-box-red roof. But as it pulled up outside some bomb-damaged homes, all could see that this was no imaginary thing. Within minutes, the van was surrounded by hordes of children and curious adults, clamouring for a better view.

Books! Stacks of them lined the van's windows and covered the shelves on its walls, more than 2,200 of them in all. This was a mobile library, filled with reading material, mostly for children and young people. The books ranged from traditional children's stories and simplified science to texts on history and personal development. Given the absence of any public libraries, in an area where few could afford to buy books, this mobile library was a joy to behold.

It may come as no surprise to learn that the project was the brainchild of Malik al-Rifaii, Muhammad Shihadeh and other evacuees from Daraya. After being shocked to discover how hard it was to get hold of books since arriving in Idlib, they decided to set up a library. Initially the idea was aimed mainly at children from Daraya who were missing the town's secret library, but it was then extended to serve local youngsters too. Honing his resourcefulness and extraordinary ability to get things done, Malik told me: 'We had learned the enormous value of reading after creating our secret library in Daraya. The way it helped build openness among us all, and filled the gaps in our knowledge which had widened during the siege. We saw how it had also brought benefits to the wider community, too. So we thought, let's try and help local children and youths by creating a library here.'

Malik told me that they had initially planned to compile the small library in one of three particularly isolated areas of rural Idlib, all of which were home to poor families who could never afford to buy books. But when more exiled people from other parts of Idlib began asking if they could have access to books too, Malik and his friends began looking at ways to expand the reach of their scheme. Many of those who contacted them were fellow evacuees from Daraya, who had been settled deep in the country-side. They, along with most locals in such isolated places, had little money and no access to transport. So, Malik told me, the solution was obvious. If they could not get to the library, the library would come to them.

To make this plan work they needed to find a vehicle to convert into a mobile library and then fill it with children's books. The problem was they had no van, no books and no money. The first obstacle was less of a problem, as the ongoing scarcity and high price of fuel meant old vans had become quite cheap. Getting hold of books was a much bigger challenge.

Malik began by asking the owner of a bookshop in Idlib if he would be willing to act as a broker and buy in a long list of titles for him. The man agreed and contacted a range of libraries and bookshops in Damascus and other regime-controlled areas of the country. A few days later, he called Malik back and told him that a deal could be done, but the books would cost more than normal and getting them to Idlib would not be cheap either. Malik had no money for the books, van or fuel but, never one to give up, he went online and searched for NGOs and charities who might be willing to fund the idea. Several weeks later, after much trawling, many failed attempts and some lengthy negotiations, the ever-resourceful Malik struck gold. A Brussels-based organisation called 'The European Endowment for Democracy' had agreed to fund the mobile library. 'Our next task,' a delighted Malik told me, 'was to order the books and then get a van to put them all in. After finding one which was just the right size, we painted it in bright colours, decorated it with stickers and installed shelves and lighting. After that we filled it full of books, and were ready to go.'

Unlike the secret library in Daraya, the fluorescent mobile library was not hidden or camouflaged; it was designed to be seen and adored. But, Malik told me, with many Islamist extremist groups in the province who disapproved of giving non-religious books to children, some precautions did have to be taken. 'We avoid visiting places where these groups are and make sure that we have the support of the local council of the town or village. We also try hard to avoid going through the extremists' checkpoints by driving along the route the day before in a normal car to see where they are.'

The first mobile library trip got on the road in July 2017 and, Malik told me proudly, it had been busy ever since. 'It is a great feeling to visit places you have never been to before in such a colourful vehicle, which brings joy to the hearts of the people after all these years of war. Every time the van turns up in a village it gets a great response, especially from children. They all get very excited when they see it arriving at their school with all these books. We open its doors and let them come over and choose whichever ones they want. I remember a child called Ghassan who lives in Kafr Halab, a village in the countryside near Aleppo. We took the mobile library there four times and on each occasion he was there. Ghassan particularly loved a book called *Atlas of the Universe and Space*. He told us that he has a passion for the planets and every time he borrows that book he learns new things which he passes on to his friends. The last time we saw him we gave him the book to keep in the hope that it will help him reach the stars someday.'

Not content to rest on their laurels, Malik and his friends invited experts on all sorts of subjects to tour with the mobile library and give talks in the villages they stopped at. He admitted that the idea was inspired by the many popular lectures held in Daraya's secret library. The speakers, he told me, would be society activists, members of the local civil defence, or career teachers and doctors, who could speak about the work they did. They also planned to hold public speaking classes for children and English lessons, as well as organising various competitions for them. 'This project,' he said, 'enables us to give something back to the local community which has helped us so much. We know that the mobile library can only give a small number of people here the chance to read, but at least it's something. Maybe the books in it will help young people here retain their hopes and dreams for the future, just like our secret library did for us in Daraya.'

I had the feeling that Amjad would have loved this project. He would have adored the children's burning enthusiasm for books and their unbridled joy as the fluorescent van pulled up before them. I can just imagine Daraya's Chief Librarian opening up the back door, clutching bundles of vividly coloured volumes, wildly extolling the delights of each one. Then, after scurrying back inside to get his pen and notebook, carefully recording who had borrowed what and when, before bidding them farewell and heading off cheerfully to the next location. All, just as before, under the ever-watchful eyes of Malik, Anas and Abdul Basit. Adored as it was, this small mobile bookstore could never truly rival the secret library in the hearts of those from Daraya, but it did help spread the same joy. In some of the villages the library went to, schools had been deprived of new books for years and many parents were illiterate. Yet out of nowhere, in the midst of war, came this library on wheels, bringing stories of adventure, fun and hope.

# Chapter Sixteen

Through the window of Abdul Basit's spartan apartment in Idlib, there was no fighting to be seen, though
the scars of war were everywhere. Cracked and crumbling
homes, some without roofs, others without walls, dotted the
skyline. Once-pleasant tree-lined streets, now blighted by
ugly gaps, like missing blackened teeth, where smart shops
and offices once stood. Continuing infighting between
rebel groups brought danger to the streets, while pro-Assad
planes dropped horrors from the skies. Yet frightening as
such perils were, they bore little comparison to the former
terrors of besieged Daraya. Traffic still flowed, people
walked the pavements and shops were open, even though
few could afford to buy the food they passed.

Abdul Basit was not alone as he stared at the scene
outside. After years of waiting, his twenty-one-year-old
fiancée, Zohour, had managed to join him in Idlib and
they had married near the end of 2016. Although we had
been in regular contact since soon after he had sent me
that joyous text declaring the happy news, our calls had
become less frequent and I often couldn't get through. He
had explained that until very recently the Internet where he
lived had been very poor and his rather battered old phone
had also been faulty, so it had been difficult speaking to
anyone outside Idlib. But now, finally, we were able to talk

properly, and I had never heard him sounding so cheerful. Nothing, I'm sure, could wipe the many horrors he had seen from his mind, nor erase his despair at the state of his country, but there was a smile in his voice, a spring in his step, a contentment, that hadn't been there before. He told me: 'The first thing I must say is that thanks to God I'm a very happily married man. The main reason for this is my wife. We share the same burdens and the same goals.'

I soon learned that Abdul Basit's joy was not derived solely from his beloved wife because, just a few days before, he had become a father. Little Muhamad, I was told in a whisper, was sleeping in the other room. How Abdul Basit's life had changed. When I asked him to tell me about his wedding day, he laughed shyly. Not because it was a silly question, or that anything funny had happened, but more because he felt I might find his description of it strange. Having seen so many Western weddings in films, he said, he knew his big day wasn't much like those, the biggest difference being that there were two ceremonies rather than one. Men celebrated in one place and women at another, so while Abdul Basit was dancing with his friends his wife was doing the same somewhere else with hers. Though, happily, they did get together in the end: 'After spending a couple of hours at the male ceremony,' he told me, 'I jumped into a car, which I'd decorated with flowers and balloons, and drove to the party where my wife was. She was wearing a lovely white dress and looked so very beautiful. I remember taking off the headscarf that brides wear, kissing her hand and then carrying her upstairs to her room. I can honestly say that I have never been so happy in all my life.'

As we talked I looked at a wedding photo Abdul Basit had sent me a few months before. He was dressed in a lightly patterned greyish-blue jacket, over what looked like a white polo shirt, smiling at the camera in an endearingly self-conscious kind of way. Like many bridegrooms on their wedding day, he seemed to be loving every second while simultaneously wishing it was over. It was strange to think, looking at him standing there so smartly, that this was taking place within a country devastated by war. A nation where more than 400,000 people lay dead and around twelve million more had been forced to flee their homes, he and his wife among them. Thankfully that day there was happiness, a welcome respite from the hatred and slaughter.

Abdul Basit wasted no time in telling me about one of the biggest joys he shares with his wife. 'Like me, she's an avid reader, she absolutely loves reading. We're already planning to read a huge number of books together. We're even planning on setting a target for how many books we will read in a month. So, yes, we both really love reading, especially novels.' Delighted to hear this and eager to know more about Zohour, I asked Abdul Basit if I could speak to his wife. A short conversation between them followed and it transpired that Zohour was a little shy and would prefer to let Abdul Basit do the talking for now. I got the feeling that Abdul Basit was concerned about her security, so this was possibly his decision as much as hers. This, if true, was hardly surprising, in a country where the higher your profile, the bigger the risks you face. He pointed out that Zohour's family had endured a traumatic time under President Bashar al-Assad's regime. Her father had been a political prisoner for more than four years and her older brother had died in Daraya during the siege. But Abdul Basit was still enthusing about a much happier topic. 'As for Zohour's love of reading,' he told me, 'as I said, this is something very special between us. I remember the first conversation we had about books, after I told her about the secret library. She thought it was wonderful. In the months that followed, I would send her updates about it. As you know, couples like to share pictures, and she would ask for photos of me in the library. We would then talk about the writers each of us loved. I realised then that this was the woman I wanted to be with for the rest of my life.'

As for the secret library, it seemed from what Abdul Basit told me, that Zohour loved it as much as he did. Even though she couldn't get to Daraya, so had never been able to set foot in it. 'During the siege she always encouraged me to go to the library and spend as much time as possible there. She thought of it as the only place that could keep me sane at such a terrible time.'

Abdul Basit and his wife had different tastes in their reading. Zohour, he told me, was especially keen on books on human development, while he was more drawn to literature. In his wife's view, he continued, Syria would need more educated women focusing on this area for the country's future development. Although not actually opposed to that thought, Abdul Basit doubted that the study of human development had answers for everything. Instead, he believed it was down to us all to decide our own paths in life. But after a sideways look at his strong-willed wife, a now grinning Abdul Basit seemed to accept that he wasn't winning this battle of beliefs. 'Thanks to the books Zohour is reading, our life is now guided by plans and schedules. She has plans for everything, including one for today. It began at 05.30 this morning and involved breakfast, a coffee break, followed by some exercises!'

Abdul Basit went on to tell me that Zohour was also very fond of reading cookery books and that having been a mathematics student she liked to further her studies by reading more on that subject too. He told me that they both loved reading the copy of *This is What Life Taught Me* that his father had given him. 'Unfortunately,' he said, 'because Zohour was living outside besieged Daraya, I wasn't able to show her this book before, though I longed to do so. But as soon as she arrived in Idlib one of the very first things I did was give it to her.' Abdul Basit reiterated what others from Daraya had told me about there being no libraries in Idlib town, and that although you could buy books there, they were very expensive. But as he and Zohour couldn't bear life without reading, they had both been saving up. So far, Abdul Basit told me, they had been able to buy two books: one on the basic principles of economy, by the Kuwaiti writer Sultan el Jassem, and one on ideas and research, by the former Syrian teacher and veteran broadcaster Ali al-Tantawi. And, as ever, Abdul Basit was certainly not leaving it there. 'We are trying our best to get more. It's not easy though, because books cost so much here, but at least it's a start. We're also continuing to work on plans to start a library here in Idlib town. We believe libraries are as important as food and water, so we're determined to start one, even if it's only very small.'

Abdul Basit was also hoping to get his hands on a copy of his favourite play, so that he could share it with his wife. 'Shakespeare's *Hamlet* is such a wonderful book. I remember reading it whenever I could back in Daraya, often during quiet moments when I was working in the hospital. Its imagery is so rich and the dialogue so captivating. But unfortunately I can't find a copy of that anywhere

here in Idlib, so my wife hasn't had the chance to read it yet.' Hearing Abdul Basit voice his love of *Hamlet* took me back several years to one of our earliest conversations in the secret library, when he had told me how he loved the book so much that he kept sneaking glimpses of it in between helping patients at the hospital. 'Abdul Basit,' he had told himself, 'this must stop!' So much had happened since then for both of us, particularly him. Here he was today, married and a father, living far away from Daraya and the secret library he so cherished. He seemed much older and our conversations, once rather formal, were those of friends, even though we had yet to actually meet. The war had gone from bad to worse, but Abdul Basit's enthusiasm for life and books remained undiminished.

Now that he had started a family, I was interested to see how he saw his future. As I asked him my mind returned to the chilling answer twelve-year-old Islam had given me when I had put the same question to her a couple of years before. She had told me then that she saw no sense in making plans for the future because she didn't think she would get out of besieged Daraya alive. Her answer still haunts me, though I had just had some very good news from Malik. He told me that Islam, her mother and siblings had managed to leave Daraya without suffering any further injuries, and were living in the neighbouring town of al-Moadamyeh. I was delighted to know that despite her darkest fears, young Islam *did* have a future after all. I hope from the bottom of my heart that it's a very happy one.

Then there was Amjad, another child whose life has been scarred by the war. While older people may feel defeated by such terrible times you expect the younger generation, imbued with the optimism and self-certainty of youth, to look forward to the future with confidence and hope. Yet even Amjad, who had once bustled around the secret library with such relentless joy and enthusiasm, now seemed lost in the past. The same, happily, could not be said of Abdul Basit.

Travel, he told me enthusiastically, was high on his and Zohour's agenda. They were hoping to go to Europe, though as tourists, not refugees. Their planned first stop was to be Andalusia in southern Spain, which was more genealogical quest than beach holiday. Abdul Basit told me he was drawn to the region because it was once ruled by the al-Ahmar family, which was his last name too. Their main aim was to get to know more about the great civilisation that had once lived in the region. After that it would be on to Saudi Arabia to go on an Islamic pilgrimage to Mecca and, that done, they wanted to finish their adventure with a trip to Malaysia. Though, again, this last leg looked set to be more of a fact-finding trip than a holiday. 'This is a nation that only thirty years ago was considered an undeveloped country. But back then its people made a plan to become part of the developed world and they are about to achieve that goal. We think that Syria could learn a lot from Malaysia's experiences and perhaps make similar progress once the war is over.' Even at this late stage, Abdul Basit seemed to believe that the revolution against President Bashar al-Assad's regime would eventually succeed. But the almost total defeat of rebel forces had made that prospect very unlikely, for the moment at least. And with the regime's army massed on Idlib's borders, I feared that avowed opponents like Abdul Basit would struggle to stay in the country, never mind play any role in rebuilding it. Yet at the same time I had a gut feeling that someday, somehow, he would indeed find a way to do that.

Abdul Basit and Zohour also hoped to spend time travelling around Idlib too. When I asked him whether he thought this might be dangerous, given the number of armed extremist groups roaming the province, he waved my concerns away. So far, he told me, he had managed to avoid any trouble with them. His confidence on this issue derived from recent brief encounters with the al-Nusra Islamist group. As soon as he mentioned where he was from, they were quite helpful. Daraya was considered a birthplace of the revolution and was lauded in most opposition circles. In fact, Abdul Basitt continued, this link with Daraya acted like a kind of passport, letting him travel through most rebel-held areas without trouble. The problem, however, was that such areas were becoming fewer and farther between as the war continued to turn in Assad's favour.

By 10 January 2018, the Syrian government's long-predicted offensive against Idlib province was well underway. In the far south of this last rebel-held province, 100,000 civilians had been forced to flee their homes as pro-regime forces advanced. Most were heading north towards Idlib city, struggling along swollen, dangerous roads, carrying, pushing or pulling all they could manage. The regime's immediate objective was the strategically important Abu al-Duhur airbase, which rebels had seized on taking control of Idlib in 2015. Soon it would fall. Meanwhile pro-Assad planes and guns continued to pound the rebel-held area of Eastern Ghouta, just outside of Damascus, home to 400,000 half-starved people. Like Daraya before its evacuation, the enclave's population has lived under siege for four long years. They too were slowly being starved into submission. Both areas had, somewhat ironically, been officially declared 'de-escalation zones'.

All through the war, those Syrians opposed to Assad had hoped that the US and its allies would intervene against the regime in as robust a way as Russia and Iran had done in support of it. That had never happened under President Obama so I was interested in whether Abdul Basit thought it might under Donald Trump. 'The previous president didn't give us much hope for the future,' he said. 'He always talked about how red lines must not be crossed by the regime, but then did nothing when they were. At least Trump did punish Assad after the chemical weapons attack here in Idlib province. But we're going to have to wait and see what else he does and whether he might offer us any further hope to cling to.' Sitting forward in his chair, as if about to impart a secret, Abdul Basit told me that he at least felt less worried on one front. He thought it was now unlikely that Assad's regime would try to retake Idlib province soon. He had thought that was coming after the evacuation of formerly rebel-held Daraya was followed by another from eastern Aleppo. But he now believed that the regime's attack on the south of the province would probably stop once they had got the Abu al-Duhur airbase back. He had become convinced, he said, that Assad's forces were simply not strong enough to march north from there and retake the whole region. Even if they did try to do this, he added, the people of Idlib would not give up easily.

While Abdul Basit and I were talking I could hear bursts of laughter and good-natured shouts and exclamations, as if some people had come into the room. Sure enough, they had and I could hear a very familiar voice calling out my name. It was Anas. Delighted, I shouted back a loud and heartfelt hello, though for a few seconds I wasn't sure if he had heard me. But he had, and a big surprise was in store for me.

'Hi, Mike,' he said, 'I would like to introduce you to my newly arrived daughter, Batoul. I am a father now!' Anas put the video-linked phone in front of a tiny little girl sitting happily in her mother's arms. Dressed in a pink Babygro with a teddy bear on the front, she stared back, her small head framed in a matching pink and white hood. This star of the show was clearly loving the limelight. Adoring words came from every corner of the room. Staring besottedly at his little daughter, who had been born just a few days before, Anas could not have looked any prouder or happier.

With great enthusiasm he told me how marriage and fatherhood had changed his life. Looking across adoringly at his wife, Asmaa, he told me what a wonderful woman she was. Just like in Abdul Basit's case, married life seemed to have done wonders for him. Anas, once described to me by Abdul Basit as a young man in clothes an older man would wear, looked younger now. Filled with new-found optimism and energy, he explained that he and Abdul Basit had been talking about returning to Daraya as soon as possible. 'The first thing we'll do when we get back,' he told me, 'is rebuild the secret library, as well as the school nearby. We want to set up educational institutions and help our country start again. But we'll be aiming at rebuilding minds rather than buildings. When people think of building a town, they normally think only of homes, shops and offices, but we want to build a nation.' Anas then added, 'If we fail to rebuild people's minds it will make no difference what buildings we put up. Without a proper foundation,' he continued, 'society will eventually collapse.' This, he insisted, had happened before, and it was why the civil war had started. After forty years of despotic rule by the Assad family, the country had fallen apart.

Much as I hated to dampen Anas's high-spirited optimism, I felt the need to point out that President Bashar al-Assad was now in the strongest position he had been in for years, largely thanks to military backing from Russia, Iran and Lebanon's Hezbollah. But he was undaunted. 'We will still continue doing our work and planning for the future. We won't give up. Even though our land is occupied and our people continue to suffer, the fight is not over. As Abdul Basit may have told you, we are hoping to set up a small library here in Idlib. Whether we succeed in this or not, I'm going to keep on reading. As I remember saying to you back in Daraya, just like the body needs food the soul needs books.'

This talk of Daraya and its treasured secret library seemed to have generated a wave of nostalgia. It washed over Anas, leaving him staring into space for a while. Then, slowly gathering his thoughts, he said: 'We had a place of sanctuary, an oasis of calm and harmony in what seemed like a world gone mad. It's not only the books I miss, it's the place I read them in. I also miss the environment of the library, the people there, I miss everything about that special place. It wasn't just a repository of books. It was another world, a world we shared together. And while outside was destruction and pain, inside was creation and hope. Despite all that was happening, I felt inspired inside those walls.'

Anas's words brought me back to those of the deeply missed Omar Abu Anas. A few days before he died, he had told me how he and his friends saw reading as the bedrock for a better future, that it would help them all rebuild their nation once the guns stopped firing. 'Brains rather than bullets are going to be needed to put this devastated country back together again.' Books, he had insisted, whether on the subject of literature, history, politics, religion, poetry or anything else, can help show the way forward and provide the building blocks for the years to come. Abdul Basit agreed: 'It is not only Anas and me,' he told me, 'many young people are just as passionate about books as we are. One day we will go back to Daraya. We will work together to build an immense library there, one that will be the heart of the town. It was our refuge, it was where we had fun, it was where we came to enjoy the magic of books. The secret library was a glimmer of hope in a very dark world. It was our spiritual sanctuary.'

While Abdul Basit and I were talking, Anas was staring at his phone. He said he was looking at a short video of the destruction in Southern Idlib and besieged rebel-held Eastern Ghouta. He passed the device to Abdul Basit, pointing to a particularly distressing scene, before later sending the video to me. A father was holding his badly injured young daughter in his arms, screaming at the camera, while white-helmeted civil defence workers struggled to dig people out of the rubble behind him. Anas became increasingly emotional as he watched the video again with his friend. 'I keep thinking that could have been my child. What if I had come back to my house to discover this? It is just so terrible. I can't imagine what the families of these children must be feeling.' Anas told me that the scene he was watching reminded him of the horrors unleashed on Daraya for so long. He had carried on as best he could in those days, refusing to be intimidated by the regime's bombs, but only now that he was a father did he understand what those with families must have gone through each day. 'If I'd had a family to look after then,' he said, 'I would have worried about them all the time. I would have been too frightened to do almost anything, I'd have been constantly fearing for their lives. I think it would have made me incapable of living my life in other ways. I can only be thankful that when I did become a father, it was here, in a safer place.'

Before Anas finished speaking, Abdul Basit had clicked on another harrowing report showing thousands of bedraggled civilians swarming along a blackened and desolate highway, heading north towards Idlib town. It made me wonder how much longer their new home-in-exile would remain safe, and whether, sooner or later, the regime would come for Idlib. Already, Anas told me, people had left Idlib town and set off for the Turkish border, hoping to escape the fighting before it came to them. I asked him if he was considering doing the same, now that he had a wife and baby to take care of.

'Some of my family and friends are trying to convince me to go to Turkey and leave Syria,' he replied, 'but I am refusing to do that. I'm determined to stay until the end. I don't want to leave my country. If every person who is against the regime does that, the regime will be free to do whatever they want with our country. So I simply have to stay here whatever happens.'

His brave and defiant words reminded me of those of Muhammad back in Daraya, when the shells were falling all around him. It is one thing to have beliefs and ideals, and quite another to stand by them in this way, risking your life and all you hold dear. These men weren't warriors in the conventional sense, they fought with words rather than weapons. To me, their quiet courage, resilience and determination was all the more remarkable for that.

When I had first tried to find people from Daraya after the evacuation, I wondered whether the secret library would still be important to them. After all, many had lost relatives and close friends, seen their homes bombed to rubble and then been uprooted to a new place far away. There they faced having to start life all over again. To find a roof over their heads, food, clothing and work to somehow pay for it all and still they weren't safe. Bombs might fall at any time and they could be besieged all over again by pro-Assad forces. Given all this, I reasoned, would the secret library now be little more than a fond but redundant memory? Inside, I knew the answer. Its books had been looted and its readers all gone, yet the extraordinary spirit of this literary sanctuary was undiminished. I cannot think of anyone who can illustrate this fact better than Abdul Basit:

> The library gave birth to a movement of knowledge and learning, and enabled us to explore new things. It was also our sanctuary, and our minaret. It guided us through all the horrors, lit the path we should take and inspired us to carry on. It taught us that a fighter without knowledge is not a hero, but a gangster. The library's many books were fuel for our souls. They gave us back our lives. While bombs rained down from the skies, we discussed new ideas, learned from the past and planned for the future. The library united us all. It was an essential part of Daraya, and what it stood for. Looking back, the secret library was not only our saviour, it was our biggest weapon against the regime.

At this point Abdul Basit went quiet. For the next few moments I heard nothing but the faint murmur of traffic and the occasional shouts of distant children. Had he no more to say? As if in answer, a deep sigh filled the void before Abdul Basit continued:

The secret library was filled with the wonderful aroma of old books and paper. It smelt of history, literature, philosophy and culture. It was a deep, rich, comforting smell. It was like when you walk in the door of your home and are guided to the kitchen by the smell of fine food. That special dish, and all its delicious ingredients, are waiting there for you. To me, the library was like that. It gave us a precious space where we could breathe hope instead of despair. It liberated us from suffering and savagery. Inside its walls the love of science, literature and ideas filled the air. This symphony of books soothed our hearts. As we entered, its aura revived us, like fresh air to a suffocating man. It was the oxygen for our souls. It was a place where angels met. Each time I stepped inside, I flew with them.

Abdul Basit's passionate eulogy, spoken as if to a long-lost lover, left the room breathless and silent. I felt shy of disturbing this near-sacred reverie, but had one remaining question. One that had played on my mind ever since seeing how Amjad seemed to have retreated into the past. Would it not be best, I asked Abdul Basit, as Assad's troops advanced by the day and Daraya lay empty, looted and dead, to forget thoughts of rebuilding the past, accept that the library was lost and build a new future around something else? Abdul Basit took his time to reply. When he did, his voice was unwavering, his tone utterly resolute. 'You suggested that our plans to go back to Daraya and rebuild our secret library are now unrealistic, given the military situation. But I am as optimistic about this as I am that the sun will rise each day. I could not be more optimistic. I promise you, I will either go back and do this, or I will die trying. My ultimate hope is that one day my wife and I will rebuild the library together. I would love this to happen. It would be a dream come true.'

Sadly, the omens do not look good. What was once a civil war has morphed into a near-global one, with most participants split along Sunni or Shia Muslim sectarian lines. Many nations have either sent fighters themselves or paid proxy armies to do battle for them. As many as half a million people are now thought to have died, 3000 of them in Daraya alone. Eleven million more have been displaced from their homes. Not long ago President Bashar al-Assad's days in office were thought to be numbered. Yet as I write these words, his blood-stained grip on power looks stronger than ever. Russian military muscle has turned his once failing war around and his forces surround Idlib, held back only by a tenuous ceasefire agreed by Ankara and Moscow. So long as his powerful allies stick by his side, and Islamist extremists continue to plague this land, there seems little hope for free speech, tolerance and other human rights in Syria. The very values upon which the now ransacked secret library was built.

Yet there is something about the people of Daraya, something about their faith in the power of books and the joy of learning, something in their community's strength, resilience and sheer sense of purpose, that utterly transcends the values of those ranged against them. An invisible something that leaves an outsider like me, welcomed among them as a faraway friend, convinced that in the end, they will succeed. I can only hope this happens. Not just for those who created this extraordinary library, but for mankind itself. To see hope triumph once more over pessimism, creation over destruction and books over bombs, would be a victory for us all.

# *Acknowledgements*

It's hard to know where to start with so many people to thank for helping to make this book possible. But I'll begin with my remarkable wife, Jane Ray, a book widow for much of the last three years. During this time, I've been an elusive, shadowy figure, hidden away in my increasingly chaotic study when not absent entirely on foreign assignments. Add to all this, the interrupted holidays, alarming skype calls and pinging nocturnal texts, sometimes bringing frightening news from Daraya. Without Jane's never-ceasing support, understanding and insightful encouragement I would have struggled to finish this book.

My limited command of Arabic has also left me deeply indebted to those who have interpreted my years of conversations with people in Syria. Stamina, patience and prolonged spells of deep concentration were required for these exchanges, many of which were barely audible over crackly, constantly failing WhatsApp and Skype lines. Sensitivity and toughness were needed too, given that some of the discussions were harrowing in nature. I would particularly like to thank Miriam El Khalef for her early translation work. Miriam's deep concern for those she was talking to, and her dedication in ensuring that their words were accurately relayed, helped forge what came to be lasting friendships. My thanks also to Steve Ali, a Syrian himself, for his calm professionalism and care with later translations.

This book has been further enriched by the vigorous

historical digging undertaken by Curtis Gallant, a re-sourceful and talented researcher and family friend. Curtis's remarkable grasp of Syrian cultural history combined with his infectious enthusiasm made him a pleasure to work with. Thanks must also go to the BBC's Bridget Harney who commissioned my radio documentary about the secret library, a broadcast that later inspired this book. Praise, too, to the Weidenfeld & Nicolson editorial team: from my initial publisher and editor, Kirsty Dunseath, a constant source of ideas and encouragement who guided me through what sometimes seemed mission impossible, to her successor, Jenny Lord, and her impressive team, Craig Lye, Jennifer Kerslake and Elizabeth Allen.

Most of all, I would like to thank the inspiring people of Daraya for enabling me to tell their extraordinary story. Even when close to starving, cut-off from their loved ones and terrorised by snipers and barrel bombs, they never tired of my endless questions, allowing me to share their often nightmarish world. Some, in particular, deserve extra special mentions. The indomitable Malik, for whom, nothing was impossible. Whether it meant finding many of the precious photographs in this book, tracking down members of the secret library team or helping me verify numerous dates, names and events. The endearing young Amjad, whose heart seemed forever pinned to his sleeve, and poetic and spiritual Abdul Basit, whose moving words and emotional honesty touched me deeply. Also, the wise and hugely respected Muhammad, who offered me advice and guidance, along with just about everyone else in besieged and bombarded Daraya. I'm grateful too, in so many ways, to Anas, Sara, Homam and Rateb, who have also become trusted and enduring friends. I have come to love and admire them all.

# References and Further Reading

1  Strathcarron, Ian, *Innocence and War: Mark Twain's Holy Land Revisited* (Courier Corporation, 2012), p.84

2  Shahid, Irfan, *Byzantium and the Arabs in the Sixth Century*, Volume 1 (Harvard University Press, 2002), p.218

3  Grove, George, 'Syrian Legends No.2 – The Grapes of Daraya', *Once a Week*, Volume 6, Eneas Sweetland Dallas, ed. (1 March 1862), p.280

4  Cobb, Paul M., *White Banners: Contention in 'Abbasid Syria, 750–880* (SUNY Press, 2001)

5  Allen, Susan Jane, and Emilie Amt, eds. *The Crusades: A Reader*, Volume 8 (University of Toronto Press, 2014), chapter 4, section 33

6  Kahf, Mohja, 'Water Bottles and Roses' (21 December 2011) www.mashallahnews.com/water-bottles-roses

7  Kahf, Mohja, 'Nonviolence in Syria', *Fellowship* 78.1–3 (2014)

8  Oweis, Khaled Yacoub, 'Local Dynamics in the Syrian Conflict: Homegrown Links in Rebel Areas Blunt Jihadist Ascendency', (Stiftung Wissenschaft und Politik, 2016)

9  Wellisch, Hans H. 'Ebla: The World's Oldest Library', *The Journal of Library History*, 6.3 (University of Texas Press, 1981), p.488

10  *Ibid.*

11  *Ibid.*
12  Rudavsky, Joseph, *To Live with Hope, to Die with Dignity: Spiritual Resistance in the Ghettos and Camps* (Jason Aronson, Inc., 1997), p.65
13  Spiritual Resistance in the Ghettos, Holocaust Encyclopedia, United States Holocaust Memorial Museum, www.ushmm.org/wlc/en/article.php?ModuleId=10005416
14  Rudavsky, p.64
15  www.pri.org/stories/2013-06-22/profiling-change-burma-secret-booklender
16  *Ibid.*
17  Tammam, Abu, 'The Sword is More Veracious', trans. Suzanne Pinckney Stetkevych, *The Poetics of Islamic Legitimacy: Myth, Gender and Ceremony in the Classical Arabic Ode* (Indiana University Press, Copyright © 2002). Reprinted with permission of Indiana University Press.
18  Al-Ma'arri, 'I No Longer Steal from Nature', trans. Reynold Alleyne Nicholson, *Translations of Eastern Poetry and Prose* (Cambridge University Press, 1922), p.107.
19  Adonis, 'A Time between Ashes and Roses', trans. Shawkat M. Toorawa, *A Time Between Ashes and Roses* (Syracuse University Press, 2004). Reprinted with permission of Syracuse University Press.
20  Al-Masri, Maram, 'Have You Seen Him?', trans. Theo Dorgan, *Liberty Walks Naked* (Southword Editions, 2018). Reprinted with permission of Southword Editions.
21  Amnesty International, 'Human Slaughterhouse' (2016) www.amnestyusa.org/sites/default/files/human_slaughterhouse.pdf

22  Amnesty International, 'Harrowing accounts of torture, inhuman conditions and mass deaths in Syria's prisons' (18 August 2016) www.amnesty.org/en/latest/news/2016/08/harrowing-accounts-of-torture-inhuman-conditions-and-mass-deaths-in-Syrias-prisons

23  Alhaji, Faisal bin Mohamad, *The Tears of Men* (Dar Al Kalam). Lines translated by Steve Ali, 2019.

# Illustration Credits

All photographs are provided courtesy of the media department of the Local Council of Daraya City, with the following exceptions:

Credit: Deiniol Buxton

**Mike Thomson** is a multi-award-winning World Affairs correspondent for the BBC. Over the last decade, his work has taken him to many of the world's most troubled places. These have included Syria, Iraq, Afghanistan, Somalia, North Korea, Darfur, DR Congo, Sierra Leone, North Sinai and the Central African Republic. He has reported undercover in places like Libya, Zimbabwe and Myanmar and covered some of the world's biggest news events including the war in Syria, the election of several US presidents, the devastating Haiti earthquake, the fall of Muammar Gaddafi and the death of Nelson Mandela.

PublicAffairs is a publishing house founded in 1997. It is a tribute to the standards, values, and flair of three persons who have served as mentors to countless reporters, writers, editors, and book people of all kinds, including me.

I. F. STONE, proprietor of *I. F. Stone's Weekly*, combined a commitment to the First Amendment with entrepreneurial zeal and reporting skill and became one of the great independent journalists in American history. At the age of eighty, Izzy published *The Trial of Socrates*, which was a national bestseller. He wrote the book after he taught himself ancient Greek.

BENJAMIN C. BRADLEE was for nearly thirty years the charismatic editorial leader of *The Washington Post*. It was Ben who gave the *Post* the range and courage to pursue such historic issues as Watergate. He supported his reporters with a tenacity that made them fearless and it is no accident that so many became authors of influential, best-selling books.

ROBERT L. BERNSTEIN, the chief executive of Random House for more than a quarter century, guided one of the nation's premier publishing houses. Bob was personally responsible for many books of political dissent and argument that challenged tyranny around the globe. He is also the founder and longtime chair of Human Rights Watch, one of the most respected human rights organizations in the world.

·       ·       ·

For fifty years, the banner of Public Affairs Press was carried by its owner Morris B. Schnapper, who published Gandhi, Nasser, Toynbee, Truman, and about 1,500 other authors. In 1983, Schnapper was described by *The Washington Post* as "a redoubtable gadfly." His legacy will endure in the books to come.

Peter Osnos, *Founder*